SACRED SPACE

The Prayer Book 2018

from the website www.sacredspace.ie

Prayer from the Irish Jesuits

Messenger Publications,
37 Lower Leeson Street, Dublin D02 W938
www.messenger.ie

First published by Loyola Press Chicago, 2017.

Cover art credit: Kathryn Seckman Kirsch

Printed by Nicholson & Bass Ltd

ISBN: 978 1 910248 751

17 18 19 20 21 Versa 10 9 8 7 6 5 4 3 2 1

Contents

Sacred Space Prayer

Bless all who worship you, almighty God,
from the rising of the sun to its setting:
from your goodness enrich us,
by your love inspire us,
by your Spirit guide us,
by your power protect us,
in your mercy receive us,
now and always.

Preface

In 1999 an Irish Jesuit named Alan McGuckian had the simple—but at the time radical—idea of bringing daily prayer to the Internet. No one imagined that his experimental project would grow into a global community with volunteers translating the prayer experience into seventeen different languages.

Millions of people, from numerous Christian traditions, visit www.sacredspace.ie each year, and what they find is an invitation to step away from their busy routine for a few minutes each day to concentrate on what is really important in their lives. Sacred Space offers its visitors the opportunity to grow in prayerful awareness of their friendship with God.

Besides the daily prayer experience, Sacred Space also offers Living Space, with commentaries on the Scripture readings for each day's Catholic Mass. The Chapel of Intentions allows people to add their own prayers, while Pray with the Pope joins the community to the international Apostleship of Prayer. In addition, Sacred Space provides Lenten and Advent retreats, often in partnership with Pray as You Go, an audio prayer service from the British Jesuits.

The contents of this printed edition, first produced in 2004, are taken directly from our Internet site. Despite the increased use of Sacred Space on mobile devices, many people want a book they can hold and carry, and this book has proven especially helpful for prayer groups.

In 2014 the Irish Jesuits entered into an apostolic agreement with the Chicago-Detroit Jesuits, and Sacred Space now operates in partnership with Loyola Press.

I am delighted to bring you the *Sacred Space* book, and I pray that your prayer life will flourish with its help.

Yours in Christ,

Paul Brian Campbell, SJ

Introduction to *Sacred Space*, 2018

Saint Ignatius of Loyola, founder of the Society of Jesus, is famously known for wanting to find God in all things. *Is that even possible?* you might ask. He believed it was, but only as a gift from God and only as the fruit of our paying attention to our experience. Ignatius developed an optimistic spiritual practice that assumed the presence of God at every moment of our existence. While we tend to think of God's presence as a "sometimes thing," Ignatius came to believe that our perception of God's presence as a sometimes occurrence is a major spiritual hindrance. Ignatius believed that God is always creating this universe, always keeping it in existence, always working to bring about God's purpose in creation, and always trying to move us to join God in the great adventure of bringing about what Jesus called the kingdom of God.

In order to experience this ever-present God, we need to develop a regular spiritual practice, a practice Ignatius had learned from his experience as a relatively untutored layman. Ignatius began to teach people and to write down the spiritual practices that helped him move toward uniting himself with God's purposes and thus toward finding God in all things. *Spiritual Exercises* is Ignatius's manual for those who want to follow his example of helping others get in touch with our ever-present God. God wants a close personal relationship with each of us, and he wants each of us to join him in the great work of bringing about a world where peace and justice prevail. Over the almost five centuries since the time of Ignatius, Jesuits and many others have found through these spiritual practices the answer to their own deepest desires.

Over the centuries, the Spiritual Exercises have been adapted in many ways. Jesuits originally followed Ignatius's own practice of giving the Exercises to individuals for thirty days. But they also used the methods of prayer suggested in the Exercises in their preaching, missions, and talks to larger groups. Eventually, houses were set aside for the giving of the Exercises to individuals and large groups. One of the adaptations suggested by Ignatius himself was to make the Exercises in daily life under the direction of someone trained in giving them. In this format, an individual maintained his or her regular daily life and work but promised to devote time every day to the spiritual practices suggested by Ignatius and to see the spiritual director once a week. In the past fifty years, this adaptation has seen a worldwide resurgence and has touched many lives. It has also been used with groups to great advantage. In modern times, the giving of the Spiritual Exercises has become something of a cottage industry in many countries.

Enter the age of the Internet. Could this new tool be used to help large numbers of people move toward finding God in all things? The answer is a resounding *yes*! Many websites, in multiple languages, try to help people become more aware of God's presence in their lives, using practices stemming from the Spiritual Exercises. One example is the book you have in your hands. In 1999 the Irish Jesuits started to offer daily prompts for prayer based on Ignatius's Exercises on the website Sacred Space (www.sacredspace.ie). The English edition was soon translated into other languages, and the site now features twenty-one languages that span the globe.

In my work as a spiritual director and in my travels, I have come across many, many people of various walks of life who use the daily prompts for prayer provided through Sacred Space. People find the site and the daily suggestions to be user-friendly, inviting, and—in keeping with Ignatian spirituality—optimistic. The suggestions help them pay attention to their experience, notice intimations of God's presence in that experience, and engage in honest conversations with God.

For each week, there is an overarching suggested theme and a method for spending time with God each day. One of the methods is to turn to the Scripture and reflections suggested for each day of the week. Each day's text is taken from the Gospel reading for Mass that day. Thus, someone who follows Sacred Space every day will, in the course of a year, work prayerfully through all four of the Gospels. No wonder that so many have been enthralled by this site.

In spite of the digital age, many of us still like the feel of a book in our hands. The book *Sacred Space*, which you now hold in your hands, was designed for the likes of us. I am very happy to introduce the book and even happier that Loyola Press, a Jesuit institution, is now the publisher. Ignatian spiritual practice has brought me closer to God, for which I am immensely grateful. Through Ignatius's spiritual practices I have experienced God's desire for my friendship, and I figure, if God wants *my* friendship, he wants *everyone's* friendship. If you take this book seriously and engage in the relationship with God that it suggests, you will, I'm sure, find as much joy in God's friendship as I have. Try it—you'll like it.

William A. Barry, SJ

How to Use This Book

During each week of the Liturgical year, begin by reading the "Something to think and pray about each day this week." Then proceed through "The Presence of God," "Freedom," and "Consciousness" steps to prepare yourself to hear the word of God in your heart. In the next step, "The Word," turn to the Scripture reading for each day of the week. Inspiration points are provided if you need them. Then return to the "Conversation" and "Conclusion" steps. Use this process every day of the year.

Please note: In Scripture text, paragraph breaks are indicated by //.

The First Week of Advent
December 3—December 9, 2017

Something to think and pray about each day this week:

Part of the Bigger Plan

I've often thought about the angel coming to Mary. Our feasts and songs and icons celebrate the Annunciation, but I'd never thought about the moment when it was all over. I can only imagine it was something like what writer Annie Dillard experienced when she looked out on what she imagined was a field of angels. "I stood in pieces," she writes, "afraid I was unable to move. Something had unhinged the world." Later she describes the grave and stricken silence, the "unbearable green" and the "God-blasted, paralyzed" fields. People always comment on the bravery of Mary's yes. I never quite understood this. Wouldn't anyone say yes to an angel? But it seems unspeakably brave when I picture that later moment, when Mary stood before the God-blasted, paralyzed day and watched the angel depart.

—Amy Andrews, *2017: A Book of Grace-Filled Days*

The Presence of God
"Be still and know that I am God." Lord, your words lead us to the calmness and greatness of your presence.

Freedom
I am free. When I look at these words in writing, they seem to create in me a feeling of awe. Yes, a wonderful feeling of freedom. Thank you, God.

Consciousness
At this moment, Lord, I turn my thoughts to you.
I will leave aside my chores and preoccupations.
I will take rest and refreshment in your presence, Lord.

The Word
The word of God comes down to us through the Scriptures. May the Holy Spirit enlighten my mind and my heart to respond to the Gospel teachings. (Please turn to the Scripture on the following pages. Inspiration points are there should you need them. When you are ready, return here to continue.)

Conversation
Begin to talk with Jesus about the Scripture you have just read. What part of it strikes a chord in you? Perhaps the words of a friend—or some story you have heard recently—will slowly rise to the surface of your consciousness. If so, does the story throw light on what the Scripture passage may be trying to say to you?

Conclusion
Glory be to the Father, and to the Son, and to the Holy Spirit,
As it was in the beginning, is now and ever shall be,
World without end. Amen.

Sunday 3rd December
First Sunday of Advent
Mark 13:33–37

Beware, keep alert; for you do not know when the time will come. It is like a man going on a journey, when he leaves home and puts his slaves in charge, each with his work, and commands the doorkeeper to be on the watch. Therefore, keep awake—for you do not know when the master of the house will come, in the evening, or at midnight, or at cockcrow, or at dawn, or else he may find you asleep when he comes suddenly. And what I say to you I say to all: Keep awake.

- Jesus is speaking of his second coming at the end of time. We must live so that it does not matter when he comes. Our life becomes a preparation for the vision of happiness.

- Do I anticipate the Lord's coming, or do I dread it? Why do I feel as I do about this?

Monday 4th December
Matthew 8:5–11

When [Jesus] entered Capernaum, a centurion came to him, appealing to him and saying, "Lord, my servant is lying at home paralyzed, in terrible distress." And he said to him, "I will come and cure him." The centurion answered, "Lord, I am not worthy to have you come under my roof; but only speak the word, and my servant will be healed. For I also am a man under authority, with soldiers under me; and I say to one, 'Go,' and he goes, and to another, 'Come,' and he comes, and to my slave, 'Do this,' and the slave does it." When Jesus heard him, he was amazed and said to those who followed him, "Truly I tell you, in no one in Israel have I found such faith. I tell you, many will come from east and west and will eat with Abraham and Isaac and Jacob in the kingdom of heaven."

- This remarkable centurion is a model of prayer. This man's faith in Jesus brought amazement and touched his heart. We too can touch the heart of Jesus when we pray with deep concern for someone in need.

- Who are the people in my life who need prayer? How might I bring their needs to Jesus?

Tuesday 5th December
Luke 10:21–24

At that same hour Jesus rejoiced in the Holy Spirit and said, "I thank you, Father, Lord of heaven and earth, because you have hidden these things from the wise and the intelligent and have revealed them to infants; yes, Father, for such was your gracious will. All things have been handed over to me by my Father; and no one knows who the Son is except the Father, or who the Father is except the Son and anyone to whom the Son chooses to reveal him."

Then turning to the disciples, Jesus said to them privately, "Blessed are the eyes that see what you see! For I tell you that many prophets and kings desired to see what you see, but did not see it, and to hear what you hear, but did not hear it."

- This lovely prayer of Jesus tells us something of the relationship he treasured with his Father through the Holy Spirit. It is his prayer of thanksgiving for the successful mission of his disciples, whom he had sent out to preach. Jesus then tells them that they are indeed blessed to have accepted the good news and to be building their lives on their relationship with God.

- Let us pray that, like the disciples, we have the "eyes to see and the ears to hear."

Wednesday 6th December
Matthew 15:29–37

After Jesus had left that place, he passed along the Sea of Galilee, and he went up the mountain, where he sat down. Great crowds came to him, bringing with them the lame, the maimed, the blind, the mute, and many others. They put them at his feet, and he cured them, so that the crowd was amazed when they saw the mute speaking, the maimed whole, the lame walking, and the blind seeing. And they praised the God of Israel. Then Jesus called his disciples to him and said, "I have compassion for the crowd, because they have been with me now for three days and have nothing to eat; and I do not want to send them away hungry, for they might faint on the way." The disciples said to him, "Where are we to get enough bread in the desert to feed so great a crowd?" Jesus asked them, "How many loaves have you?" They said, "Seven, and a few small fish."

Then ordering the crowd to sit down on the ground, he took the seven loaves and the fish; and after giving thanks he broke them and gave them to the disciples, and the disciples gave them to the crowds. And all of them ate and were filled; and they took up the broken pieces left over, seven baskets full.

- Lord, you are the one who notices when we are hungry, tired, or disorganized, and without making a fuss you reach out to our needs. The crowds wore you out, bringing you the maimed, the mute, and the blind. Again and again in the Gospels, you are the one who feeds the hungry and gives them strength for their journey. You are the bread of life.

- What resources do I have that, today, Jesus might use to help others?

Thursday 7th December
Matthew 7:21, 24–27

[Jesus said to the people,] "Not everyone who says to me, 'Lord, Lord,' will enter the kingdom of heaven, but only one who does the will of my Father in heaven. . . . Everyone then who hears these words of mine and acts on them will be like a wise man who built his house on rock. The rain fell, the floods came, and the winds blew and beat on that house, but it did not fall, because it had been founded on rock. And everyone who hears these words of mine and does not act on them will be like a foolish man who built his house on sand. The rain fell, and the floods came, and the winds blew and beat against that house, and it fell—and great was its fall!"

- The Lord is the everlasting Rock, says the prophet Isaiah, so trust in the Lord forever. "For he has brought low the inhabitants of the height; the lofty city he lays low." . . . But the faithful ones, on the other hand, can say, "he sets up victory like walls and bulwarks . . . we have a strong city" (Isaiah 26). Any moment now, he's going to come and surround us with protection.

- It is the Lord who is "the rock of ages"—a still point, though the centuries swirl around. The Lord is a solid center on which we can build our life. If we are faithful to the Lord, the Lord is faithful to us.

Friday 8th December
The Immaculate Conception of the Blessed Virgin Mary
Luke 1:26–38

In the sixth month the angel Gabriel was sent by God to a town in Galilee called Nazareth, to a virgin engaged to a man whose name was Joseph, of the house of David. The virgin's name was Mary. And he came to her and said, "Greetings, favored one! The Lord is with you." But she was much perplexed by his words and pondered what sort of greeting this might be. The angel said to her, "Do not be afraid, Mary, for you have found favor with God. And now, you will conceive in your womb and bear a son, and you will name him Jesus. He will be great, and will be called the Son of the Most High, and the Lord God will give to him the throne of his ancestor David. He will reign over the house of Jacob forever, and of his kingdom there will be no end." Mary said to the angel, "How can this be, since I am a virgin?" The angel said to her, "The Holy Spirit will come upon you, and the power of the Most High will overshadow you; therefore the child to be born will be holy; he will be called Son of God. And now, your relative Elizabeth in her old age has also conceived a son; and this is the sixth month for her who was said to be barren. For nothing will be impossible with God." Then Mary said, "Here am I, the servant of the Lord; let it be with me according to your word." Then the angel departed from her.

- Scripture leaves us in no doubt about God being a long-range planner; he can determine that a whole series of events come to maturity in his own good time. In fact, he has done this for the benefit of us all—planning, even before the beginning of the world, for us to become sisters and brothers of Jesus.

- For the grand plan to come to completion, the cooperation of Mary was needed. God still asks for our cooperation in the overall plan of his kingdom here on earth. Where do I fit in that plan today, or this week?

Saturday 9th December

Matthew 9:35—10:1, 5a, 6–8

Then Jesus went about all the cities and villages, teaching in their synagogues, and proclaiming the good news of the kingdom, and curing every disease and every sickness. When he saw the crowds, he had compassion for them, because they were harassed and helpless, like sheep without a shepherd. Then he said to his disciples, "The harvest is plentiful, but the laborers are few; therefore, ask the Lord of the harvest to send out laborers into his harvest." Then Jesus summoned his twelve disciples and gave them authority over unclean spirits, to cast them out, and to cure every disease and every sickness. These twelve Jesus sent out with the following instructions: "Go nowhere among the Gentiles, and enter no town of the Samaritans, but go rather to the lost sheep of the house of Israel. As you go, proclaim the good news, 'The kingdom of heaven has come near.' Cure the sick, raise the dead, cleanse the lepers, cast out demons. You received without payment; give without payment."

- The Twelve are to perform cures, to cast out devils—and even to raise the dead. (All in the day's work, as it were.) Indeed, something totally new must be stirring!

- A shepherd-king has suddenly arrived: Jesus, full of compassion, is bringing heaven close to earth. I have the power, through the Holy Spirit, to express that compassion in my situations and relationships this very day.

The Second Week of Advent
December 10—December 16, 2017

Something to think and pray about each day this week:

Signs of the Savior
When I was in my early twenties, I backpacked around Scotland. At my northernmost destination, I stayed at a sheep farm. I remember waking up in the middle of the night, checking my watch, only four o'clock, and being shocked to see the sun outside my window blazing down on the fields. Since I'd expected darkness, the sun seemed unbearably bright. Later, on the Isle of Skye, I watched the sun go down at ten at night and the sky gradually grow a darker blue but never turn black. I'm sure the natives barely noticed, but to me this perpetual daylight seemed like a sign. Though we sometimes turn away from brightness, preferring dark, the light is out there burning always, pouring through the universe at the greatest possible speed, forever coming, light upon light, dawning through the darkness.

—Amy Andrews, *2017: A Book of Grace-Filled Days*

The Presence of God

"Come to me, all you who are weary and are carrying heavy burdens, and I will give you rest." Here I am, Lord. I come to seek your presence. I long for your healing power.

Freedom

"In these days, God taught me as a schoolteacher teaches a pupil" (Saint Ignatius).

I remind myself that there are things God has to teach me yet, and I ask for the grace to hear those things and let them change me.

Consciousness

Help me, Lord, to be more conscious of your presence. Teach me to recognize your presence in others.

Fill my heart with gratitude for the times your love has been shown to me through the care of others.

The Word

God speaks to each of us individually. I listen attentively, to hear what he is saying to me. Read the text a few times, then listen. (Please turn to the Scripture on the following pages. Inspiration points are there should you need them. When you are ready, return here to continue.)

Conversation

Conversation requires talking and listening.

As I talk to Jesus, may I also learn to be still and listen.

I picture the gentleness in his eyes and the smile full of love as he gazes on me.

I can be totally honest with Jesus as I tell him of my worries and my cares.

I will open my heart to him as I tell him of my fears and my doubts.

I will ask him to help me place myself fully in his care and to abandon myself to him, knowing that he always wants what is best for me.

Conclusion

I thank God for these moments we have spent together and for any insights I have been given concerning the text.

Sunday 10th December
Second Sunday of Advent

Mark 1:1–8

The beginning of the good news of Jesus Christ, the Son of God.

As it is written by the prophet Isaiah,

"See, I am sending my messenger ahead of you, who will prepare
   your way;
the voice of one crying out in the wilderness: 'Prepare the way of the
   Lord, make his paths straight,'"

John the baptizer appeared in the wilderness, proclaiming a baptism of repentance for the forgiveness of sins. And people from the whole Judean countryside and all the people of Jerusalem were going out to him, and were baptized by him in the river Jordan, confessing their sins. Now John was clothed with camel's hair, with a leather belt around his waist, and he ate locusts and wild honey. He proclaimed, "The one who is more powerful than I is coming after me; I am not worthy to stoop down and untie the thong of his sandals. I have baptized you with water; but he will baptize you with the Holy Spirit."

- Imagine yourself witnessing this scene, perhaps standing in the shallows with the water flowing around your ankles. Allow the scene to unfold. What is it like? The young man from Nazareth joins those waiting for John's baptism: a symbol of purification but also of birth—coming up out of the waters of the womb into a new life as God's beloved child.

- Lord, when I realize that you love me, it is like the start of a new life. As I hear your voice, I know that I have a purpose and a destiny.

Monday 11th December

Luke 5:17–26

One day, while he was teaching, Pharisees and teachers of the law were sitting nearby (they had come from every village of Galilee and Judea and from Jerusalem); and the power of the Lord was with him to heal. Just then some men came, carrying a paralyzed man on a bed. They were trying to bring him in and lay him before Jesus; but finding no way to bring him in because of the crowd, they went up on the roof and let him down with his bed through the tiles into the middle of the crowd in front of Jesus. When he saw their faith, he said, "Friend, your sins are forgiven you." Then the scribes and the Pharisees began to question, "Who is this who is speaking blasphemies? Who can forgive sins but God alone?" When Jesus perceived their questionings, he answered them, "Why do you raise such questions in your hearts? Which is easier, to say, 'Your sins are forgiven you,' or to say, 'Stand up and walk'? But so that you may know that the Son of Man has authority on earth to forgive sins"—he said to the one who was paralyzed—"I say to you, stand up and take your bed and go to your home." Immediately he stood up before them, took what he had been lying on, and went to his home, glorifying God. Amazement seized all of them, and they glorified God and were filled with awe, saying, "We have seen strange things today."

- Jesus is the newly arrived kingdom, personified in his very self. Not only has he power to cure the paralyzed man, he also lays claim to forgive the man's sins—and this requires nothing less than God's own power.

- "We have seen strange things today," say the onlookers. Nothing had prepared them for this. But this precisely is what our Advent season is about. We are commemorating the first coming of a Savior, and we are also preparing a welcome for this Savior in our own hearts and in the world of today.

Tuesday 12th December
Luke 1:39–47

In those days Mary set out and went with haste to a Judean town in the hill country, where she entered the house of Zechariah and greeted Elizabeth. When Elizabeth heard Mary's greeting, the child leapt in her womb. And Elizabeth was filled with the Holy Spirit and exclaimed with a loud cry, "Blessed are you among women, and blessed is the fruit of your womb. And why has this happened to me, that the mother of my Lord comes to me? For as soon as I heard the sound of your greeting, the child in my womb leapt for joy. And blessed is she who believed that there would be a fulfillment of what was spoken to her by the Lord."

And Mary said,

"My soul magnifies the Lord, and my spirit rejoices in God my Savior"

- I marvel at the instincts and insight of mothers. While husband Zechariah is baffled and struck dumb and foster-father Joseph has misgivings, it is a woman, Elizabeth, herself pregnant, who recognizes the action of the Lord in her young cousin. She is given the special grace of an intimate appreciation of what is happening and who is really present.

- In daily life, do I always appreciate what is happening and who is really present?

Wednesday 13th December
Matthew 11:28–30

[Jesus said,] "Come to me, all you that are weary and are carrying heavy burdens, and I will give you rest. Take my yoke upon you, and learn from me; for I am gentle and humble in heart, and you will find rest for your souls. For my yoke is easy, and my burden is light."

- The reign of the coming Savior king will not just bring security and welcome to anyone who feels lost and abandoned. Jesus' kingdom also promises relief and support to those who simply feel that life has become too much for them.

- Jesus understands each of us better than we understand ourselves. His heart, gentle and humble, goes out to us. What burdens of mine does he offer to help me with today?

Thursday 14th December
Matthew 11:11–15

Jesus said, "Truly I tell you, among those born of women no one has arisen greater than John the Baptist; yet the least in the kingdom of heaven is greater than he. From the days of John the Baptist until now the kingdom of heaven has suffered violence, and the violent take it by force. For all the prophets and the law prophesied until John came; and if you are willing to accept it, he is Elijah who is to come. Let anyone with ears listen!"

- What was it that placed John the Baptist below the least in the kingdom of heaven? He had preached the justice of God and the need for repentance; but he had not lived to see Jesus crucified and, in that, to see the unbelievable extent of God's love for us.

- "If you are willing to accept it, he is Elijah . . ." Has God revealed anything to me lately that I felt unwilling to accept? When do we know that we are willing, or not willing, to receive God's revelation?

Friday 15th December
Matthew 11:16–19

[Jesus spoke to the crowds,] "But to what will I compare this generation? It is like children sitting in the marketplaces and calling to one another,

> 'We played the flute for you, and you did not dance;
> we wailed, and you did not mourn.'

For John came neither eating nor drinking, and they say, 'He has a demon;' the Son of Man came eating and drinking, and they say, 'Look, a glutton and a drunkard, a friend of tax collectors and sinners!' Yet wisdom is vindicated by her deeds."

- The Lord has always wanted to shower his people with gifts. But often when the offer was made (through the mouth of his messengers, the prophets), the people turned their backs. In fact, even as Jesus prepared to begin his public ministry, this was still happening. The people refused the message of John the Baptist; it was no surprise that Jesus himself met opposition.

- Jesus has arrived offering the gift of new life in abundance, but we remain choosy about the way his message comes to us; it is "too churchy" on the one hand or "too worldly" on the other. May we pray during this season that our hearts become more open.

Saturday 16th December
Matthew 17:9a, 10–13

As they were coming down the mountain, Jesus ordered them, "Tell no one about the vision until after the Son of Man has been raised from the dead." And the disciples asked him, "Why, then, do the scribes say that Elijah must come first?" He replied, "Elijah is indeed coming and will restore all things; but I tell you that Elijah has already come, and they did not recognize him, but they did to him whatever they pleased. So also the Son of Man is about to suffer at their hands." Then the disciples understood that he was speaking to them about John the Baptist.

- The Jewish faith looked forward to the 'last days' or end time when the Lord would come in glory and finally wrap up the affairs of this world. And a conviction had arisen that the approach of the end time would be signaled by a forerunner; the figure of the larger-than-life prophet Elijah would make a renewed appearance. The coming of Jesus was meant to bring about the kingdom of God on earth with the offer of salvation for all, but the people struck out against the bearer of the message.

- By our prayer this Christmas, we can ensure that the newly born Jesus is welcome in our lives, even if his message turns some of our values on their heads.

The Third Week of Advent
December 17—December 23, 2017

Something to think and pray about each day this week:

Preparing Our Hearts
The great purge of every nook and cranny of our home has begun. We are in the process of sharing our toys, outgrown clothes, and superfluous belongings. We are letting go of the things we have held onto "just in case" and other things that have cluttered our lives just because we haven't had the time to clear things out on a regular basis. The resulting space that we are recovering in our home is freeing. There is more room to move and more room to live. There is more space to focus on the things that really matter—and those things are *not things*.

As we clear the clutter from our home, I am reminded that Advent is a great time to clear the spiritual clutter as well. I ask myself, when Jesus comes, will there be room for him to stay, or will he find my heart and soul too cluttered? Am I hanging onto things I don't need out of that "just in case" type of fear? Or, do I trust him enough to let everything go? Have I taken the necessary time to free up space for him? Is my priority, in fact, Jesus, or is it things or other attachments? When he comes, will I be able to respond to him freely, or will my movements be impeded by stuff that's holding me back? My soul-cleaning goal is to be able to fling open the door to my heart and fearlessly let go of all of those things that might get in the way of his entry. Can I do this?

—Rebecca Ruiz on *dotMagis*, the blog of *IgnatianSpirituality.com*

The Presence of God

"I am standing at the door, knocking," says the Lord. What a wonderful privilege that the Lord of all creation desires to come to me. I welcome his presence.

Freedom

Leave me here freely all alone / In cell where never sunlight shone / should no one ever speak to me. / This golden silence makes me free.

—Part of a poem written by a prisoner at
Dachau concentration camp

Consciousness

How am I really feeling? Lighthearted? Heavy-hearted? I may be very much at peace, happy to be here. Equally, I may be frustrated, worried, or angry.
I acknowledge how I really am. It is the real me whom the Lord loves.

The Word

I take my time to read the word of God slowly, a few times, allowing myself to dwell on anything that strikes me. (Please turn to the Scripture on the following pages. Inspiration points are there should you need them. When you are ready, return here to continue.)

Conversation

Do I notice myself reacting as I pray with the word of God? Do I feel challenged, comforted, angry? Imagining Jesus sitting or standing by me, I speak out my feelings, as one trusted friend to another.

Conclusion

Glory be to the Father, and to the Son, and to the Holy Spirit,
As it was in the beginning, is now and ever shall be,
World without end. Amen.

Sunday 17th December
Third Sunday of Advent
John 1:6–8, 19–28

There was a man sent from God, whose name was John. He came as a witness to testify to the light, so that all might believe through him. He himself was not the light, but he came to testify to the light. . . . This is the testimony given by John when the Jews sent priests and Levites from Jerusalem to ask him, "Who are you?" He confessed and did not deny it, but confessed, "I am not the Messiah." And they asked him, "What then? Are you Elijah?" He said, "I am not." "Are you the prophet?" He answered, "No." Then they said to him, "Who are you? Let us have an answer for those who sent us. What do you say about yourself?" He said,

"I am the voice of one crying out in the wilderness,
'Make straight the way of the Lord,'"
as the prophet Isaiah said.

Now they had been sent from the Pharisees. They asked him, "Why then are you baptizing if you are neither the Messiah, nor Elijah, nor the prophet?" John answered them, "I baptize with water. Among you stands one whom you do not know, the one who is coming after me; I am not worthy to untie the thong of his sandal." This took place in Bethany across the Jordan where John was baptizing.

- Here are questions we can ask about ourselves: Who am I? What is my purpose in God's scheme?
- Lord, I think of you beside me, seeing the good and the promise in me. This is what I want to say about myself: I am called into being by God, who loves me.

Monday 18th December
Matthew 1:18–25

Now the birth of Jesus the Messiah took place in this way. When his mother Mary had been engaged to Joseph, but before they lived together, she was found to be with child from the Holy Spirit. Her husband Joseph, being a righteous man and unwilling to expose her to public disgrace, planned to dismiss her quietly. But just when he had resolved to do this, an angel of the Lord appeared to him in a dream and said, "Joseph, son of

David, do not be afraid to take Mary as your wife, for the child conceived in her is from the Holy Spirit. She will bear a son, and you are to name him Jesus, for he will save his people from their sins." All this took place to fulfill what had been spoken by the Lord through the prophet:

"Look, the virgin shall conceive and bear a son, and they shall name
    him Emmanuel,"

which means, "God is with us." When Joseph awoke from sleep, he did as the angel of the Lord commanded him; he took her as his wife, but had no marital relations with her until she had borne a son; and he named him Jesus.

- Jean Paul Sartre, philosopher and atheist, once wrote a Christmas play, *Bariona*. In it he tries to imagine Joseph in Bethlehem: "He [Joseph] feels himself slightly out of it. He suffers because he sees how much this woman whom he loves resembles God; how she is already at the side of God. For God has burst like a bomb into the intimacy of this family. Joseph and Mary are separated forever by this explosion of light. And I imagine that all through his life Joseph will be learning to accept this."
- There is a model here for making decisions and dealing with doubts. Pray about it, carry it as a question, pester God about it. This is the story of Joseph's utterly unique vocation, as foster-father of the Son of God.

Tuesday 19th December
Luke 1:5–25

In the days of King Herod of Judea, there was a priest named Zechariah, who belonged to the priestly order of Abijah. His wife was a descendant of Aaron, and her name was Elizabeth. Both of them were righteous before God, living blamelessly according to all the commandments and regulations of the Lord. But they had no children, because Elizabeth was barren, and both were getting on in years. Once when he was serving as priest before God and his section was on duty, he was chosen by lot, according to the custom of the priesthood, to enter the sanctuary of the Lord and offer incense. Now at the time of the incense offering, the whole assembly of the people was praying outside. Then there appeared to him an angel of the Lord, standing at the right side of the altar of incense. When

Zechariah saw him, he was terrified; and fear overwhelmed him. But the angel said to him, "Do not be afraid, Zechariah, for your prayer has been heard. Your wife Elizabeth will bear you a son, and you will name him John. You will have joy and gladness, and many will rejoice at his birth, for he will be great in the sight of the Lord. He must never drink wine or strong drink; even before his birth he will be filled with the Holy Spirit. He will turn many of the people of Israel to the Lord their God. With the spirit and power of Elijah he will go before him, to turn the hearts of parents to their children, and the disobedient to the wisdom of the righteous, to make ready a people prepared for the Lord." Zechariah said to the angel, "How will I know that this is so? For I am an old man, and my wife is getting on in years." The angel replied, "I am Gabriel. I stand in the presence of God, and I have been sent to speak to you and to bring you this good news. But now, because you did not believe my words, which will be fulfilled in their time, you will become mute, unable to speak, until the day these things occur." Meanwhile the people were waiting for Zechariah, and wondered at his delay in the sanctuary. When he did come out, he could not speak to them, and they realized that he had seen a vision in the sanctuary. He kept motioning to them and remained unable to speak. When his time of service was ended, he went to his home.

After those days his wife Elizabeth conceived, and for five months she remained in seclusion. She said, "This is what the Lord has done for me when he looked favorably on me and took away the disgrace I have endured among my people."

- On the basis of their faithfulness to God, Zechariah and Elizabeth could be rated as being "one in a thousand." But, to the external view, both were unknown and just like a thousand others. Harder still, they were childless, which was seen in those days to indicate the absence of God's favor. But they were already in God's plan for the world's coming Savior.

- Certainly, God's ways are not our ways, and the very people who have tried to remain fully loyal to the Lord are sometimes going to find themselves called to deeper faith—involving an ever more privileged closeness to God. We might ask, in what ways is my faith being called upon to grow?

Wednesday 20 December

Luke 1:26–38

In the sixth month the angel Gabriel was sent by God to a town in Galilee called Nazareth, to a virgin engaged to a man whose name was Joseph, of the house of David. The virgin's name was Mary. And he came to her and said, "Greetings, favored one! The Lord is with you." But she was much perplexed by his words and pondered what sort of greeting this might be. The angel said to her, "Do not be afraid, Mary, for you have found favor with God. And now, you will conceive in your womb and bear a son, and you will name him Jesus. He will be great, and will be called the Son of the Most High, and the Lord God will give to him the throne of his ancestor David. He will reign over the house of Jacob forever, and of his kingdom there will be no end." Mary said to the angel, "How can this be, since I am a virgin?" The angel said to her, "The Holy Spirit will come upon you, and the power of the Most High will overshadow you; therefore the child to be born will be holy; he will be called Son of God. And now, your relative Elizabeth in her old age has also conceived a son; and this is the sixth month for her who was said to be barren. For nothing will be impossible with God." Then Mary said, "Here am I, the servant of the Lord; let it be with me according to your word." Then the angel departed from her.

- For any young woman of Israel, the gift of a child—fruitfulness—was a special mark of God's favor. But before Mary even has time to take in this news, she is confronted by the announcement that her future son will be "savior" (the meaning of *Jesus*)—successor to the kingship of David—Son of the Most High. Still trying to come to terms with it all, imagine her consternation as she realizes that not even a first step is in place; she is as yet no more than betrothed. Then the announcing angel compounds her wonder by speaking of God's action in bestowing a son on the aged Elizabeth.

- Is there such a thing as being overwhelmed with good news? It appears that this was the case with the young, yet willing, Mary. Am I willing to be overwhelmed by the potential God has placed in my life?

Thursday 21st December
Luke 1:39–45

In those days Mary set out and went with haste to a Judean town in the hill country, where she entered the house of Zechariah and greeted Elizabeth. When Elizabeth heard Mary's greeting, the child leaped in her womb. And Elizabeth was filled with the Holy Spirit and exclaimed with a loud cry, "Blessed are you among women, and blessed is the fruit of your womb. And why has this happened to me, that the mother of my Lord comes to me? For as soon as I heard the sound of your greeting, the child in my womb leaped for joy. And blessed is she who believed that there would be a fulfillment of what was spoken to her by the Lord."

- Jesus, the child that Mary is carrying, is recognized by the child in Elizabeth's womb; John leaps in recognition of the one both mothers revere as "Lord" (John himself being of miraculous origin from an elderly mother). Not only is this a confirmation for both women, but their miraculous situations bring them together in a special sort of faith community.

- And above and beyond what is happening to each mother, the Lord (long awaited) has finally come to visit his people, to be victorious over enemies, to exult with joy over those who are his own. We can rest in the confidence that our individual stories are always part of a larger, eternal story.

Friday 22nd December
Luke 1:46–56

And Mary said,

"My soul magnifies the Lord,
and my spirit rejoices in God my Savior,
for he has looked with favor on the lowliness of his servant.
    Surely, from now on all generations will call me blessed;
for the Mighty One has done great things for me, and holy is his name.
His mercy is for those who fear him from generation to generation.
He has shown strength with his arm;
    he has scattered the proud in the thoughts of their hearts.
He has brought down the powerful from their thrones,

and lifted up the lowly;
he has filled the hungry with good things,
    and sent the rich away empty.
He has helped his servant Israel,
    in remembrance of his mercy,
according to the promise he made to our ancestors,
    to Abraham and to his descendants forever."

And Mary remained with [Elizabeth] about three months and then returned to her home.

• Although Mary is giving thanks for the honor accorded her, this is
  a self-effacing prayer. It is a hymn of praise for everything the Lord
  has done for his people—the people as a whole (descendants of
  Abraham)—as well as anyone anywhere who truly reveres [fears] God.
  There is joy and exultation which the angels around Bethlehem will
  also give voice to at the coming of salvation.

• As I look at my life this day, what blessings do I see? And how do my
  personal blessings connect with what God is doing for the whole world?

Saturday 23rd December
Luke 1:57–66

Now the time came for Elizabeth to give birth, and she bore a son. Her
neighbors and relatives heard that the Lord had shown his great mercy to
her, and they rejoiced with her.
On the eighth day they came to circumcise the child, and they were going
to name him Zechariah after his father. But his mother said, "No; he is to
be called John." They said to her, "None of your relatives has this name."
Then they began motioning to his father to find out what name he wanted to give him. He asked for a writing tablet and wrote, "His name is
John." And all of them were amazed. Immediately his mouth was opened
and his tongue freed, and he began to speak, praising God. Fear came
over all their neighbors, and all these things were talked about throughout the entire hill country of Judea. All who heard them pondered them
and said, "What then will this child become?" For, indeed, the hand of
the Lord was with him.

- Zechariah and Elizabeth have been blessed with this new life in their declining years. And through the miracle of the unexpected birth—and of the binding and loosing of Zechariah's tongue—the people realize that here God is taking a very direct hand in events. They know that they are on the threshold of mystery.

- My life, too, is reason for rejoicing because God has planted within it a purpose that is unique to my situation, my history, and my gifts. May I thank God for all of this and offer it back to him.

The Fourth Week of Advent/Christmas
December 24—December 30, 2017

Something to think and pray about each day this week:

What Are We Expecting?
I don't believe that Christianity is a departure from all that came before.
I don't believe, in some sense, that there is anything new under the sun.
And yet the birth of Jesus changed everything. Before he came, there was
a great yearning expressed in the myths, in philosophy, in the words of the
prophets. These voices cried out their hope that God would not abandon
us to death, that there was meaning beyond life. On Christmas Day the
life that would answer these voices was again made visible. It came not
as a new thing but as a confirmation, a proclamation that what had long
been hoped for, theorized, prophesied now lay under the sun as real as
you and I.

—Amy Andrews, *2017: A Book of Grace-Filled Days*

The Presence of God

"Be still, and know that I am God!" Lord, may your spirit guide me to seek your loving presence more and more for it is there I find rest and refreshment from this busy world.

Freedom

By God's grace I was born to live in freedom. Free to enjoy the pleasures he created for me. Dear Lord, grant that I may live as you intended, with complete confidence in your loving care.

Consciousness

How am I today?
Where am I with God? With others?
Do I have something to be grateful for? Then I give thanks.
Is there something I am sorry for? Then I ask forgiveness.

The Word

God speaks to each of us individually. I need to listen, to hear what he is saying to me. Read the text a few times, then listen. (Please turn to the Scripture on the following pages. Inspiration points are there should you need them. When you are ready, return here to continue.)

Conversation

How has God's word moved me? Has it left me cold?
Has it consoled me or moved me to act in a new way?
I imagine Jesus standing or sitting beside me.
I turn and share my feelings with him.

Conclusion

I thank God for these moments we have spent together and for any insights I have been given concerning the text.

Sunday 24th December
Fourth Sunday of Advent

Luke 1:26–38

In the sixth month the angel Gabriel was sent by God to a town in Galilee called Nazareth, to a virgin engaged to a man whose name was Joseph, of the house of David. The virgin's name was Mary. And he came to her and said, "Greetings, favored one! The Lord is with you." But she was much perplexed by his words and pondered what sort of greeting this might be. The angel said to her, "Do not be afraid, Mary, for you have found favor with God. And now, you will conceive in your womb and bear a son, and you will name him Jesus. He will be great, and will be called the Son of the Most High, and the Lord God will give to him the throne of his ancestor David. He will reign over the house of Jacob forever, and of his kingdom there will be no end." Mary said to the angel, "How can this be, since I am a virgin?" The angel said to her, "The Holy Spirit will come upon you, and the power of the Most High will overshadow you; therefore the child to be born will be holy; he will be called Son of God. And now, your relative Elizabeth in her old age has also conceived a son; and this is the sixth month for her who was said to be barren. For nothing will be impossible with God." Then Mary said, "Here am I, the servant of the Lord; let it be with me according to your word." Then the angel departed from her.

- When a woman in the crowd cried to Jesus, "Blessed is the womb that bore you," he replied, "Blessed rather are those who hear the word of God and obey it." The first of these was his mother, who said "Let it be with me according to your word." We remember her words whenever we pray the Angelus.

- Lord, this is not an easy prayer to make. You prayed it yourself in Gethsemane in a sweat of blood, "not my will but yours be done." Help me make it the pattern of my life. What issues of surrender and trust does it raise for me?

Monday 25th December
The Nativity of the Lord (Christmas)
John 1:1–18

In the beginning was the Word, and the Word was with God, and the Word was God. He was in the beginning with God. All things came into being through him, and without him not one thing came into being. What has come into being in him was life, and the life was the light of all people. The light shines in the darkness, and the darkness did not overcome it.

There was a man sent from God, whose name was John. He came as a witness to testify to the light, so that all might believe through him. He himself was not the light, but he came to testify to the light. The true light, which enlightens everyone, was coming into the world.

He was in the world, and the world came into being through him; yet the world did not know him. He came to what was his own, and his own people did not accept him. But to all who received him, who believed in his name, he gave power to become children of God, who were born, not of blood or of the will of the flesh or of the will of man, but of God.

And the Word became flesh and lived among us, and we have seen his glory, the glory as of a father's only son, full of grace and truth. (John testified to him and cried out, "This was he of whom I said, 'He who comes after me ranks ahead of me because he was before me.'") From his fullness we have all received, grace upon grace. The law indeed was given through Moses; grace and truth came through Jesus Christ. No one has ever seen God. It is God the only Son, who is close to the Father's heart, who has made him known.

- In this hymn, which introduces the fourth Gospel, John proclaims the faith that marks us as Christian. We believe that Jesus is the word of God, his perfect expression. "No one has ever seen God. It is God the only Son, who is close to the Father's heart, who has made him known."

- Lord, in the year that starts tonight, let me grow in the knowledge of God. May I receive of your fullness, grace upon grace. You took on this mortal flesh for me and lived among us. May this coming year bring me closer to you.

Tuesday 26th December

Matthew 10:17–22

Beware of them, for they will hand you over to councils and flog you in
their synagogues; and you will be dragged before governors and kings
because of me, as a testimony to them and the Gentiles. When they hand
you over, do not worry about how you are to speak or what you are to say;
for what you are to say will be given to you at that time; for it is not you
who speak, but the Spirit of your Father speaking through you. Brother
will betray brother to death, and a father his child, and children will rise
against parents and have them put to death; and you will be hated by all
because of my name. But the one who endures to the end will be saved.

- Jesus gave up heaven's glory to join our life on earth. And the Christian,
  in turn, often must give up earth's privileges, even the freedom to live,
  to be worthy of joining the life of heaven. Martyrdom happened to
  Stephen, and we cannot rule out its happening to any of us.

- How often do I expect special privileges in this life because I'm a
  Christian? When have I needed to give up privilege to live as God
  asked me to live?

Wednesday 27th December

John 20:1a, 2–8

Early on the first day of the week, while it was still dark, Mary Magdalene
came to the tomb and saw that the stone had been removed from the
tomb.

So she ran and went to Simon Peter and the other disciple, the one
whom Jesus loved, and said to them, "They have taken the Lord out of the
tomb, and we do not know where they have laid him." Then Peter and the
other disciple set out and went towards the tomb. The two were running
together, but the other disciple outran Peter and reached the tomb first.
He bent down to look in and saw the linen wrappings lying there, but
he did not go in. Then Simon Peter came, following him, and went into
the tomb. He saw the linen wrappings lying there, and the cloth that had
been on Jesus' head, not lying with the linen wrappings but rolled up in
a place by itself. Then the other disciple, who reached the tomb first, also
went in, and he saw and believed.

- It may be unfair to say that one person is "better" at believing than another; but today's Gospel passage gives us a portrait of two followers of Jesus. The strong point of one of them (Peter) is, you might say, action; and the strong point of the other (the apostle John, today's saint) is believing. Perhaps that's why John—seemingly more attuned to the inner sense of things—is called "the one whom Jesus loved."

- In the words of one Gospel petitioner, we say, "I believe; Help my unbelief!" I give myself permission to pray this prayer. The praying itself will prepare my life for more faith.

Thursday 28th December
Matthew 2:13–18

Now after they had left, an angel of the Lord appeared to Joseph in a dream and said, "Get up, take the child and his mother, and flee to Egypt, and remain there until I tell you; for Herod is about to search for the child, to destroy him." Then Joseph got up, took the child and his mother by night, and went to Egypt, and remained there until the death of Herod. This was to fulfill what had been spoken by the Lord through the prophet, "Out of Egypt I have called my son."
When Herod saw that he had been tricked by the wise men, he was infuriated, and he sent and killed all the children in and around Bethlehem who were two years old or under, according to the time that he had learned from the wise men. Then was fulfilled what had been spoken through the prophet Jeremiah:

"A voice was heard in Ramah,
     wailing and loud lamentation,
Rachel weeping for her children;
     she refused to be consoled, because they are no more."

- When we reflect on the scene of the Holy Family forced to flee into Egypt, we remember the Jewish people once found themselves in captivity in Egypt. They were eventually released by the Pharaoh after the blood of a child flowed in every house of his people.

- Mothers who are separated from their children by death or exile will mourn continuously. I pray for those families, that they will find comfort in the ever-present compassion of God.

Friday 29th December

Luke 2:22–35

When the time came for their purification according to the law of Moses, they brought him up to Jerusalem to present him to the Lord (as it is written in the law of the Lord, "Every firstborn male shall be designated as holy to the Lord"), and they offered a sacrifice according to what is stated in the law of the Lord, "a pair of turtledoves or two young pigeons."

Now there was a man in Jerusalem whose name was Simeon; this man was righteous and devout, looking forward to the consolation of Israel, and the Holy Spirit rested on him. It had been revealed to him by the Holy Spirit that he would not see death before he had seen the Lord's Messiah. Guided by the Spirit, Simeon came into the temple; and when the parents brought in the child Jesus, to do for him what was customary under the law, Simeon took him in his arms and praised God, saying,

"Master, now you are dismissing your servant in peace,
    according to your word;
for my eyes have seen your salvation,
    which you have prepared in the presence of all peoples,
a light for revelation to the Gentiles
    and for glory to your people Israel."

And the child's father and mother were amazed at what was being said about him. Then Simeon blessed them and said to his mother Mary, "This child is destined for the falling and the rising of many in Israel, and to be a sign that will be opposed so that the inner thoughts of many will be revealed—and a sword will pierce your own soul too."

- The Scripture readings in the season of Christmas often emphasize how the coming of Jesus was the end point of all the initiatives God had taken in the interests of the people he had chosen. And today we're reminded that this was true for the whole non-Jewish world as well. But we are warned not to be complacent. Jesus is not going to force himself on anybody. There will always be the choice to accept him or to reject him.

- In my prayer today, I rely on the Holy Spirit to help me as I make choices. I have a destiny, too, but God honors my ability to say yes or no.

Saturday 30th December

Luke 2:36–40

There was also a prophet, Anna the daughter of Phanuel, of the tribe of Asher. She was of a great age, having lived with her husband seven years after her marriage, then as a widow to the age of eighty-four. She never left the temple but worshipped there with fasting and prayer night and day. At that moment she came, and began to praise God and to speak about the child to all who were looking for the redemption of Jerusalem.

When they had finished everything required by the law of the Lord, they returned to Galilee, to their own town of Nazareth. The child grew and became strong, filled with wisdom; and the favor of God was upon him.

- As Anna took the baby in her arms and her eyes lit up, how Mary must have warmed to her! Here was yet another confirmation of this child's destiny as the chosen one. Mary had no way of knowing that Anna had waited many years to see this one child. Anna did not know who the child would be—or who the child's parents would be—until they appeared that day. Yet all were ready to see God's revelation when it appeared.

- Lord, you are telling me that I don't have to know the details of how your grace will come about in my life. I need only to be ready to recognize it when the time comes.

First Week of Christmas
December 31, 2017—January 6, 2018

Something to think and pray about each day this week:

True Gift Giving
There are countless stories and legends about the deeds of St. Nicholas, a bishop of Myra in what's now Turkey, back in the fourth century. I suppose the most well-known story is that of the dowry. A man was too poor to provide dowries for his daughters, so Bishop Nicholas found ways to get the needed funds to the family, in secret. The thing I like about the story is that Nicholas was so determined to be anonymous in his giving that, for the last daughter, he supposedly dropped the bag of cash down the chimney. It gives me something to think about. In this season of gift giving, is my heart truly centered on others, or do I give in order to impress?

—Amy Welborn, *A Catholic Woman's Book of Days*

The Presence of God

As I sit here, the beating of my heart,
the ebb and flow of my breathing, the movements of my mind
are all signs of God's ongoing creation of me.
I pause for a moment and become aware
of this presence of God within me.

Freedom

Everything has the potential to draw from me a fuller love and life.
Yet my desires are often fixed, caught, on illusions of fulfillment.
I ask that God, through my freedom, may orchestrate my desires in a
vibrant loving melody rich in harmony.

Consciousness

I ask, how am I within myself today? Am I particularly tired, stressed,
or off-form? If any of these characteristics apply, can I try to let go of the
concerns that disturb me?

The Word

I read the word of God slowly, a few times over, and I listen to what
God is saying to me. (Please turn to the Scripture on the following pages.
Inspiration points are there should you need them. When you are ready,
return here to continue.)

Conversation

I begin to talk with Jesus about the Scripture I have just read. What part
of it strikes a chord in me? Perhaps the words of a friend or a story I have
heard recently will slowly rise to the surface of my consciousness. If so,
does the story throw light on what the Scripture passage may be trying
to say to me?

Conclusion

Glory be to the Father, and to the Son, and to the Holy Spirit,
As it was in the beginning, is now and ever shall be,
World without end. Amen.

Sunday 31st December
The Holy Family of Jesus, Mary, and Joseph
Luke 2:22–40

When the time came for their purification according to the law of Moses, they brought him up to Jerusalem to present him to the Lord (as it is written in the law of the Lord, "Every firstborn male shall be designated as holy to the Lord"), and they offered a sacrifice according to what is stated in the law of the Lord, "a pair of turtle-doves or two young pigeons." Now there was a man in Jerusalem whose name was Simeon; this man was righteous and devout, looking forward to the consolation of Israel, and the Holy Spirit rested on him. It had been revealed to him by the Holy Spirit that he would not see death before he had seen the Lord's Messiah. Guided by the Spirit, Simeon came into the temple; and when the parents brought in the child Jesus, to do for him what was customary under the law, Simeon took him in his arms and praised God, saying,

"Master, now you are dismissing your servant in peace,
according to your word;
for my eyes have seen your salvation,
which you have prepared in the presence of all peoples,
a light for revelation to the Gentiles
and for glory to your people Israel."

And the child's father and mother were amazed at what was being said about him. Then Simeon blessed them and said to his mother Mary, "This child is destined for the falling and the rising of many in Israel, and to be a sign that will be opposed so that the inner thoughts of many will be revealed—and a sword will pierce your own soul too."

There was also a prophet, Anna the daughter of Phanuel, of the tribe of Asher. She was of a great age, having lived with her husband for seven years after her marriage, then as a widow to the age of eighty-four. She never left the temple but worshipped there with fasting and prayer night and day. At that moment she came, and began to praise God and to speak about the child to all who were looking for the redemption of Jerusalem.

When they had finished everything required by the law of the Lord, they returned to Galilee, to their own town of Nazareth. The child grew and became strong, filled with wisdom; and the favor of God was upon him.

- Jesus comes not in splendor, but as a baby in his mother's arms. Lord, I see you here in the vulnerable flesh of a child, a sign that will be spoken against. Already the shadow of Calvary falls on Mary as Simeon tells her that a sword will pierce her soul.

- Jesus, you share my humanity in every way. Like you, I want to grow and become strong, filled with wisdom. I still have miles to go before I sleep. May the favor of God be with me as with you.

Monday 1st January
The Solemnity of Mary, The Holy Mother of God
Luke 2:16–21

So they went with haste and found Mary and Joseph, and the child lying in the manger. When they saw this, they made known what had been told them about this child; and all who heard it were amazed at what the shepherds told them. But Mary treasured all these words and pondered them in her heart. The shepherds returned, glorifying and praising God for all they had heard and seen, as it had been told them.

After eight days had passed, it was time to circumcise the child; and he was called Jesus, the name given by the angel before he was conceived in the womb.

- We start the year, as we start our life, under the protection of a mother. Today we celebrate the most passionate and enduring of all human relationships, that of mother and child. As Mary looked at her baby and gave him her breast, she knew that there was a dimension here beyond her imagining.

- Christians contemplated Mary for three centuries before the Council of Ephesus, when they dared to consecrate the title *theotokos*, Mother of God. Like Mary, I treasure the words spoken about Jesus, and ponder them in my heart.

Tuesday 2nd January
John 1:19–28

This is the testimony given by John when the Jews sent priests and Levites from Jerusalem to ask him, "Who are you?" He confessed and did not deny it, but confessed, "I am not the Messiah." And they asked him, "What then? Are you Elijah?" He said, "I am not." "Are you the prophet?"

He answered, "No." Then they said to him, "Who are you? Let us have an answer for those who sent us. What do you say about yourself?" He said,

"I am the voice of one crying out in the wilderness,
'Make straight the way of the Lord,'"
as the prophet Isaiah said.

Now they had been sent from the Pharisees. They asked him, "Why then are you baptizing if you are neither the Messiah, nor Elijah, nor the prophet?" John answered them, "I baptize with water. Among you stands one whom you do not know, the one who is coming after me; I am not worthy to untie the thong of his sandal." This took place in Bethany across the Jordan where John was baptizing.

- John understood who he was—and who he wasn't. He had a strong sense of the role he played in God's plan. He could not allow his own ego or others' expectations to distract or distort his mission.

- God, I want a better sense of who I am—and who I am not. I want to embrace fully the mission you have for me. I do not want my own ego or others' expectations to get in the way of my walking the path you have set before me.

Wednesday 3rd January
John 1:29–34

The next day he saw Jesus coming towards him and declared, "Here is the Lamb of God who takes away the sin of the world! This is he of whom I said, 'After me comes a man who ranks ahead of me because he was before me.' I myself did not know him; but I came baptizing with water for this reason, that he might be revealed to Israel." And John testified, "I saw the Spirit descending from heaven like a dove, and it remained on him. I myself did not know him, but the one who sent me to baptize with water said to me, 'He on whom you see the Spirit descend and remain is the one who baptizes with the Holy Spirit.' And I myself have seen and have testified that this is the Son of God."

- "Lamb of God" evokes Old Testament passages: of the Passover lamb, and of the suffering servant in Isaiah, led like a lamb to the slaughter, bearing our sins.

- Lord, whenever I hear of some atrocious barbarism and of the injustice and pain people suffer through others' wickedness, I remember that this is the world you entered, the burden you took on yourself. You had a strong back to carry the evil that is in the world. Remind me to rely on your strength and compassion.

Thursday 4th January

John 1:35–42

The next day John again was standing with two of his disciples, and as he watched Jesus walk by, he exclaimed, "Look, here is the Lamb of God!" The two disciples heard him say this, and they followed Jesus. When Jesus turned and saw them following, he said to them, "What are you looking for?" They said to him, "Rabbi" (which translated means Teacher), "where are you staying?" He said to them, "Come and see." They came and saw where he was staying, and they remained with him that day. It was about four o'clock in the afternoon. One of the two who heard John speak and followed him was Andrew, Simon Peter's brother. He first found his brother Simon and said to him, "We have found the Messiah" (which is translated Anointed). He brought Simon to Jesus, who looked at him and said, "You are Simon son of John. You are to be called Cephas" (which is translated Peter).

- "What are you looking for?" Such a searching question that is! Many would say, "I'm not looking for anything. I am just trying to survive." But in sober moments we realize that we would like our lives to amount to more than just getting and spending, eating and sleeping.

- Lord, I want you to look at me as you looked at Simon. Invite me to see where you are to be found and to remain with you.

Friday 5th January

John 1:43–51

The next day Jesus decided to go to Galilee. He found Philip and said to him, "Follow me." Now Philip was from Bethsaida, the city of Andrew and Peter. Philip found Nathanael and said to him, "We have found him about whom Moses in the law and also the prophets wrote, Jesus son of Joseph from Nazareth." Nathanael said to him, "Can anything good come out of Nazareth?" Philip said to him, "Come and see." When Jesus saw Nathanael coming toward him, he said of him, "Here is truly an Israelite in whom there is no deceit!" Nathanael asked him, "Where did you get to know me?" Jesus answered, "I saw you under the fig tree before Philip called you." Nathanael replied, "Rabbi, you are the Son of God! You are the King of Israel!" Jesus answered, "Do you believe because I told you that I saw you under the fig tree? You will see greater things than these." And he said to him, "Very truly, I tell you, you will see heaven opened and the angels of God ascending and descending upon the Son of Man."

- "Can anything good come out of Nazareth?" Nathanael (identified with Bartholomew from the ninth century on) could have missed the chance to meet Jesus, but he heard Philip's gentle invitation, "Come and see."

- How often, Lord, have I tried to pigeon-hole people by looking down at their gender, origin, race, or family. Save me from the stupidity of those who try to seem smart by despising others. May I heed Philip and "come and see" who you are and what you offer me.

Saturday 6th January
Mark 1:7–11

[John] proclaimed, "The one who is more powerful than I is coming after me; I am not worthy to stoop down and untie the thong of his sandals. I have baptized you with water; but he will baptize you with the Holy Spirit."

In those days Jesus came from Nazareth of Galilee and was baptized by John in the Jordan. And just as he was coming up out of the water, he saw the heavens torn apart and the Spirit descending like a dove on him. And a voice came from heaven, "You are my Son, the Beloved; with you I am well pleased."

- Do we ever consider that Jesus needed to hear these words from his heavenly Father—"You are my Son, the Beloved; with you I am well pleased"? He was about to embark on his ministry. In fact, from this place of baptism he would first be severely tempted in the wilderness. He was divine but also human, and these words from heaven came at the right time.

- Lord, when I realize that you love me and are well pleased with me, I experience true freedom. I can do anything you ask. I can endure whatever is required. I can grow strong in faith and hope and love.

The Epiphany of The Lord/The First Week of Ordinary Time
January 7—January 13

Something to think and pray about each day this week:

A Simple Plan

Rather than compose elaborate resolutions for the year to come, simply do, in some small way, what you intend to do all year:

- Say "Thank you" to at least one person.
- Make one healthy choice about your body—food or drink or rest or motion.
- Do one generous act, big or small.
- Say "yes" to the day's gifts.
- Get quiet for five minutes, just to be still.
- Let one person know that you appreciate him or her.
- Do one creative act, big or small.
- Allow yourself to consider what someone else is going through.
- Do one thing well and with full attention.
- Open your arms—and your heart—to God.

If you did it today, you can do it again, and again.

—Vinita Hampton Wright on *dotMagis*, the blog of
IgnatianSpirituality.com

The Presence of God
Dear Jesus, I come to you today longing for your presence. I desire to love you as you love me. May nothing ever separate me from you.

Freedom
Lord, grant me the grace to be free from the excesses of this life. Let me not get caught up with the desire for wealth. Keep my heart and mind free to love and serve you.

Consciousness
Where do I sense hope, encouragement, and growth in my life? By looking back over the past few months, I may be able to see which activities and occasions have produced rich fruit. If I do notice such areas, I will determine to give those areas both time and space in the future.

The Word
God speaks to each of us individually. I listen attentively, to hear what he is saying to me. Read the text a few times, then listen. (Please turn to the Scripture on the following pages. Inspiration points are there should you need them. When you are ready, return here to continue.)

Conversation
What is stirring in me as I pray? Am I consoled, troubled, left cold? I imagine Jesus standing or sitting at my side, and I share my feelings with him.

Conclusion
Glory be to the Father, and to the Son, and to the Holy Spirit,
As it was in the beginning, is now and ever shall be,
World without end. Amen.

Sunday 7th January
The Epiphany of the Lord
Matthew 2:1–12

In the time of King Herod, after Jesus was born in Bethlehem of Judea, wise men from the East came to Jerusalem, asking, "Where is the child who has been born king of the Jews? For we observed his star at its rising, and have come to pay him homage." When King Herod heard this, he was frightened, and all Jerusalem with him; and calling together all the chief priests and scribes of the people, he inquired of them where the Messiah was to be born. They told him, "In Bethlehem of Judea; for so it has been written by the prophet:

'And you, Bethlehem, in the land of Judah,
    are by no means least among the rulers of Judah;
for from you shall come a ruler
    who is to shepherd my people Israel.'

Then Herod secretly called for the wise men and learned from them the exact time when the star had appeared. Then he sent them to Bethlehem, saying, "Go and search diligently for the child; and when you have found him, bring me word so that I may also go and pay him homage." When they had heard the king, they set out; and there, ahead of them, went the star that they had seen at its rising, until it stopped over the place where the child was. When they saw that the star had stopped, they were overwhelmed with joy. On entering the house, they saw the child with Mary his mother; and they knelt down and paid him homage. Then, opening their treasure chests, they offered him gifts of gold, frankincense, and myrrh. And having been warned in a dream not to return to Herod, they left for their own country by another road.

- There is a Bavarian custom of chalking G M B (Gaspar, Melchior, Balthasar) on the wall of each room of the house on Epiphany morning. These are the names that tradition assigns to the Magi, representing all the nations of the world. More and more, the nations of the world move to our shores and come into our homes. If the Magi arrived here today, would they be welcome?

- When people come to my home, Lord, do they discover you there? If justice and love are to be found in my home, then visitors, like the Magi, will be overwhelmed with joy, and they will pay you homage.

Monday 8th January
The Baptism of the Lord
Mark 1:7–11

John proclaimed, "The one who is more powerful than I is coming after me; I am not worthy to stoop down and untie the thong of his sandals. I have baptised you with water; but he will baptize you with the Holy Spirit." In those days Jesus came from Nazareth of Galilee and was baptized by John in the Jordan. And just as he was coming up out of the water, he saw the heavens torn apart and the Spirit descending like a dove on him. And a voice came from heaven, "You are my Son, the Beloved; with you I am well pleased."

- Imagine yourself witnessing the scene, perhaps standing in the shallows, the water flowing around your ankles. Picture the scene and allow it to unfold. What is it like? The young man from Nazareth joins the queue waiting for John's baptism: a symbol of purifying but also of birth—coming up out of the waters of the womb into a new life as God's beloved child.

- Lord, when I realize that you love me and are well pleased with me, it is like the start of a new life. As I hear your voice, I know that I have a purpose and a destiny.

Tuesday 9th January
Mark 1:21–28

When the sabbath came, Jesus entered the synagogue and taught. They were astounded at his teaching, for he taught them as one having authority, and not as the scribes. Just then there was in their synagogue a man with an unclean spirit, and he cried out, "What have you to do with us, Jesus of Nazareth? Have you come to destroy us? I know who you are, the Holy One of God." But Jesus rebuked him, saying, "Be silent, and come out of him!" And the unclean spirit, convulsing him and crying with a loud voice, came out of him. They were all amazed, and they kept on asking one another, "What is this? A new teaching—with authority!

He commands even the unclean spirits, and they obey him." At once his fame began to spread throughout the surrounding region of Galilee.

• At some point in their lives, people may feel themselves being brought to their knees by urges and forces that are too strong for them. They need to turn to a power above and beyond themselves.

• Jesus, with that above-and-beyond power, you come close to us—in your teaching, in the Christian community, and in the church. Remind me to ask for your help as I face other powers that seek to hold me back from your love and grace.

Wednesday 10th January
Mark 1:29–39

As soon as they left the synagogue, they entered the house of Simon and Andrew, with James and John. Now Simon's mother-in-law was in bed with a fever, and they told him about her at once. He came and took her by the hand and lifted her up. Then the fever left her, and she began to serve them. // That evening, at sunset, they brought to him all who were sick or possessed with demons. And the whole city was gathered around the door. And he cured many who were sick with various diseases, and cast out many demons; and he would not permit the demons to speak, because they knew him. // In the morning, while it was still very dark, he got up and went out to a deserted place, and there he prayed. And Simon and his companions hunted for him. When they found him, they said to him, "Everyone is searching for you." He answered, "Let us go on to the neighboring towns, so that I may proclaim the message there also; for that is what I came out to do." And he went throughout Galilee, proclaiming the message in their synagogues and casting out demons.

• Jesus does his tour, preaching and casting out devils. And we're given to understand that these two are practically the same thing—and that, were it not for the devils (who here want to find their voice!), even disease and sickness would disappear. Jesus is going into battle, head to head, with the kingdom of evil.

• When I feel powerless before outside events, and before wayward tendencies in my own heart—I ask Jesus, the strong one, to come to my side.

Thursday 11th January
Mark 1:40–45

A leper came to him begging him, and kneeling he said to him, "If you choose, you can make me clean." Moved with pity, Jesus stretched out his hand and touched him, and said to him, "I do choose. Be made clean!" Immediately the leprosy left him, and he was made clean. After sternly warning him he sent him away at once, saying to him, "See that you say nothing to anyone; but go, show yourself to the priest, and offer for your cleansing what Moses commanded, as a testimony to them." But he went out and began to proclaim it freely, and to spread the word, so that Jesus could no longer go into a town openly, but stayed out in the country; and people came to him from every quarter.

- The leper doesn't think, *I've tried others for a cure; now I'll try Jesus.* No, he just knows that Jesus has the power. His only worry is: *Will he use that power for me?* Jesus looks at me, too, ready to use his power for my good.

- Finally, the leper is so thankful that he can't stop telling people. I, too, can be aware of great things that have been done for me and can express gratitude for them in my prayer.

Friday 12th January
Mark 2:1–12

When Jesus returned to Capernaum after some days, it was reported that he was at home. So many gathered around that there was no longer room for them, not even in front of the door; and he was speaking the word to them. Then some people came, bringing to him a paralyzed man, carried by four of them. And when they could not bring him to Jesus because of the crowd, they removed the roof above him; and after having dug through it, they let down the mat on which the paralytic lay. When Jesus saw their faith, he said to the paralytic, "Son, your sins are forgiven." Now some of the scribes were sitting there, questioning in their hearts, "Why does this fellow speak in this way? It is blasphemy! Who can forgive sins but God alone?" At once Jesus perceived in his spirit that they were discussing these questions among themselves; and he said to them, "Why do you raise such questions in your hearts? Which is easier, to say to the paralytic, 'Your sins are forgiven,' or to say, 'Stand up and take your mat and walk'? But so that you may know that the Son of Man has authority on earth to forgive sins"—he said to the paralytic—"I say to you, stand up, take your mat and go to your home." And he stood up, and immediately took the mat and went out before all of them; so that they were all amazed and glorified God, saying, "We have never seen anything like this!"

- I too sometimes feel paralyzed by fears or by lack of energy. And I come before Jesus, not disguising my helplessness. I allow the strength of Jesus to take over.

- Jesus also puts my neediness in proportion; he wants me to see that his support is not just for me; it is also there for the whole world.

Saturday 13th January
Mark 2:13–17

Jesus went out again beside the sea; the whole crowd gathered around him, and he taught them. As he was walking along, he saw Levi son of Alphaeus sitting at the tax booth, and he said to him, "Follow me." And he got up and followed him. And as he sat at dinner in Levi's house, many tax collectors and sinners were also sitting with Jesus and his disciples—for there were many who followed him. When the scribes of the Pharisees saw that he was eating with sinners and tax collectors, they said to his disciples, "Why does he eat with tax collectors and sinners?" When Jesus heard this, he said to them, "Those who are well have no need of a physician, but those who are sick; I have come to call not the righteous but sinners."

- As Jesus preached by the lakeside, his words had a different impact from person to person. For some he was just a novelty. Others, perhaps, were half-interested. But the reports reaching Levi sitting in his office-booth nearby must have stirred his heart, for when Jesus invited him to be a coworker for the kingdom, Levi rose immediately with not even a thought for the career he was leaving behind.

- Levi's job—collecting the taxes for the occupying Roman government—did not endear him to his countrymen. Yet it was he who had the more attuned ear for the changed relationship with God ushered in by Jesus of Nazareth. May my heart be as well tuned, in this time and place, to what God is doing.

The Second Week of Ordinary Time
January 14—January 20

Something to think and pray about each day this week:

Thinking of the Gray
When I think of gray I think of gloom, of low clouds and cold and rain. Perhaps we get what we expect, and I need to adjust my expectations. Perhaps the presence of gray can invite us into solitude to reflect, offering time and space for a good book, a life-giving conversation. Perhaps it can open the gateway to a whole spectrum of subtle colors that we never expected to find hiding in the gray.

Everyday life can feel gray for months at a time, especially in the winter season. But what if that drab exterior holds a wealth of unknown possibilities within it? A kind word resonates gently through our day. A time of reflection draws us into deeper reaches of ourselves. A good book opens up vistas invisible in the brighter light.

—Margaret Silf in *Daily Inspiration for Women*

The Presence of God

"I am standing at the door, knocking", says the Lord. What a wonderful privilege that the Lord of all creation desires to come to me. I welcome his presence.

Freedom

I will ask God's help
to be free from my own preoccupations,
to be open to God in this time of prayer,
to come to know, love, and serve God more.

Consciousness

In God's loving presence I unwind the past day,
starting from now and looking back, moment by moment.
I gather in all the goodness and light, in gratitude.
I attend to the shadows and what they say to me,
seeking healing, courage, forgiveness.

The Word

Now I turn to the Scripture set out for me this day. I read slowly over the words and see if any sentence or sentiment appeals to me. (Please turn to the Scripture on the following pages. Inspiration points are there should you need them. When you are ready, return here to continue.)

Conversation

Sometimes I wonder what I might say if I were to meet you in person, Lord.
I think I might say "Thank you" because you are always there for me.

Conclusion

I thank God for these moments we have spent together and for any insights I have been given concerning the text.

Sunday 14th January
Second Sunday in Ordinary Time
John 1:35–42

The next day John again was standing with two of his disciples, and as he watched Jesus walk by, he exclaimed, "Look, here is the Lamb of God!" The two disciples heard him say this, and they followed Jesus. When Jesus turned and saw them following, he said to them, "What are you looking for?" They said to him, "Rabbi" (which translated means Teacher), "where are you staying?" He said to them, "Come and see." They came and saw where he was staying, and they remained with him that day. It was about four o'clock in the afternoon. One of the two who heard John speak and followed him was Andrew, Simon Peter's brother. He first found his brother Simon and said to him, "We have found the Messiah" (which is translated Anointed). He brought Simon to Jesus, who looked at him and said, "You are Simon son of John. You are to be called Cephas" (which is translated Peter).

• Andrew and his companion set aside their day to be in Jesus' company. Impressed, they decided to be his followers. When we meet a new person, we must first give ourselves a chance to get to know them. Then, if we like what we see, we are attracted by everything they stand for.

• Do we give Jesus a chance in our busy lives so that the attraction of his person can work on us?

Monday 15th January
Mark 2:18–22

Now John's disciples and the Pharisees were fasting; and people came and said to Jesus, "Why do John's disciples and the disciples of the Pharisees fast, but your disciples do not fast?" Jesus said to them, "The wedding guests cannot fast while the bridegroom is with them, can they? As long as they have the bridegroom with them, they cannot fast. The days will come when the bridegroom is taken away from them, and then they will fast on that day. // "No one sews a piece of unshrunk cloth on an old cloak; otherwise, the patch pulls away from it, the new from the old, and a worse tear is made. And no one puts new wine into old wineskins; otherwise, the wine will burst the skins, and the wine is lost, and so are the skins; but one puts new wine into fresh wineskins."

- Jesus joined our human race to raise it, by adoption, to the sphere of God in heaven. At the first Christmas, heaven was wedded to earth. The arrival of Jesus and the announcement of this great offer, then, was an occasion for deep rejoicing—just as any wedding is.

- Joy and celebration are key to the Christian life. Am I as focused on joy as I am on the "duties" of my faith?

Tuesday 16th January
Mark 2:23–28

One sabbath Jesus was going through the grainfields; and as they made their way his disciples began to pluck heads of grain. The Pharisees said to him, "Look, why are they doing what is not lawful on the sabbath?" And he said to them, "Have you never read what David did when he and his companions were hungry and in need of food? He entered the house of God, when Abiathar was high priest, and ate the bread of the Presence, which it is not lawful for any but the priests to eat, and he gave some to his companions." Then he said to them, "The sabbath was made for humankind, and not humankind for the sabbath; so the Son of Man is lord even of the sabbath."

- The Sabbath was meant to be a day of rest, when people would be free to think of God, to give thanks for God's gifts, and to take care of health and well-being. But some religious authorities gradually encroached on the Sabbath with so many regulations that it risked no longer serving its purpose.

- Do we sometimes seek security by exercising too much control over other people's lives (and perhaps too little control over our own)? By contrast, perhaps we can trust ourselves to that freedom we enjoy as God's sons and daughters, as sisters and brothers of Jesus. What might that freedom look like this day?

Wednesday 17th January
Mark 3:1–6

Jesus entered the synagogue, and a man was there who had a withered hand. They watched him to see whether he would cure him on the sabbath, so that they might accuse him. And he said to the man who had the withered hand, "Come forward." Then he said to them, "Is it lawful to do good or to do harm on the sabbath, to save life or to kill?" But they were silent. He looked around at them with anger; he was grieved at their hardness of heart and said to the man, "Stretch out your hand." He stretched it out, and his hand was restored. The Pharisees went out and immediately conspired with the Herodians against him, how to destroy him.

- Perhaps when I'm in difficulty and looking for help, people might not always go out of their way for me; they can hide behind "red tape" and regulations. But Jesus cuts through the red tape, as he did here in the synagogue, and is always ready to help me.

- Jesus can heal me. But am I an obstacle to the healing, or open to his help?

Thursday 18th January
Mark 3:7–12

Jesus departed with his disciples to the sea, and a great multitude from Galilee followed him; hearing all that he was doing, they came to him in great numbers from Judea, Jerusalem, Idumea, beyond the Jordan, and the region around Tyre and Sidon. He told his disciples to have a boat ready for him because of the crowd, so that they would not crush him; for he had cured many, so that all who had diseases pressed upon him to touch him. Whenever the unclean spirits saw him, they fell down before him and shouted, "You are the Son of God!" But he sternly ordered them not to make him known.

- Jesus finds himself suddenly a "sensation," mobbed by onlookers who have come even from foreign parts. They're satisfied with nothing less than getting to touch him.

- We, in our day, touch Jesus in many ways, including in prayer with this *Sacred Space* book, which can help us connect with him and his presence in our lives today.

Friday 19th January
Mark 3:13–19

Jesus went up the mountain and called to him those whom he wanted, and they came to him. And he appointed twelve, whom he also named apostles, to be with him, and to be sent out to proclaim the message, and to have authority to cast out demons. So he appointed the twelve: Simon (to whom he gave the name Peter); James son of Zebedee and John the brother of James (to whom he gave the name Boanerges, that is, Sons of Thunder); and Andrew, and Philip, and Bartholomew, and Matthew, and Thomas, and James son of Alphaeus, and Thaddaeus, and Simon the Cananaean, and Judas Iscariot, who betrayed him. Then he went home.

- If being a preacher of the kingdom also included the power to cast out devils, then this was a role people could not just take upon themselves. It involved a direct sharing in Jesus' own power; they had to be hand-picked and invited to it. Whenever Jesus wished to converse with his Father in prayer, as in this case, he went up into the hills. This shows how important the choosing of his twelve coworkers was to him.

- Each one of us in our own way is picked by Jesus for some task that is appointed for us and special to him. Do I know what Jesus has hand-picked me for today, at this point in my life?

Saturday 20th January
Mark 3:20–21

Then Jesus went home; and the crowd came together again, so that they could not even eat. When his family heard it, they went out to restrain him, for people were saying, "He has gone out of his mind."

- One of the most painful experiences for any person is to be let down by their nearest and dearest. With Jesus being mobbed all day by the crowds eager for his message and his help, his family were caught off guard. They just couldn't get their heads around the vast change introduced into their everyday world by his new movement, namely, Jesus' preaching of God's kingdom.

- Sometimes the urgent claims of the kingdom can turn our everyday world upside down. Sometimes kingdom work doesn't make much sense. Can I stay with Jesus and trust that everything will fall into place?

The Third Week of Ordinary Time
January 21—January 27

Something to think and pray about each day this week:

Seen Less, Not More

We followers of Christ did not come to church striving for efficiency or results, or to swagger and preen and lord it over the rest of the world. We came as sinners, as beggars. We came hungering and thirsting. We came: the blind, the deaf, the halt, the leprous, the demoniacs, the desperate, the lost, the lonely. We did not have our political views to offer; we had Christ. We did not have convincing arguments; we had our wounds, our holy longing, our groping in the dark. We didn't have clever op-eds; we had our bodies, our puny desire to be good, our lurching, guaranteed-to-fall-short striving for purity.

Here's how I knew I was very, very slowly becoming a follower of Christ. I was willing to be seen less, not more. I began to want to be quieter, not louder. I found myself making tiny sacrifices: fasting from meat for a day or giving the three bucks I would have spent at Starbucks to a homeless person. I found myself experiencing tiny moments of joy. I found myself mysteriously, ever more deeply drawn to Confession, to Mass. More and more I asked different questions from those the world asked. I looked for a different kind of result. I served a different master.

—Heather King, *Stripped: At the Intersection of Cancer, Culture, and Christ*

The Presence of God

At any time of the day or night we can call on Jesus.
He is always waiting, listening for our call.
What a wonderful blessing.
No phone needed, no emails, just a whisper.

Freedom

If God were trying to tell me something, would I know?
If God were reassuring me or challenging me, would I notice?
I ask for the grace to be free of my own preoccupations
and open to what God may be saying to me.

Consciousness

Help me, Lord, become more conscious of your presence. Teach me to recognize your presence in others. Fill my heart with gratitude for the times your love has been shown to me through the care of others.

The Word

In this expectant state of mind, please turn to the text for the day with confidence. Believe that the Holy Spirit is present and may reveal whatever the passage has to say to you. Read reflectively, listening with a third ear to what may be going on in your heart. (Please turn to the Scripture on the following pages. Inspiration points are there should you need them. When you are ready, return here to continue.)

Conversation

Conversation requires talking and listening.
As I talk to Jesus, may I also learn to pause and listen.
I picture the gentleness in his eyes and the love in his smile.
I can be totally honest with Jesus as I tell him my worries and cares.
I will open my heart to Jesus as I tell him my fears and doubts.
I will ask him to help me place myself fully in his care, knowing that he always desires good for me.

Conclusion

I thank God for these moments we have spent together and for any insights I have been given concerning the text.

Sunday 21st January
Third Sunday in Ordinary Time
Mark 1:14–20

Now after John was arrested, Jesus came to Galilee, proclaiming the good news of God, and saying, "The time is fulfilled, and the kingdom of God has come near; repent, and believe in the good news." As Jesus passed along the Sea of Galilee, he saw Simon and his brother Andrew casting a net into the sea—for they were fishermen. And Jesus said to them, "Follow me and I will make you fish for people." And immediately they left their nets and followed him. As he went a little farther, he saw James son of Zebedee and his brother John, who were in their boat mending the nets. Immediately he called them; and they left their father Zebedee in the boat with the hired men, and followed him.

• Had Simon and Andrew, James and John already been in the audience—in the synagogue, or at their mooring by the lakeshore—when Jesus first preached the coming of God's kingdom? Had they already in some way sensed what Jesus was about? Did they already realize that in his work he was going to need followers? Whatever the case, when Jesus called them, they needed no second invitation.

• Is there something prompting me, telling me how I too could do more for Christ's kingdom?

Monday 22nd January
Mark 3:22–30

And the scribes who came down from Jerusalem said, "He has Beelzebul, and by the ruler of the demons he casts out demons." And he called them to him, and spoke to them in parables, "How can Satan cast out Satan? If a kingdom is divided against itself, that kingdom cannot stand. And if a house is divided against itself, that house will not be able to stand. And if Satan has risen up against himself and is divided, he cannot stand, but his end has come. But no one can enter a strong man's house and plunder his property without first tying up the strong man; then indeed the house can be plundered. // "Truly I tell you, people will be forgiven for their sins and whatever blasphemies they utter; but whoever blasphemes against the Holy Spirit can never have forgiveness, but is guilty of an eternal sin"—for they had said, "He has an unclean spirit."

- How easy it is to accuse one you do not understand or like of being evil. The scribes could not understand Jesus; therefore, he must be working by the power of Beelzebul. This is not as extreme as it sounds. When was the last time I suggested that someone—perhaps a public figure I really dislike—was horrible, stupid, or out to hurt others?

- Jesus speaks to the scribes in a no-nonsense, logical way. They are, after all, the attorneys of that day; they need a rational explanation. In my life, too, Lord, you speak to me in ways that make sense to me, in ways I can hear you. Thank you.

Tuesday 23rd January
Mark 3:31–35

Then Jesus' mother and his brothers came; and standing outside, they sent to him and called him. A crowd was sitting around him; and they said to him, "Your mother and brothers and sisters are outside, asking for you." And he replied, "Who are my mother and my brothers?" And looking at those who sat around him, he said, "Here are my mother and my brothers! Whoever does the will of God is my brother and sister and mother."

- We can picture members of the crowd, no doubt more eager to hear what he had to say, ranging themselves in a circle round Jesus. Would Jesus leave them to go see his family? Would he introduce them to his mother and brothers? Wasn't his response rather harsh? Was he disrespecting his mother?

- Jesus had already been inviting those who heard him to the totally new life of members of the kingdom of heaven. Then, born into that new life, *they* would be his brothers and sisters in a new way. And this bond would become even deeper than the normal ties of family. This is the invitation Jesus still extends to all of us.

Wednesday 24th January
Mark 4:1–20

Again Jesus began to teach beside the sea. Such a very large crowd gathered around him that he got into a boat on the sea and sat there, while the whole crowd was beside the sea on the land. He began to teach them many things in parables, and in his teaching he said to them: "Listen! A sower went out to sow. And as he sowed, some seed fell on the path, and the birds came and ate it up. Other seed fell on rocky ground, where it did not have much soil, and it sprang up quickly, since it had no depth of soil. And when the sun rose, it was scorched; and since it had no root, it withered away. Other seed fell among thorns, and the thorns grew up and choked it, and it yielded no grain. Other seed fell into good soil and brought forth grain, growing up and increasing and yielding thirty and sixty and a hundredfold." And he said, "Let anyone with ears to hear listen!" When he was alone, those who were around him along with the twelve asked him about the parables. And he said to them, "To you has been given the secret of the kingdom of God, but for those outside, everything comes in parables; in order that 'they may indeed look, but not perceive, and may indeed listen, but not understand; so that they may not turn again and be forgiven.'" And he said to them, "Do you not understand this parable? Then how will you understand all the parables? The sower sows the word. These are the ones on the path where the word is sown: when they hear, Satan immediately comes and takes away the word that is sown in them. And these are the ones sown on rocky ground: when they hear the word, they immediately receive it with joy. But they have no root, and endure only for a while; then, when trouble or persecution arises on account of the word, immediately they fall away. And others are those sown among the thorns: these are the ones who hear the word, but the cares of the world, and the lure of wealth, and the desire for other things come in and choke the word, and it yields nothing. And these are the ones sown on the good soil: they hear the word and accept it and bear fruit, thirty and sixty and a hundredfold."

• I try to take to heart the words of Jesus, and Jesus is more eager still for that message to take root in my heart. Sometimes, perhaps, I may just admire his teaching from a distance, treat it as a novelty. Or there can be days when I'm easily diverted by some other attraction or competing values and interests in my life.

• Lord, give me the grace to allow the word of God to take root in my heart, and bear fruit in my words and actions.

Thursday 25th January
Mark 16:15–18

And he said to them, "Go into all the world and proclaim the good news to the whole creation. The one who believes and is baptized will be saved; but the one who does not believe will be condemned. And these signs will accompany those who believe: by using my name they will cast out demons; they will speak in new tongues; they will pick up snakes in their hands, and if they drink any deadly thing, it will not hurt them; they will lay their hands on the sick, and they will recover."

- At one point Jesus said that it was to the "lost sheep of the house of Israel" (of the Jewish people) that he had been sent. But in this scene, as he leaves this earth and ascends into heaven, he tells his followers to set no bounds to their preaching—they are to "take on" the whole pagan world.

- Saint Paul was to be the great example of this. We celebrate today this special "call" which followed his conversion to the cause of Christ. From now on, nobody is to be considered "out of bounds" when it comes to spreading Jesus' message.

Friday 26th January
Mark 4:26–34

Jesus also said, "The kingdom of God is as if someone would scatter seed on the ground, and would sleep and rise night and day, and the seed would sprout and grow, he does not know how. The earth produces of itself, first the stalk, then the head, then the full grain in the head. But when the grain is ripe, at once he goes in with his sickle, because the harvest has come." He also said, "With what can we compare the kingdom of God, or what parable will we use for it? It is like a mustard seed, which, when sown upon the ground, is the smallest of all the seeds on earth; yet when it is sown it grows up and becomes the greatest of all shrubs, and puts forth large branches, so that the birds of the air can make nests in its shade." With many such parables he spoke the word to them, as they were able to hear it; he did not speak to them except in parables, but he explained everything in private to his disciples.

- Whenever we think of a "miracle," what comes to mind is an instant miracle. But there's also a slow-motion miracle: the miracle of growth.

This may not be a one-off event that is being concluded before our eyes, but over time it's still a real happening. And God's hidden hand is giving it direction.

• My life is God's "project." I must leave God free to keep working on me. Then I'll be God's work of art.

Saturday 27th January
Mark 4:35–41

On that day, when evening had come, Jesus said to the disciples, "Let us go across to the other side." And leaving the crowd behind, they took him with them in the boat, just as he was. Other boats were with him. A great windstorm arose, and the waves beat into the boat, so that the boat was already being swamped. But he was in the stern, asleep on the cushion; and they woke him up and said to him, "Teacher, do you not care that we are perishing?" He woke up and rebuked the wind, and said to the sea, "Peace! Be still!" Then the wind ceased, and there was a dead calm. He said to them, "Why are you afraid? Have you still no faith?" And they were filled with great awe and said to one another, "Who then is this, that even the wind and the sea obey him?"

• Jesus rebukes the storm, with all the authority of a trainer bringing an unruly animal to heel. The disciples now have to totally revise their view of what they are dealing with in Jesus.

• Jesus is always looking out for my needs, even if he seems to be asleep.

The Fourth Week of Ordinary Time
January 28—February 3

Something to think and pray about each day this week:

Living Lightly

Your life is an overflowing closet. You know it is. There are sweatshirts folded up in a corner of your mind where your children's birthdays should be stored. That worry about the rust on the car is taking up the space that you had reserved for a slow cup of tea in the morning. I know how you feel. And guess what? There's a way to get stuff back where it belongs: let go of some of it.

Living lightly is not just about the stuff we accumulate, and it's not just for people in the second half of life. It's about an attitude of living with fewer burdens and encumbrances, whether you're twenty-one or sixty-five. When done with honest self-awareness, the journey toward living more lightly has moved me to realize that I am blessed by less. Less stuff and worries have opened space to live with more contentment and meaning. Living lightly reminds me that my existence is more than accumulating possessions and status. Ultimately, I am on a spiritual pilgrimage.

As I continue to strip away the unnecessary stuff in my closets and mind, I've been able to see more clearly how much is enough and how much is more than enough. It's a delicate dance to balance my own genuine needs with those of others. The spiritual paradox is that the less tightly I cling to my stuff, my way, and my concerns, the happier and more blessed I feel. Once I have enough, less is more.

—Susan V. Vogt, *Blessed by Less*

The Presence of God

As I sit here, the beating of my heart,
the ebb and flow of my breathing, the movements of my mind
are all signs of God's ongoing creation of me.
I pause for a moment and become aware
of this presence of God within me.

Freedom

It is so easy to get caught up
with the trappings of wealth in this life.
Grant, O Lord, that I may be free
from greed and selfishness.
Remind me that the best things in life are free:
Love, laughter, caring, and sharing.

Consciousness

Knowing that God loves me unconditionally, I can afford to be honest
about how I am.
How has the day been, and how do I feel now? I share my feelings openly
with the Lord.

The Word

Lord Jesus, you became human to communicate with me.
You walked and worked on this earth.
You endured the heat and struggled with the cold.
All your time on this earth was spent in caring for humanity.
You healed the sick, you raised the dead.
Most important of all, you saved me from death.
(Please turn to the Scripture on the following pages. Inspiration points
are there should you need them. When you are ready, return here to
continue.)

Conversation

Sometimes I wonder what I might say if I were to meet you in person,
Lord.
I think I might say "Thank you" because you are always there for me

Conclusion

I thank God for these moments we have spent together and for any insights I have been given concerning the text.

Sunday 28th January
Fourth Sunday in Ordinary Time
Mark 1:21–28

When the sabbath came, Jesus entered the synagogue and taught. They were astounded at his teaching, for he taught them as one having authority, and not as the scribes. Just then there was in their synagogue a man with an unclean spirit, and he cried out, "What have you to do with us, Jesus of Nazareth? Have you come to destroy us? I know who you are, the Holy One of God." But Jesus rebuked him, saying, "Be silent, and come out of him!" And the unclean spirit, convulsing him and crying with a loud voice, came out of him. They were all amazed, and they kept on asking one another, "What is this? A new teaching—with authority! He commands even the unclean spirits, and they obey him." At once his fame began to spread throughout the surrounding region of Galilee.

- At some point in their lives people may feel themselves being brought to their knees by urges and forces that are too strong for them. They need to turn to a power above and beyond themselves.

- Jesus, with that power behind him, comes close to each one of us—in his teaching, in the Christian community, in the church.

Monday 29th January
Mark 5:1–20

They came to the other side of the sea, to the country of the Gerasenes. And when he had stepped out of the boat, immediately a man out of the tombs with an unclean spirit met him. He lived among the tombs; and no one could restrain him any more, even with a chain; for he had often been restrained with shackles and chains, but the chains he wrenched apart, and the shackles he broke in pieces; and no one had the strength to subdue him. Night and day among the tombs and on the mountains he was always howling and bruising himself with stones. When he saw Jesus from a distance, he ran and bowed down before him; and he shouted at the top of his voice, "What have you to do with me, Jesus, Son of the Most High God? I adjure you by God, do not torment me." For he had said to him, "Come out of the man, you unclean spirit!" Then Jesus asked him, "What is your name?" He replied, "My name is Legion; for we are many." He begged him earnestly not to send them out of the country.

Now there on the hillside a great herd of swine was feeding; and the unclean spirits begged him, "Send us into the swine; let us enter them." So he gave them permission. And the unclean spirits came out and entered the swine; and the herd, numbering about two thousand, rushed down the steep bank into the sea, and were drowned in the sea. The swineherds ran off and told it in the city and in the country. Then people came to see what it was that had happened. They came to Jesus and saw the demoniac sitting there, clothed and in his right mind, the very man who had had the legion; and they were afraid. Those who had seen what had happened to the demoniac and to the swine reported it. Then they began to beg Jesus to leave their neighborhood. As he was getting into the boat, the man who had been possessed by demons begged him that he might be with him. But Jesus refused, and said to him, "Go home to your friends, and tell them how much the Lord has done for you, and what mercy he has shown you." And he went away and began to proclaim in the Decapolis how much Jesus had done for him; and everyone was amazed.

- There is drama in this exorcism. It pits the demon, who torments the possessed man, against the calm power of Jesus. The demon recognizes Jesus' power and authority, and obeys his command to go out of the man. Lord, when I fear the forces of evil, in others or in myself, I remember that you took on the demons and defeated them. In you I have a Savior against whom the devil is powerless.

- The healed man had asked to go with Jesus but, at Jesus' request, he stays in his own place to announce the gospel. Our call to work with Jesus and our partnership with him is on Jesus' initiative. As disciples, we wait to be told what to do and where to minister. In prayer, we may sense his call to take part with him in his work.

Tuesday 30th January
Mark 5:21–43

When Jesus had crossed again in the boat to the other side, a great crowd gathered round him; and he was by the sea. Then one of the leaders of the synagogue named Jairus came and, when he saw him, fell at his feet and begged him repeatedly, "My little daughter is at the point of death. Come and lay your hands on her, so that she may be made well, and live." So he went with him. And a large crowd followed him and pressed in on him. Now there was a woman who had been suffering from hemorrhages for twelve years. She had endured much under many physicians, and had spent all that she had; and she was no better, but rather grew worse. She had heard about Jesus, and came up behind him in the crowd and touched his cloak, for she said, "If I but touch his clothes, I will be made well." Immediately her hemorrhage stopped; and she felt in her body that she was healed of her disease. Immediately aware that power had gone forth from him, Jesus turned about in the crowd and said, "Who touched my clothes?" And his disciples said to him, "You see the crowd pressing in on you; how can you say, 'Who touched me?'" He looked all round to see who had done it. But the woman, knowing what had happened to her, came in fear and trembling, fell down before him, and told him the whole truth. He said to her, "Daughter, your faith has made you well; go in peace, and be healed of your disease." // While he was still speaking, some people came from the leader's house to say, "Your daughter is dead. Why trouble the teacher any further?" But overhearing what they said, Jesus said to the leader of the synagogue, "Do not fear, only believe." He allowed no one to follow him except Peter, James, and John, the brother of James. When they came to the house of the leader of the synagogue, he saw a commotion, people weeping and wailing loudly. When he had entered, he said to them, "Why do you make a commotion and weep? The child is not dead but sleeping." And they laughed at him. Then he put them all outside, and took the child's father and mother and those who were with him, and went in where the child was. He took her by the hand and said to her, "Talitha cum," which means, "Little girl, get up!" And immediately the girl got up and began to walk about (she was twelve years of age). At this they were overcome with amazement. He strictly ordered them that no one should know this, and told them to give her something to eat.

- Here we find situations where human solutions fail. "She is at the point of death" . . . "She grew worse" . . . "She is dead." But Jesus confronts human hopelessness. The needs of the sick and the faith of those concerned evoke a compassionate response from him. He is tender to the two women. He calls one, "Daughter!" and the other, "Little girl" (literally "Little lamb").

- In my need, I too can turn to Jesus and find healing. That healing will focus on my heart: my negativity, bad moods, hurtful responses, and hardness. He is always trying to help me grow in love. Then I can in turn become a tender and healing presence to those around me.

Wednesday 31st January
Mark 6:1–6

Jesus left that place and came to his hometown, and his disciples followed him. On the sabbath he began to teach in the synagogue, and many who heard him were astounded. They said, "Where did this man get all this? What is this wisdom that has been given to him? What deeds of power are being done by his hands! Is not this the carpenter, the son of Mary and brother of James and Joses and Judas and Simon, and are not his sisters here with us?" And they took offense at him. Then Jesus said to them, "Prophets are not without honor, except in their hometown, and among their own kin, and in their own house." And he could do no deed of power there, except that he laid his hands on a few sick people and cured them. And he was amazed at their unbelief. Then he went about among the villages teaching.

- Francois Mauriac wrote in his life of Jesus: "It is baffling to record that, for a period of thirty years, the Son of Man did not appear to be anything other than a man. Those who lived with him thought they knew him. He fixed their tables and chairs. They ate and drank with his extended family. When he stepped outside the role they had fixed for him, they put him down as just a workman."

- Lord, there are depths in each of us, even those we think we know well, that only you can glimpse. A put-down tells more about the speaker than about the victim. Save me, Lord, from such folly.

Thursday 1st February
Mark 6:7–13

Jesus called the twelve and began to send them out two by two, and gave them authority over the unclean spirits. He ordered them to take nothing for their journey except a staff; no bread, no bag, no money in their belts; but to wear sandals and not to put on two tunics. He said to them, "Wherever you enter a house, stay there until you leave the place. If any place will not welcome you and they refuse to hear you, as you leave, shake off the dust that is on your feet as a testimony against them." So they went out and proclaimed that all should repent. They cast out many demons, and anointed with oil many who were sick and cured them.

- These instructions in Mark's Gospel indicate the way of proceeding for the disciples whom Jesus sent out. Communication of the good news had to be by word of mouth, and it depended on travelling missionaries. Many listeners could not read, and Jesus stressed not so much the message as the medium—the lifestyle of the preachers.

- Then as now, people judged the message of Christ by the life of the messengers more than by the words they spoke. Dom Helder Camara, the saintly Brazilian bishop of the dispossessed, used to tell his catechists, who were speaking to illiterate people: "Sisters and brothers, watch how you live. Your lives may be the only gospel your listeners will ever read." Forgive me, Lord, for the times when my lifestyle distorted your gospel.

Friday 2nd February
The Presentation of the Lord
Luke 2:22–40

When the time came for their purification according to the law of Moses, they brought him up to Jerusalem to present him to the Lord (as it is written in the law of the Lord, "Every firstborn male shall be designated as holy to the Lord"), and they offered a sacrifice according to what is stated in the law of the Lord, "a pair of turtle-doves or two young pigeons." // Now there was a man in Jerusalem whose name was Simeon; this man was righteous and devout, looking forward to the consolation of Israel, and the Holy Spirit rested on him. It had been revealed to him by the Holy Spirit that he would not see death before he had seen the Lord's Messiah. Guided by the Spirit, Simeon came into the temple; and when the parents brought in the child Jesus, to do for him what was customary under the law, Simeon took him in his arms and praised God, saying,

"Master, now you are dismissing your servant in peace,
    according to your word;

for my eyes have seen your salvation,
  which you have prepared in the presence of all peoples,
a light for revelation to the Gentiles
  and for glory to your people Israel."

And the child's father and mother were amazed at what was being said about him. Then Simeon blessed them and said to his mother Mary, "This child is destined for the falling and the rising of many in Israel, and to be a sign that will be opposed so that the inner thoughts of many will be revealed—and a sword will pierce your own soul too." // There was also a prophet, Anna the daughter of Phanuel, of the tribe of Asher. She was of a great age, having lived with her husband for seven years after her marriage, then as a widow to the age of eighty-four. She never left the temple but worshipped there with fasting and prayer night and day. At that moment she came, and began to praise God and to speak about the child to all who were looking for the redemption of Jerusalem. // When they had finished everything required by the law of the Lord, they returned to Galilee, to their own town of Nazareth. The child grew and became strong, filled with wisdom; and the favor of God was upon him.

- At the presentation in the temple, Mary and Joseph made "the offering of the poor": two pigeons instead of the lamb, which was the offering of wealthier people. They met Simeon, one of "the quiet in the land" Jews who awaited God's coming to his people in a spirit of prayer and quiet watchfulness, rather than the expectation of a triumphant warlord. In my prayer, I join Mary in listening to Simeon's lovely but loaded message.

- As I meditate on the story of the presentation in the temple, I let God speak to me especially through the words of Simeon.

Saturday 3rd February
Mark 6:30–34

The apostles gathered around Jesus, and told him all that they had done and taught. He said to them, "Come away to a deserted place all by yourselves and rest a while." For many were coming and going, and they had no leisure even to eat. And they went away in the boat to a deserted place by themselves. Now many saw them going and recognized them, and they hurried there on foot from all the towns and arrived ahead of them. As he went ashore, he saw a great crowd; and he had compassion for them, because they were like sheep without a shepherd; and he began to teach them many things.

• As you read today's material from this book, you are answering Jesus' invitation to come away to a deserted place and rest a while. Do not be afraid of being alone. Fear rather the opposite: as Blaise Pascal wrote, "The sole cause of man's unhappiness is that he does not know how to stay quietly in his room."

• Lord, there are times when I want to get away from the crowds, when I feel oppressed by company. There are other times when I just wish somebody knew that I exist; I can have too much of aloneness. If I can reach you in prayer and know that you are more central to me than my own thoughts, I feel at peace, as the apostles must have felt.

The Fifth Week of Ordinary Time
February 4—February 10

Something to think and pray about each day this week:

The Divine in Life

If we believe that a Divine Presence brought all of creation into being and it was good, then it follows that this God loves us unconditionally and sees our goodness despite our human failings. God's love for us is not dependent on our possessions, appearance, or accomplishments.

St. Ignatius of Loyola, who gave us the Spiritual Exercises that have been used to help people's spiritual formation for nearly five centuries, describes these attributes of a spiritually healthy and balanced life as follows:

- Detachment from the things and worries of this world.

- Spiritual freedom from all that might distract us from the ultimate purpose of our life in order to focus on what is essential—a deeper relationship with God.

- The practiced ability to find God's presence "in all things"—in our ordinary situations.

As we seek to recognize the Divine in all of life, we humans grow in the awareness that it's not all about me. We start to see more clearly what is important and what our personal false gods may be. Our human and planetary lives need many things to survive, but the more we can free ourselves from undue attachment to things that will pass away, the deeper our happiness will be.

—Susan V. Vogt, *Blessed by Less*

The Presence of God

"Come to me, all you who are weary and are carrying heavy burdens, and I will give you rest." Here I am, Lord. I come to seek your presence. I long for your healing power.

Freedom

God is not foreign to my freedom. The Spirit breathes life into my most intimate desires, gently nudging me toward all that is good. I ask for the grace to let myself be enfolded by the Spirit.

Consciousness

I remind myself that I am in the presence of the Lord. I will take refuge in his loving heart. He is my strength in times of weakness. He is my comforter in times of sorrow.

The Word

I take my time to read the word of God slowly, a few times, allowing myself to dwell on anything that strikes me. (Please turn to the Scripture on the following pages. Inspiration points are there should you need them. When you are ready, return here to continue.)

Conversation

Jesus, you always welcomed little children when you walked on this earth. Teach me to have a childlike trust in you. Teach me to live in the knowledge that you will never abandon me.

Conclusion

Glory be to the Father, and to the Son, and to the Holy Spirit,
As it was in the beginning, is now and ever shall be,
World without end. Amen.

Sunday 4th February
Fifth Sunday in Ordinary Time
Mark 1:29–39

As soon as they left the synagogue, they entered the house of Simon and Andrew, with James and John. Now Simon's mother-in-law was in bed with a fever, and they told him about her at once. He came and took her by the hand and lifted her up. Then the fever left her, and she began to serve them. // That evening, at sunset, they brought to him all who were sick or possessed with demons. And the whole city was gathered around the door. And he cured many who were sick with various diseases, and cast out many demons; and he would not permit the demons to speak, because they knew him. // In the morning, while it was still very dark, he got up and went out to a deserted place, and there he prayed. And Simon and his companions hunted for him. When they found him, they said to him, 'Everyone is searching for you.' He answered, 'Let us go on to the neighboring towns, so that I may proclaim the message there also; for that is what I came out to do.' And he went throughout Galilee, proclaiming the message in their synagogues and casting out demons."

• Jesus does his tour preaching and casting out devils. And we're given to understand that these two are practically the same thing—and that, were it not for the devils (who here want to find their voice!), even disease and sickness would disappear. Jesus is going into battle, head to head, with the kingdom of evil.

• When I feel powerless before outside events, and before wayward tendencies in my own heart, I ask Jesus, the strong one, to come to my side.

Monday 5th February
Mark 6:53–56

When Jesus and the disciples had crossed over, they came to land at Gennesaret and moored the boat. When they got out of the boat, people at once recognized him, and rushed about that whole region and began to bring the sick on mats to wherever they heard he was. And wherever he went, into villages or cities or farms, they laid the sick in the market-places, and begged him that they might touch even the fringe of his cloak; and all who touched it were healed.

- Lord Jesus, I would not like to be thought of as a user—someone who in a selfish way exploits family, friends, church, or even God. If I feel I am being used, I resent it. But in this scene, you are being used to the point of exhaustion, and you react as you urged us to react, without a trace of resentment.

- Help me, great Healer, to see the crowds as people in need, as ones you love. May I see their need for you more than their demands on me.

Tuesday 6th February
Mark 7:1–13

Now when the Pharisees and some of the scribes who had come from Jerusalem gathered around him, they noticed that some of his disciples were eating with defiled hands, that is, without washing them. (For the Pharisees, and all the Jews, do not eat unless they thoroughly wash their hands, thus observing the tradition of the elders; and they do not eat anything from the market unless they wash it; and there are also many other traditions that they observe, the washing of cups, pots, and bronze kettles.) So the Pharisees and the scribes asked him, "Why do your disciples not live according to the tradition of the elders, but eat with defiled hands?" He said to them, "Isaiah prophesied rightly about you hypocrites, as it is written,

'This people honors me with their lips,
    but their hearts are far from me;
in vain do they worship me,
    teaching human precepts as doctrines.'

You abandon the commandment of God and hold to human tradition." // Then he said to them, "You have a fine way of rejecting the commandment of God in order to keep your tradition! For Moses said, 'Honor your father and your mother'; and, 'Whoever speaks evil of father or mother must surely die.' But you say that if anyone tells father or mother, 'Whatever support you might have had from me is Corban' (that is, an offering to God)—then you no longer permit doing anything for a father or mother, thus making void the word of God through your tradition that you have handed on. And you do many things like this."

- Jesus, with his uneducated disciples, is mixing with sophisticated Pharisees from Jerusalem, men who have mastered the intricate rules about ritual purity and who look down on those who are ignorant of them. As Christians, we can set up our own norms of what is god-fearing and respectable and forget that it is the heart that matters.

- Jesus, you always see through the externals of behavior to the love and goodness that may lie beneath. Give me such vision as I deal with the various people I encounter.

Wednesday 7th February
Mark 7:14–23

Then he called the crowd again and said to them, "Listen to me, all of you, and understand: there is nothing outside a person that by going in can defile, but the things that come out are what defile." // When he had left the crowd and entered the house, his disciples asked him about the parable. He said to them, "Then do you also fail to understand? Do you not see that whatever goes into a person from outside cannot defile, since it enters, not the heart but the stomach, and goes out into the sewer?" (Thus he declared all foods clean.) And he said, "It is what comes out of a person that defiles. For it is from within, from the human heart, that evil intentions come: fornication, theft, murder, adultery, avarice, wickedness, deceit, licentiousness, envy, slander, pride, folly. All these evil things come from within, and they defile a person."

- For Jesus, the battlefield between good and evil is the human heart, and my heart is included! How clean is my heart? In Psalm 51, I ask God to create in me a clean heart. It is not something I can do on my own, much as I try to be respectable before I meet with God in prayer.

- We know the difference between clean and sticky fingers, and our hearts can be sticky too. We can be grasping, spoil things for others, and leave our smudge on them. We can make things difficult for others, humiliate them, and reduce them to tears. Lord, you list twelve evil intentions that defile a person. Reveal to me the one I need to address right now!

Thursday 8th February
Mark 7:24–30

From there Jesus set out and went away to the region of Tyre. He entered a house and did not want anyone to know he was there. Yet he could not escape notice, but a woman whose little daughter had an unclean spirit immediately heard about him, and she came and bowed down at his feet. Now the woman was a Gentile, of Syrophoenician origin. She begged him to cast the demon out of her daughter. He said to her, "Let the children be fed first, for it is not fair to take the children's food and throw it to the dogs." But she answered him, "Sir, even the dogs under the table eat the children's crumbs." Then he said to her, "For saying that, you may go— the demon has left your daughter." So she went home, found the child lying on the bed, and the demon gone.

- In all the Gospels, only this non-Jewish lady gets the better of Jesus. A decisive woman, she goes into action as soon as she hears about him. She has a strong sense of herself; his dismissive remark does not diminish her. She sticks to what she wants: the cure of her little daughter. The dialogue teaches me something about the directness of prayer. It is to be an interpersonal encounter.

- It seems that the early church needed reminding that it was meant to reach out to the Gentiles. Hence this tale is recorded. Pope Francis today tells us that everyone must be an evangelizer, reaching out to the alienated. Jesus' horizons are enlarged in this scene; in what ways might my horizons expand in this place and time?

Friday 9th February
Mark 7:31–37

Then Jesus returned from the region of Tyre, and went by way of Sidon towards the Sea of Galilee, in the region of the Decapolis. They brought to him a deaf man who had an impediment in his speech; and they begged him to lay his hand on him. He took him aside in private, away from the crowd, and put his fingers into his ears, and he spat and touched his tongue. Then looking up to heaven, he sighed and said to him, "Ephphatha," that is, "Be opened." And immediately his ears were opened, his tongue was released, and he spoke plainly. Then Jesus ordered them to tell no one; but the more he ordered them, the more zealously they proclaimed it. They were astounded beyond measure, saying, "He has done everything well; he even makes the deaf to hear and the mute to speak."

- "They brought to him a deaf man." I often bring others to God's attention, asking that they may be healed, and that is good. Can I also allow others to bring me before God? Do I ask others to pray for me?

- Let me spend a few moments with that man. I imagine myself before Jesus, gazing at him but unable to hear him, unable to speak. I can only see, so I follow him to a quiet spot, feel his fingers in my ears and on my tongue. Suddenly the world of sound opens to me, and my tongue is freed. What are my first words?

Saturday 10th February
Mark 8:1–10

In those days when there was again a great crowd without anything to eat, he called his disciples and said to them, "I have compassion for the crowd, because they have been with me now for three days and have nothing to eat. If I send them away hungry to their homes, they will faint on the way—and some of them have come from a great distance." His disciples replied, "How can one feed these people with bread here in the desert?" He asked them, "How many loaves do you have?" They said, "Seven." Then he ordered the crowd to sit down on the ground; and he took the seven loaves, and after giving thanks he broke them and gave them to his disciples to distribute; and they distributed them to the crowd. They had also a few small fish; and after blessing them, he ordered that these too should be distributed. They ate and were filled; and they took up the broken pieces left over, seven baskets full. Now there were about four thousand people. And he sent them away. And immediately he got into the boat with his disciples and went to the district of Dalmanutha.

- "I have compassion," says Jesus. I need to have it too. Compassion means that when faced with misery, you are moved "to the very guts," and you try to help. Have I ever experienced deep compassion from someone—a parent, a friend, a nurse, a teacher? Do I sense God's compassion toward me? But of course, if I do not acknowledge my needs, the compassion of others will be irrelevant.

- "How can one feed these people?" The disciples do not yet understand that nothing is impossible to God. Jesus does not scold them; instead, he provides bread in abundance. Our God is a lavish God. Later, in the Passion, it will be he himself who, like the bread, is taken, blessed, broken, and given. The pattern of my life is to be the same. I am to be taken, blessed, broken, and given, until, like Jesus, I am emptied out, and yet mysteriously filled with love.

The Sixth Week of Ordinary Time
February 11—February 17

Something to think and pray about each day this week:

Preparing for Lent
The preparation before prayer is important. It allows us to physically carve out space in our day for prayer, and it allows our minds to be mentally ready for prayer. The same idea of preparation that St. Ignatius suggests can be helpful in our preparation for Lent.

- Have we physically set aside a prayer space for our Lenten journey?

- What time of day will we pray during Lent?

- What are the "exercises" or prayer methods we will be using during Lent?

In our preparatory prayer, we pray for specific graces. What is the grace we desire to deepen within us during Lent?

- To deepen our understanding of Jesus' Passion?

- To walk with Jesus through his Passion and Resurrection?

- To work on overcoming a temptation that keeps us from fully entering into life with Christ?

- To foster a new spiritual practice to ignite or inflame our relationship with Jesus?

In this week of Ash Wednesday, I invite us to begin our preparatory prayer. We can turn to Jesus and ask, "What is the grace you desire to deepen within me over these next 40 days?"

—Becky Eldredge on *dotMagis*, the blog of *IgnatianSpirituality.com*
http://www.ignatianspirituality.com/15261/preparation-for-lent

The Presence of God

What is present to me is what has a hold on my becoming.
I reflect on the presence of God always there in love,
amidst the many things that have a hold on me.
I pause and pray that I may let God
affect my becoming in this precise moment.

Freedom

By God's grace I was born to live in freedom. Free to enjoy the pleasures
he created for me. Dear Lord, grant that I may live as you intended, with
complete confidence in your loving care.

Consciousness

I exist in a web of relationships: links to nature, people, God.
I trace out these links, giving thanks for the life that flows through them.
Some links are twisted or broken; I may feel regret, anger, disappointment.
I pray for the gift of acceptance and forgiveness.

The Word

God speaks to each of us individually. I listen attentively, to hear what he
is saying to me. Read the text a few times, then listen. (Please turn to the
Scripture on the following pages. Inspiration points are there should you
need them. When you are ready, return here to continue.)

Conversation

I begin to talk with Jesus about the Scripture I have just read. What part
of it strikes a chord in me? Perhaps the words of a friend—or some story
I have heard recently—will rise to the surface in my consciousness. If so,
does the story throw light on what the Scripture passage may be saying
to me?

Conclusion

Glory be to the Father, and to the Son, and to the Holy Spirit,
As it was in the beginning, is now and ever shall be,
World without end. Amen.

Sunday 11th February
Sixth Sunday in Ordinary Time
Mark 1:40–45

A leper came to him begging him, and kneeling he said to him, "If you choose, you can make me clean." Moved with pity, Jesus stretched out his hand and touched him, and said to him, "I do choose. Be made clean!" Immediately the leprosy left him, and he was made clean. After sternly warning him he sent him away at once, saying to him, "See that you say nothing to anyone; but go, show yourself to the priest, and offer for your cleansing what Moses commanded, as a testimony to them." But he went out and began to proclaim it freely, and to spread the word, so that Jesus could no longer go into a town openly, but stayed out in the country; and people came to him from every quarter.

- The leper wonders if he is worthy of Jesus' help. He knows Jesus has the power to do anything—but will that power be directed to an outcast leper? We know God loves and heals. But do I expect that, today, God's love and healing are meant for me?

- Finally, the leper is so thankful that he can't stop telling people. How do I express my gratitude? Do I freely talk about the ways in which God touches my life?

Monday 12th February
Mark 8:11–13

The Pharisees came and began to argue with Jesus, asking him for a sign from heaven, to test him. And he sighed deeply in his spirit and said, "Why does this generation ask for a sign? Truly I tell you, no sign will be given to this generation." And he left them, and getting into the boat again, he went across to the other side.

- It was customary for Pharisees to debate about the meaning of the Law and aspects of the Jewish faith. But here, they have become hostile toward Jesus. From now on in the Gospel they will be testing him, trying to find his weaknesses so that they can do away with him. Nothing he does will satisfy them: their hearts are closed. God does test us at times, but to bring out the best in us, to make our faith and love grow deeper.

- Do I sometimes make Jesus sigh deeply? Am I waiting for him to do something spectacular for me? Is it not enough for him to have given his life to save the world?

Tuesday 13th February
Mark 8:14–21

Now the disciples had forgotten to bring any bread; and they had only one loaf with them in the boat. And he cautioned them, saying, "Watch out—beware of the yeast of the Pharisees and the yeast of Herod." They said to one another, "It is because we have no bread." And becoming aware of it, Jesus said to them, "Why are you talking about having no bread? Do you still not perceive or understand? Are your hearts hardened? Do you have eyes, and fail to see? Do you have ears, and fail to hear? And do you not remember? When I broke the five loaves for the five thousand, how many baskets full of broken pieces did you collect?" They said to him, "Twelve." "And the seven for the four thousand, how many baskets full of broken pieces did you collect?" And they said to him, "Seven." Then he said to them, "Do you not yet understand?"

- Jesus channels his anger in a constructive and challenging way. He asks the poor disciples nine pointed questions. Like the disciples, I too can be dull, mediocre, half-alive, confused. The divine drama is being played out around me, but I do not seem to know my God-given part in it.

- I take these moments of prayer and ask Jesus to be honest with me. What questions does he ask me as his lackluster disciple? "If you want to be alive, why not follow me closely? You are limitlessly loved—do you know that? You are my friend and I want us to be close, but do you? Can you believe that the world needs you? I am offering you a new way of living: let's go!" Do I respond: "Jesus, do in me what needs to be done to set my heart on fire"?

Wednesday 14th February
Ash Wednesday
Matthew 6:1–6, 16–18

"Beware of practicing your piety before others in order to be seen by them; for then you have no reward from your Father in heaven. So whenever you give alms, do not sound a trumpet before you, as the hypocrites do in the synagogues and in the streets, so that they may be praised by others. Truly I tell you, they have received their reward. But when you give alms, do not let your left hand know what your right hand is doing, so that your alms may be done in secret; and your Father who sees in secret will reward you. And whenever you pray, do not be like the hypocrites; for they love to stand and pray in the synagogues and at the street corners, so that they may be seen by others. Truly I tell you, they have received their reward. But whenever you pray, go into your room and shut the door and pray to your Father who is in secret; and your Father who sees in secret will reward you. // "And whenever you fast, do not look dismal, like the hypocrites, for they disfigure their faces so as to show others that they are fasting. Truly I tell you, they have received their reward. But when you fast, put oil on your head and wash your face, so that your fasting may be seen not by others but by your Father who is in secret; and your Father who sees in secret will reward you."

- We are entering that season of the Christian year when the church invites us to test our inner freedom. We ask such questions as, "Can I do this, or choose not to do it?" This can be hard to do with gossip, gambling, pornography, or complaining. What habits make me hard to live with?

- Lent is about regaining control of our own lives, especially in those areas that damage other people. We don't admire those whose appetites or habits lead them by the nose. At the same time, our purifying is to be accomplished, not out in the public eye to impress others, but in that private space where we dwell with God alone.

Thursday 15th February
Luke 9:22–25

Jesus said to his disciples: "The Son of Man must undergo great suffering, and be rejected by the elders, chief priests, and scribes, and be killed, and on the third day be raised." // Then he said to them all, "If any want to become my followers, let them deny themselves and take up their cross daily and follow me. For those who want to save their life will lose it, and those who lose their life for my sake will save it. What does it profit them if they gain the whole world, but lose or forfeit themselves?

- "Deny yourself and take up your cross daily." Lord, I used to think this meant looking for mortifications. You have taught me that my cross is myself, my ego, the pains in my body, my awkwardness, my mistakes. To follow you is to move beyond ego trips. It means coping with the business of life without trampling on others or making them suffer. There is a world here to be explored this Lent.

- To deny myself means: to reach a point where my self is no longer the most important thing in the world; to be able to take a back seat comfortably; to be happy to listen; to accept without resentment the diminishments that come to me through time or circumstances; and to see your hand, Lord, in both the bright and dark places of my life.

Friday 16th February
Matthew 9:14–15

Then the disciples of John came to him, saying, "Why do we and the Pharisees fast often, but your disciples do not fast?" And Jesus said to them, "The wedding guests cannot mourn as long as the bridegroom is with them, can they? The days will come when the bridegroom is taken away from them, and then they will fast."

- Lord, when I sense how John's disciples viewed you, I feel relieved. John the Baptist was admirable, but you are my model, and people saw you as a man given to joy and celebration. People were high-spirited in your company, as at a wedding feast. The feast would not last forever; you had no illusion and would not encourage illusions. But long faces do not suit your companions.

- On most days, is my focus joy and celebration of God's gifts?

Saturday 17th February
Luke 5:27–32

After this he went out and saw a tax collector named Levi, sitting at the tax booth; and he said to him, "Follow me." And he got up, left everything, and followed him. // Then Levi gave a great banquet for him in his house; and there was a large crowd of tax collectors and others sitting at the table with them. The Pharisees and their scribes were complaining to his disciples, saying, "Why do you eat and drink with tax collectors and sinners?" Jesus answered, "Those who are well have no need of a physician, but those who are sick; I have come to call not the righteous but sinners to repentance."

- Who are the Levis in our world, hated and despised by the public? Not the tax collectors—it is quite respectable now to work for the Internal Revenue Service. The tabloid newspapers have different objects of hate today: addicts, drug dealers, rapists, pedophiles. You would sit with them, Lord. They too need your grace.

- Lord, on whom do I focus as I walk through a day? Those who are most like me? Or those who are already judged and found wanting?

The First Week of Lent
February 18—February 24

Something to think and pray about each day this week:

The Desert—for Jesus and for Us

Desert time is vital to a mature relationship with God. If we are committed men and women of faith, then God is going to bring us to the desert at some point to look deeply at ourselves and see all of us the way God sees us. This means we will have to confront the dark spots of our lives and the things we do our best to hide from God and from the rest of the world.

Jesus was no different. He was "led by the Spirit in the wilderness, where for forty days he was tempted by the devil" (Luke 4:1–2). Jesus faced Satan and "then the devil left him, and suddenly angels came and waited on him" (Matthew 4:11). We face Satan and our own temptations in our desert time, just as Jesus did. And just as Jesus was not alone in his desert battle, we are not alone either.

As we continue on our Lenten journey, let us be led by the Spirit to have the courage to head into the desert as Jesus did. We pray that during these weeks of Lent, God will strengthen us in our weakness the way Jesus was strengthened. As St. Paul reminds us, "My grace is sufficient for you, for power is made perfect in weakness" (2 Corinthians 12:9).

Jesus' time in the desert prepared him to begin his public ministry. When we leave our desert time and confront our demons with God's help, we are stronger. It is in the desert time—our time of prayer, solitude, and aloneness with God—that God readies us for our next steps.

—Becky Eldredge on *dotMagis*, the blog of *IgnatianSpirituality.com*
http://www.ignatianspirituality.com/20689/desert-time

The Presence of God
"Be still and know that I am God!" Lord, your words lead us to the calmness and greatness of your presence.

Freedom
"In these days, God taught me as a schoolteacher teaches a pupil" (Saint Ignatius). I remind myself that there are things God has to teach me yet, and I ask for the grace to hear them and let them change me.

Consciousness
How am I really feeling? Lighthearted? Heavyhearted? I may be very much at peace, happy to be here.
Equally, I may be frustrated, worried, or angry.
I acknowledge how I really am. It is the real me whom the Lord loves.

The Word
God speaks to each of us individually. I listen attentively, to hear what he is saying to me. Read the text a few times, then listen. (Please turn to the Scripture on the following pages. Inspiration points are there should you need them. When you are ready, return here to continue.)

Conversation
Do I notice myself reacting as I pray with the word of God? Do I feel challenged, comforted, angry? Imagining Jesus sitting or standing by me, I speak out my feelings, as one trusted friend to another.

Conclusion
I thank God for these moments we have spent together and for any insights I have been given concerning the text.

Sunday 18th February
First Sunday of Lent
Mark 1:12–15

And the Spirit immediately drove him out into the wilderness. He was in the wilderness forty days, tempted by Satan; and he was with the wild beasts; and the angels waited on him. Now after John was arrested, Jesus came to Galilee, proclaiming the good news of God, and saying, "The time is fulfilled, and the kingdom of God has come near; repent, and believe in the good news."

- What spirit drives me in the things I do? Is my heart a home for the Spirit? Could the Holy Spirit be inviting me to take more quiet space? In the Bible, the "wilderness" is a place of revelation and of intimacy with God. I need to put secondary things aside to meet God. God is found in emptiness as well as in fullness. I can find him in the emptiness of sickness, old age, disappointment, failure, and solitude.

- As Lent begins, I might promise God that I will be faithful to the quiet space and time that Sacred Space offers me. I want the kingdom of God to come near me. I want to believe more deeply in the good news.

Monday 19th February
Matthew 25:31–46

Jesus said, "When the Son of Man comes in his glory, and all the angels with him, then he will sit on the throne of his glory. All the nations will be gathered before him, and he will separate people one from another as a shepherd separates the sheep from the goats, and he will put the sheep at his right hand and the goats at the left. Then the king will say to those at his right hand, 'Come, you that are blessed by my Father, inherit the kingdom prepared for you from the foundation of the world; for I was hungry and you gave me food, I was thirsty and you gave me something to drink, I was a stranger and you welcomed me, I was naked and you gave me clothing, I was sick and you took care of me, I was in prison and you visited me.' Then the righteous will answer him, 'Lord, when was it that we saw you hungry and gave you food, or thirsty and gave you something to drink? And when was it that we saw you a stranger and welcomed you, or naked and gave you clothing? And when was it that we saw you sick or in prison and visited you?' And the king will answer them, 'Truly

I tell you, just as you did it to one of the least of these who are members of my family, you did it to me.' Then he will say to those at his left hand, 'You that are accursed, depart from me into the eternal fire prepared for the devil and his angels; for I was hungry and you gave me no food, I was thirsty and you gave me nothing to drink, I was a stranger and you did not welcome me, naked and you did not give me clothing, sick and in prison and you did not visit me.' Then they also will answer, 'Lord, when was it that we saw you hungry or thirsty or a stranger or naked or sick or in prison, and did not take care of you?' Then he will answer them, 'Truly I tell you, just as you did not do it to one of the least of these, you did not do it to me.' And these will go away into eternal punishment, but the righteous into eternal life."

- This message is simple, Lord. You will judge me on my love and service of others. You are there in the poor, the sick, the prisoners, the strangers. May I recognize your face in them.

- Where are the hungry, the naked, the homeless who would call on me if they could reach me? Or have I so organized my life that the needy never impinge on me? Lord, you have made this the sole criterion of judgment. How will I measure up?

Tuesday 20th February
Matthew 6:7–15

Jesus said, "When you are praying, do not heap up empty phrases as the Gentiles do; for they think that they will be heard because of their many words. Do not be like them, for your Father knows what you need before you ask him. // "Pray then in this way:

Our Father in heaven,
   hallowed be your name.
   Your kingdom come.
   Your will be done,
      on earth as it is in heaven.
Give us this day our daily bread.
And forgive us our debts,
   as we also have forgiven our debtors.
And do not bring us to the time of trial,
   but rescue us from the evil one.

For if you forgive others their trespasses, your heavenly Father will also forgive you; but if you do not forgive others, neither will your Father forgive your trespasses."

- One teacher's advice on learning to pray is this: Say the Lord's Prayer, and take an hour to say it. There is no word or phrase in it that does not repay you if you mine it for meaning, and savor it. For instance: "Our"—not just my father, for I share God with the human race. Is there anyone whom I feel uneasy to claim as a sister or brother?

- Father, as I turn to you in prayer, you already know what I need. I do not change you by asking; I change myself. I love to reflect on Jesus' words: that I may call God my father and work to make his name known and revered. I shall be forgiven as I forgive others. I beg for nourishment enough for the day, and for deliverance from evil.

Wednesday 21st February
Luke 11:29–32

When the crowds were increasing, Jesus began to say, "This generation is an evil generation; it asks for a sign, but no sign will be given to it except the sign of Jonah. For just as Jonah became a sign to the people of Nineveh, so the Son of Man will be to this generation. The queen of the South will rise at the judgment with the people of this generation and condemn them, because she came from the ends of the earth to listen to the wisdom of Solomon, and see, something greater than Solomon is here! The people of Nineveh will rise up at the judgment with this generation and condemn it, because they repented at the proclamation of Jonah, and see, something greater than Jonah is here!"

- Jonah converted the great city of Nineveh by his godliness and his preaching, not by miracles. Holiness is a greater marvel than special effects, but less easily recognized. The spectacular is what draws the crowds. Lord, your hand is more evident in saintliness than in extraordinary signs. Open my eyes to your work in my sisters and brothers.

- So often, I ask God for more information—a new revelation or some reassurance of what has already been communicated. But what do I do with the information I already have? Am I living out what God has revealed to me thus far?

Thursday 22nd February
Matthew 16:13–19

Now when Jesus came into the district of Caesarea Philippi, he asked his disciples, "Who do people say that the Son of Man is?" And they said, "Some say John the Baptist, but others Elijah, and still others Jeremiah or one of the prophets." He said to them, "But who do you say that I am?" Simon Peter answered, "You are the Messiah, the Son of the living God." And Jesus answered him, "Blessed are you, Simon son of Jonah! For flesh and blood has not revealed this to you, but my Father in heaven. And I tell you, you are Peter, and on this rock I will build my church, and the gates of Hades will not prevail against it. I will give you the keys of the kingdom of heaven, and whatever you bind on earth will be bound in heaven, and whatever you loose on earth will be loosed in heaven."

- No Gospel text has been scrutinized more carefully than this, because it describes Jesus founding a church and giving primacy to Peter. Let me imagine myself in that setting, under the cliff face in Caesarea Philippi, as Jesus asks his momentous question: "Who do you say that I am?" Suddenly the dimensions of his mission expand. He is handing over to us (the *ecclesia*, or people of God) the task of continuing his mission. We are not, as is sometimes phrased, "followers of the church." We *are* the church, served by bishops and others, but with our own wisdom.

- Lord, you did not leave us orphans. We are the people of God, with a leader and the support of the Holy Spirit. I am not alone.

Friday 23rd February
Matthew 5:20–26

For I tell you, unless your righteousness exceeds that of the scribes and Pharisees, you will never enter the kingdom of heaven. "You have heard that it was said to those of ancient times, 'You shall not murder'; and 'whoever murders shall be liable to judgement.' But I say to you that if you are angry with a brother or sister, you will be liable to judgement; and if you insult a brother or sister, you will be liable to the council; and if you say, 'You fool,' you will be liable to the hell of fire. So when you are offering your gift at the altar, if you remember that your brother or sister has something against you, leave your gift there before the altar and go;

first be reconciled to your brother or sister, and then come and offer your gift. Come to terms quickly with your accuser while you are on the way to court with him, or your accuser may hand you over to the judge, and the judge to the guard, and you will be thrown into prison. Truly I tell you, you will never get out until you have paid the last penny."

- You are speaking to my heart, Lord. I cannot be reconciled to you unless I am reconciled to my neighbor. Forgiveness requires contrition and atonement. If I have stolen, I cannot ask God's forgiveness unless I have given back what I stole. If I feel a barrier in talking to you, Lord, it may be because I have not tackled the barrier between me and my neighbor.

- Lord, you are pushing my conscience inward. I will be judged not just by what I have done in the external forum but also by the voluntary movements of my heart. God sees the heart, and sees how far I go along with feelings of hatred, lust, or pride. In other words, I should be of one piece, responding more to God's gaze than to other people's.

Saturday 24th February
Matthew 5:43–48

Jesus said to the disciples, "You have heard that it was said, 'You shall love your neighbor and hate your enemy.' But I say to you, Love your enemies and pray for those who persecute you, so that you may be children of your Father in heaven; for he makes his sun rise on the evil and on the good, and sends rain on the righteous and on the unrighteous. For if you love those who love you, what reward do you have? Do not even the tax collectors do the same? And if you greet only your brothers and sisters, what more are you doing than others? Do not even the Gentiles do the same? Be perfect, therefore, as your heavenly Father is perfect."

- Lord, you warn us against tribal or racial exclusiveness: that is where we love only our kith and kin, and reject outsiders. For you there are no outsiders. Your sun shines and your rain falls on all alike. We are to open our hearts even to those who hate us.

- This is not hopeless idealism but a wise strategy for overcoming the persecutor. Aggression is changed into a strategy for winning through the wisdom of love.

The Second Week of Lent
February 25—March 3

Something to think and pray about each day this week:

Bringing Us Light
When we ask God for light, we are asking to know as God knows: good, bad, up, down, all of it.

A good prayer is to ask the Father to let me know myself the way the Holy Spirit knows me, "for the Spirit searches the depths of everything, even the depths of God" (1 Corinthians 2:10).

God does everything to bring us light. In our turn, each of us must get ready to accept God's illumination. One important way to get ready for God's light is to pray to be unafraid of what we see.

We can ask God to shed light on our routines and habits. Is a good habit growing stronger? Is a certain habit more harmful than I admit? We need our usual ways of doing things. Without routines we'd take all day just to have breakfast. At the same time, almost any habit can either enable our freedom or impede our freedom. We have to watch.

And habits can turn into harmful attachments. We can hold on to things or ideas so tightly that we are no longer really free. So we beg God for light to see when an attachment is leading us to sin. God sees it for what it is; we ask to share that insight.

Finally, when we ask for light, we need to be ready to accept what God gives us.

—Joseph Tetlow, SJ, on *dotMagis*, the blog of *IgnatianSpirituality.com*
http://www.ignatianspirituality.com/15390/pray-for-light-with-the-examen

The Presence of God
I remind myself that, as I sit here now,
God is gazing on me with love and holding me in being.
I pause for a moment and think of this.

Freedom
"There are very few people who realize what God would make of them
if they abandoned themselves into his hands, and let themselves be formed
by his grace" (Saint Ignatius). I ask for the grace to trust myself totally to
God's love.

Consciousness
Where do I sense hope, encouragement, and growth in my life? By looking back over the past few months, I may be able to see which activities
and occasions have produced rich fruit. If I do notice such areas, I will
determine to give those areas both time and space in the future.

The Word
Lord Jesus, you became human to communicate with me.
You walked and worked on this earth.
You endured the heat and struggled with the cold.
All your time on this earth was spent in caring for humanity.
You healed the sick, you raised the dead.
Most important of all, you saved me from death.
(Please turn to the Scripture on the following pages. Inspiration points
are there should you need them. When you are ready, return here to
continue.)

Conversation
What is stirring in me as I pray? Am I consoled, troubled, left cold? I imagine Jesus standing or sitting at my side, and I share my feelings with him.

Conclusion
Glory be to the Father, and to the Son, and to the Holy Spirit,
As it was in the beginning, is now and ever shall be,
World without end. Amen.

Sunday 25th February
Second Sunday of Lent
Mark 9:2–10

Six days later, Jesus took with him Peter and James and John, and led them up a high mountain apart, by themselves. And he was transfigured before them, and his clothes became dazzling white, such as no one on earth could bleach them. And there appeared to them Elijah with Moses, who were talking with Jesus. Then Peter said to Jesus, "Rabbi, it is good for us to be here; let us make three dwellings, one for you, one for Moses, and one for Elijah." He did not know what to say, for they were terrified. Then a cloud overshadowed them, and from the cloud there came a voice, "This is my Son, the Beloved; listen to him!" Suddenly when they looked around, they saw no one with them any more, but only Jesus. // As they were coming down the mountain, he ordered them to tell no one about what they had seen, until after the Son of Man had risen from the dead. So they kept the matter to themselves, questioning what this rising from the dead could mean.

- In our journey to God, we have peak moments, when the ground is holy. Like Peter, we want them to last forever. But Jesus brings us down the mountain and prepares us for the hard times ahead, during which we live on the memory of brief transfigurations. Can I recall any of my peak moments?

- There was glory in this experience, but also fear. I want God's presence and revelation, but am I willing to stand in places that are unfamiliar to me?

Monday 26th February
Luke 6:36–38

Jesus said to the disciples, "Be merciful, just as your Father is merciful. Do not judge, and you will not be judged; do not condemn, and you will not be condemned. Forgive, and you will be forgiven; give, and it will be given to you. A good measure, pressed down, shaken together, running over, will be put into your lap; for the measure you give will be the measure you get back."

- Lord, my lap and my hands are open to receive from you; you tell me they will not be able to contain the cascade of blessings from your hand, provided my hands are open to give as well as to receive. You respond in a superabundant way when we generously share what we have. I remember the old Dean in *Babette's Feast*: "The only things which we may take with us from our life on earth are those which we have given away."

- "Do not judge." It can take a lifetime to unlearn this habit, can't it? Holy Spirit, alert me when my mind and heart revert to this damaging response toward others.

Tuesday 27th February
Matthew 23:1–12

Then Jesus said to the crowds and to his disciples, "The scribes and the Pharisees sit on Moses' seat; therefore, do whatever they teach you and follow it; but do not do as they do, for they do not practice what they teach. They tie up heavy burdens, hard to bear, and lay them on the shoulders of others; but they themselves are unwilling to lift a finger to move them. They do all their deeds to be seen by others; for they make their phylacteries broad and their fringes long. They love to have the place of honor at banquets and the best seats in the synagogues, and to be greeted with respect in the marketplaces, and to have people call them rabbi. But you are not to be called rabbi, for you have one teacher, and you are all students. And call no one your father on earth, for you have one Father—the one in heaven. Nor are you to be called instructors, for you have one instructor, the Messiah. The greatest among you will be your servant. All who exalt themselves will be humbled, and all who humble themselves will be exalted."

- Lord, you pick out the manifestations of vanity and self-importance. "You are all students," you say. In the mysterious way that Scripture works, I am growing daily in knowledge of God's ways. You, Lord, are my teacher.

- The Christian identity is servant, disciple, humble follower. Greatness is seen in love, in our willingness to serve others as Jesus did. Many cultures and groups of people honor success, wealth, and self-importance. Remember in prayer a moment when you felt humbled as you served somebody or did something truly relevant for them. Offer this memory to God in thanks.

Wednesday 28th February
Matthew 20:17–28

While Jesus was going up to Jerusalem, he took the twelve disciples aside by themselves, and said to them on the way, "See, we are going up to Jerusalem, and the Son of Man will be handed over to the chief priests and scribes, and they will condemn him to death; then they will hand him over to the Gentiles to be mocked and flogged and crucified; and on the third day he will be raised." // Then the mother of the sons of Zebedee came to him with her sons, and kneeling before him, she asked a favor of him. And he said to her, "What do you want?" She said to him, "Declare that these two sons of mine will sit, one at your right hand and one at your left, in your kingdom." But Jesus answered, "You do not know what you are asking. Are you able to drink the cup that I am about to drink? They said to him, "We are able." He said to them, "You will indeed drink my cup, but to sit at my right hand and at my left, this is not mine to grant, but it is for those for whom it has been prepared by my Father." // When the ten heard it, they were angry with the two brothers. But Jesus called them to him and said, "You know that the rulers of the Gentiles lord it over them, and their great ones are tyrants over them. It will not be so among you; but whoever wishes to be great among you must be your servant, and whoever wishes to be first among you must be your slave; just as the Son of Man came not to be served but to serve, and to give his life a ransom for many."

• Perhaps, when they heard of Jesus' impending death, these two men and their mother were thinking, *Who will succeed Jesus? What is going to happen?* After so much time with Jesus, his disciples still thought more in terms of an earthly kind of kingdom and power. How often do I slip into this way of thinking?

• Jesus does not present a positive picture of "the Gentiles"; he refers to a style of ruling over others that was never meant to be found among God's people, going all the way back to the prophets and kings of Israel. What would a "servant" look like in my time and culture, and how could I behave more like a servant?

Thursday 1st March
Luke 16:19–31

Jesus said to the Pharisees, "There was a rich man who was dressed in purple and fine linen and who feasted sumptuously every day. And at his gate lay a poor man named Lazarus, covered with sores, who longed to satisfy his hunger with what fell from the rich man's table; even the dogs would come and lick his sores. The poor man died and was carried away by the angels to be with Abraham. The rich man also died and was buried. In Hades, where he was being tormented, he looked up and saw Abraham far away with Lazarus by his side. He called out, 'Father Abraham, have mercy on me, and send Lazarus to dip the tip of his finger in water and cool my tongue; for I am in agony in these flames.' But Abraham said, 'Child, remember that during your lifetime you received your good things, and Lazarus in like manner evil things; but now he is comforted here, and you are in agony. Besides all this, between you and us a great chasm has been fixed, so that those who might want to pass from here to you cannot do so, and no one can cross from there to us.' He said, 'Then, father, I beg you to send him to my father's house—for I have five brothers—that he may warn them, so that they will not also come into this place of torment.' Abraham replied, 'They have Moses and the prophets; they should listen to them.' He said, 'No, father Abraham; but if someone goes to them from the dead, they will repent.' He said to him, 'If they do not listen to Moses and the prophets, neither will they be convinced even if someone rises from the dead.'"

- This is a parable of startling contrasts, but its central message is simple: be alert to the needs under your nose. It is not concerned with patterns of good living on the part of Lazarus, nor of evil-doing on the part of the rich man. But the latter closed his eyes to the needy at his gate.

- Without an eye for those in need around us, our life becomes self-centered and callous. Jesus is asking his listeners to open their eyes to what is right in front of them and to open their ears to the simple command of the Gospel: love your neighbor.

Friday 2nd March

Matthew 21:33–43, 45–46

Jesus said: "Listen to another parable. There was a landowner who planted a vineyard, put a fence around it, dug a wine press in it, and built a
watchtower. Then he leased it to tenants and went to another country.
When the harvest time had come, he sent his slaves to the tenants to
collect his produce. But the tenants seized his slaves and beat one, killed
another, and stoned another. Again he sent other slaves, more than the
first; and they treated them in the same way. Finally he sent his son to
them, saying, 'They will respect my son.' But when the tenants saw the
son, they said to themselves, 'This is the heir; come, let us kill him and
get his inheritance.' So they seized him, threw him out of the vineyard,
and killed him. Now when the owner of the vineyard comes, what will he
do to those tenants?" They said to him, "He will put those wretches to a
miserable death, and lease the vineyard to other tenants who will give him
the produce at the harvest time." // Jesus said to them, "Have you never
read in the scriptures:

'The stone that the builders rejected
      has become the cornerstone;
this was the Lord's doing,
      and it is amazing in our eyes'?

Therefore I tell you, the kingdom of God will be taken away from you
and given to a people that produces the fruits of the kingdom. When the
chief priests and the Pharisees heard his parables, they realized that he
was speaking about them. They wanted to arrest him, but they feared the
crowds, because they regarded him as a prophet.

- Lord, this parable is about the Jews rejecting Jesus as Messiah. But it
  is also about me. I am the tenant of your vineyard. For me you have
  planted and protected a crop, and from me you expect some harvest.
  The fruit is for you, not for me. I may feel annoyed when you ask, but
  you are right to expect something of me.

- As I look at my life today, what do I see that God has entrusted to me?
  What might God expect from me? And what is my response?

Saturday 3rd March

Luke 15:1–3, 11–32

Now all the tax-collectors and sinners were coming near to listen to him. And the Pharisees and the scribes were grumbling and saying, "This fellow welcomes sinners and eats with them." So he told them this parable: // "There was a man who had two sons. The younger of them said to his father, 'Father, give me the share of the property that will belong to me.' So he divided his property between them. A few days later the younger son gathered all he had and travelled to a distant country, and there he squandered his property in dissolute living. When he had spent everything, a severe famine took place throughout that country, and he began to be in need. So he went and hired himself out to one of the citizens of that country, who sent him to his fields to feed the pigs. He would gladly have filled himself with the pods that the pigs were eating; and no one gave him anything. But when he came to himself he said, 'How many of my father's hired hands have bread enough and to spare, but here I am dying of hunger! I will get up and go to my father, and I will say to him, "Father, I have sinned against heaven and before you; I am no longer worthy to be called your son; treat me like one of your hired hands."' So he set off and went to his father. But while he was still far off, his father saw him and was filled with compassion; he ran and put his arms around him and kissed him. Then the son said to him, 'Father, I have sinned against heaven and before you; I am no longer worthy to be called your son.' But the father said to his slaves, 'Quickly, bring out a robe—the best one—and put it on him; put a ring on his finger and sandals on his feet. And get the fatted calf and kill it, and let us eat and celebrate; for this son of mine was dead and is alive again; he was lost and is found!' And they began to celebrate. // "Now his elder son was in the field; and when he came and approached the house, he heard music and dancing. He called one of the slaves and asked what was going on. He replied, 'Your brother has come, and your father has killed the fatted calf, because he has got him back safe and sound.' Then he became angry and refused to go in. His father came out and began to plead with him. But he answered his father, 'Listen! For all these years I have been working like a slave for you, and I have never disobeyed your command; yet you have never given me even a young goat so that I might celebrate with my friends. But when this son of yours came back, who has devoured your property with prostitutes, you killed the fatted calf for him!' Then the father said to him, 'Son, you are always with me, and all that is mine is yours. But we had to celebrate and rejoice, because this brother of yours was dead and has come to life; he was lost and has been found.'"

- The parable of the prodigal son gives me a picture of the steadfast love of God. There, Lord, you show how your heavenly father would appear in human form. When he welcomes back his lost son with tears of delight, kills the fatted calf, brings out the best robe, and throws a great party, it is not to please other people, but to give expression to his own overwhelming pleasure that his child has come home.

- Can I believe that God delights in me as much as he delights in the lost son of this parable?

The Third Week of Lent
March 4—March 10

Something to think and pray about each day this week:

Our Inheritance

[In the parable of the forgiving father, the younger son returned home and] was welcomed, forgiven, and restored to full sonship . . . The son had been lost and found. Now he knew what it meant to be his father's son. He was home! The father was overjoyed: "My son has come to life; let the celebration begin!"

No sooner had the music and dancing begun than the other, older son stormed in and confronted their father. However disappointed the father may have been by the older son's resentment and ill will, he had the wisdom not to take sides. He may have sensed that the older son was suffering an alienation of his own. The older son's attitudes had distanced him from his brother to such an extent that he referred to him not as "my brother" but as "this son of yours." His self-righteous attitudes had prevented him from entering into a loving relationship, not only with his brother but also with his father. The elder son, too, was lost; he was lost in a foreign land of his own making.

The father responded as he had with his younger son. He was compassionate. He did not ridicule his son, but rebuked him gently. "You are always with me, and all that is mine is yours." All the father was able to do was invite the son to confront his negativity, accept his own position, and enter into the joy of his brother's return.

As sons and daughters of our Father, we are invited to claim the reality of our inheritance as sons and daughters of a loving and merciful God. The banquet is prepared. Will you enter into the joy of your Father?

—Jacqueline Syrup Bergan and Sister Marie Schwan, CSJ,
Forgiveness: A Guide for Prayer

The Presence of God

I pause for a moment
and reflect on God's life-giving presence
in every part of my body,
in everything around me,
in the whole of my life.

Freedom

Many countries are at this moment suffering the agonies of war. I bow my head in thanksgiving for my freedom. I pray for all prisoners and captives.

Consciousness

Knowing that God loves me unconditionally, I look honestly over the past day, its events, and my feelings. Do I have something to be grateful for? Then I give thanks. Is there something I am sorry for? Then I ask forgiveness.

The Word

Now I turn to the Scripture set out for me this day. I read slowly over the words and see if any sentence or sentiment appeals to me. (Please turn to the Scripture on the following pages. Inspiration points are there should you need them. When you are ready, return here to continue.)

Conversation

I know with certainty that there were times when you carried me, Lord. There were times when it was through your strength that I got through the dark times in my life.

Conclusion

Glory be to the Father, and to the Son, and to the Holy Spirit,
As it was in the beginning, is now and ever shall be,
World without end. Amen.

Sunday 4th March
Third Sunday of Lent
John 2:13–25

The Passover of the Jews was near, and Jesus went up to Jerusalem. In the temple he found people selling cattle, sheep, and doves, and the money changers seated at their tables. Making a whip of cords, he drove all of them out of the temple, both the sheep and the cattle. He also poured out the coins of the money changers and overturned their tables. He told those who were selling the doves, "Take these things out of here! Stop making my Father's house a marketplace!" His disciples remembered that it was written, "Zeal for your house will consume me." The Jews then said to him, "What sign can you show us for doing this?" Jesus answered them, "Destroy this temple, and in three days I will raise it up." The Jews then said, "This temple has been under construction for forty-six years, and will you raise it up in three days?" But he was speaking of the temple of his body. After he was raised from the dead, his disciples remembered that he had said this; and they believed the scripture and the word that Jesus had spoken. // When he was in Jerusalem during the Passover festival, many believed in his name because they saw the signs that he was doing. But Jesus on his part would not entrust himself to them, because he knew all people and needed no one to testify about anyone; for he himself knew what was in everyone.

- I imagine myself visiting the temple when Jesus enters. I am accustomed to the money changers and to the hucksters who convenience worshippers by selling cattle, sheep, and doves for the ritual sacrifices. The fury of Jesus startles and upsets me, makes me think. Surely these guys are making honest money?

- But this is the house of God. When money creeps in, it tends to take over. Is there any of the Christian sacraments untouched by commercialism? Christening parties, first communion money, confirmation dances, and wedding feasts—they are meant to be the touch of God at key moments in our lives; but can God get a hearing amid the clatter of coins?

Monday 5th March
Luke 4:24–30

And he said, "Truly I tell you, no prophet is accepted in the prophet's hometown. But the truth is, there were many widows in Israel in the time of Elijah, when the heaven was shut up three years and six months, and there was a severe famine over all the land; yet Elijah was sent to none of them except to a widow at Zarephath in Sidon. There were also many lepers in Israel in the time of the prophet Elisha, and none of them was cleansed except Naaman the Syrian." When they heard this, all in the synagogue were filled with rage. They got up, drove him out of the town, and led him to the brow of the hill on which their town was built, so that they might hurl him off the cliff. But he passed through the midst of them and went on his way.

- This is about the expectation of miracles and cures. The self-important Naaman felt he had been slighted: he met only a messenger, not the prophet himself; and the cure depended on Naaman washing himself in the river, instead of receiving hands-on treatment by Elisha.

- I am the same, Lord. Even in my neediness my ego pushes through. I want to be not just a victim but a celebrity victim. I want not just a cure, but to be the center of attention. Help me center on you, not myself.

Tuesday 6th March
Matthew 18:21–35

Then Peter came and said to him, "Lord, if another member of the church sins against me, how often should I forgive? As many as seven times?" Jesus said to him, "Not seven times, but, I tell you, seventy-seven times." // "For this reason the kingdom of heaven may be compared to a king who wished to settle accounts with his slaves. When he began the reckoning, one who owed him ten thousand talents was brought to him; and, as he could not pay, his lord ordered him to be sold, together with his wife and children and all his possessions, and payment to be made. So the slave fell on his knees before him, saying, 'Have patience with me, and I will pay you everything.' And out of pity for him, the lord of that slave released him and forgave him the debt. But that same slave, as he went out, came upon one of his fellow slaves who owed him a hundred denarii; and seizing him by the throat, he said, 'Pay what you owe.' Then his fellow slave fell down and pleaded with him, 'Have patience with me, and I will pay you.' But he refused; then he went and threw him into prison until he would pay the debt. When his fellow slaves saw what had happened, they were greatly distressed, and they went and reported to their lord all that had taken place. Then his lord summoned him and said to him, 'You wicked slave! I forgave you all that debt because you pleaded with me. Should you not have had mercy on your fellow slave, as I had mercy on you?' And in anger his lord handed him over to be tortured until he would pay his entire debt. So my heavenly Father will also do to every one of you, if you do not forgive your brother or sister from your heart."

- There is no limit to the number of times we are called to forgive. This is one of the most demanding aspects of Christ's teaching. Yet forgiveness is a grace for the one offering it as well as for the one receiving it.

- When is it most difficult for me to be merciful? Do I feel that a person must somehow deserve my mercy?

Wednesday 7th March
Matthew 5:17–19

"Do not think that I have come to abolish the law or the prophets; I have come not to abolish but to fulfill. For truly I tell you, until heaven and earth pass away, not one letter, not one stroke of a letter, will pass from the law until all is accomplished. Therefore, whoever breaks one of the least of these commandments, and teaches others to do the same, will be called least in the kingdom of heaven; but whoever does them and teaches them will be called great in the kingdom of heaven."

- What role do the law and the prophets play in the new covenant instituted by Jesus? This issue was critical for Jewish converts in the early church, as Matthew realized. It is still relevant for us today. Jesus speaks of fulfilling rather than abolishing the law and the prophets. What does that mean exactly?

- God of both law and grace, sometimes I'd like to think that spiritual laws and rules don't really apply to me. After all, we are saved through faith, not our good works. Yet the laws and instructions in both Old and New Testaments had purpose, and they were important to Jesus. Show me how to understand them in my life.

Thursday 8th March
Luke 11:14–23

Now he was casting out a demon that was mute; when the demon had gone out, the one who had been mute spoke, and the crowds were amazed. But some of them said, "He casts out demons by Beelzebul, the ruler of the demons." Others, to test him, kept demanding from him a sign from heaven. But he knew what they were thinking and said to them, "Every kingdom divided against itself becomes a desert, and house falls on house. If Satan also is divided against himself, how will his kingdom stand?—for you say that I cast out the demons by Beelzebul. Now if I cast out the demons by Beelzebul, by whom do your exorcists cast them out? Therefore they will be your judges. But if it is by the finger of God that I cast out the demons, then the kingdom of God has come to you. When a strong man, fully armed, guards his castle, his property is safe. But when one stronger than he attacks him and overpowers him, he takes away his armor in which he trusted and divides his plunder. Whoever is not with me is against me, and whoever does not gather with me scatters.

- The core issue here is the source of Jesus' power when he expels demons from people. Is he tapping into the power of Beelzebul, the ruler of the demons, or is he calling on the power of God? If you were present, what would you have thought?

- Notice how Jesus points to his exorcisms (carried out with the power of God) as signs that the kingdom of God has come among us. This is true of all his miracles. Am I open to miracles in my life here and now? Do I truly want God's power to be evident?

Friday 9th March
Mark 12:28–34

One of the scribes came near and heard them disputing with one another, and seeing that Jesus answered them well, he asked him, "Which commandment is the first of all?" Jesus answered, "The first is, 'Hear, O Israel: the Lord our God, the Lord is one; you shall love the Lord your God with all your heart, and with all your soul, and with all your mind, and with all your strength.' The second is this, 'You shall love your neighbor as yourself.' There is no other commandment greater than these." Then the scribe said to him, "You are right, Teacher; you have truly said that 'he is one, and besides him there is no other'; and 'to love him with all the heart, and with all the understanding, and with all the strength,' and 'to love one's neighbor as oneself,'—this is much more important than all whole burnt offerings and sacrifices." When Jesus saw that he answered wisely, he said to him, "You are not far from the kingdom of God." After that no one dared to ask him any question.

- Loving God with our whole being, and loving our neighbor as we love ourselves—these two commitments, taken together, have greater priority than any and all other offerings. Love has priority over all other virtues.

- Are you comfortable with the designation of love as a *commandment*? The word can sound cold and legalistic whereas the word *love* evokes warmth and freedom. Could you suggest an alternative to "command-ment"? Or would you want to?

Saturday 10th March
Luke 18:9–14

Jesus also told this parable to some who trusted in themselves that they were righteous and regarded others with contempt: "Two men went up to the temple to pray, one a Pharisee and the other a tax collector. The Pharisee, standing by himself, was praying thus, 'God, I thank you that I am not like other people: thieves, rogues, adulterers, or even like this tax collector. I fast twice a week; I give a tenth of all my income.' But the tax collector, standing far off, would not even look up to heaven, but was beating his breast and saying, 'God, be merciful to me, a sinner!' I tell you, this man went down to his home justified rather than the other; for all who exalt themselves will be humbled, but all who humble themselves will be exalted."

- This is a beautifully crafted parable whose meaning leaps off the page for us. Yet there is always more to learn from praying on it and asking Jesus to reveal its hidden depths. There may be some detail we had not noticed before or we may see how it applies to ourselves in a new light.

- It can be helpful to use our imagination and "become" one or the other of the characters. Notice how comfortable or uncomfortable we feel in his clothes. Try saying the prayer of each in turn. What is that like for you? Experience tells us that no one is wholly "Pharisee" (hypocrite) or wholly "tax collector" (truthfully self-aware).

The Fourth Week of Lent
March 11—March 17

Something to think and pray about each day this week:

Building the Kingdom

The Beatitudes are an insider's guide to the Christian life, inasmuch as they describe what it's like to be on mission in the world. Every customary marker of success, Jesus suggests, is wrong—and what appears to be difficult may in fact be a sign of fidelity to building God's kingdom.

I imagine what it might be like to be part of a great team embarking on a hoped-for championship season. The coach tells the team members of the hardships they will face, the struggles they will have to overcome in order to achieve victory. A good coach will be honest about what the team members must face so that they will not lose heart when, inevitably, things don't always go as hoped.

In the Beatitudes, Christ takes a similar approach, suggesting that the distant hope for building the kingdom will involve highs and lows. He tells his students that this mission will be arduous but that the reward will be heaven itself.

You'll know that you're building God's kingdom, Jesus says, when people "hate you, and when they exclude you, revile you, and defame you" (Luke 6:22), just as people did to the prophets. People hate those sent by God because such people always sting the consciences of the self-righteous. Jesus upset things through his outreach to lepers, to women, and to tax collectors and sinners. Today, Christians sting consciences through outreach to the poor, children yet to be born, immigrants and refugees, families, the sick, and many others.

Whose good is Christ calling you to serve? Are you willing to be reviled for the work to which Christ has called you? Are you willing to take a stand on behalf of those who have not the power to stand for themselves, and work tirelessly in the face of harassment? If so, Jesus says, you are blessed.

—Tim Muldoon, *The Ignatian Workout for Lent*

The Presence of God
I pause for a moment and think of the love and the grace that God showers on me. I am created in the image and likeness of God; I am God's dwelling place.

Freedom
Lord, you granted me the great gift of freedom. In these times, O Lord, grant that I may be free from any form of racism or intolerance. Remind me that we are all equal in your loving eyes.

Consciousness
Knowing that God loves me unconditionally, I can afford to be honest about how I am.
How has the day been, and how do I feel now? I share my feelings openly with the Lord.

The Word
I take my time to read the word of God slowly, a few times, allowing myself to dwell on anything that strikes me. (Please turn to the Scripture on the following pages. Inspiration points are there should you need them. When you are ready, return here to continue.)

Conversation
Sometimes I wonder what I might say if I were to meet you in person, Lord.
I think I might say "Thank you" because you are always there for me.

Conclusion
I thank God for these moments we have spent together and for any insights I have been given concerning the text.

Sunday 11th March
Fourth Sunday of Lent
John 3:14–21

Jesus said, "And just as Moses lifted up the serpent in the wilderness, so must the Son of Man be lifted up, that whoever believes in him may have eternal life. For God so loved the world that he gave his only Son, so that everyone who believes in him may not perish but may have eternal life. Indeed, God did not send the Son into the world to condemn the world, but in order that the world might be saved through him. Those who believe in him are not condemned; but those who do not believe are condemned already, because they have not believed in the name of the only Son of God. And this is the judgement, that the light has come into the world, and people loved darkness rather than light because their deeds were evil. For all who do evil hate the light and do not come to the light, so that their deeds may not be exposed. But those who do what is true come to the light, so that it may be clearly seen that their deeds have been done in God."

- God loved the world. This is my faith, Lord. Sometimes it seems to go against the evidence, when floods, earthquakes, droughts, and tsunamis devastate poor people. Central to my faith is the figure of Jesus, lifted on the Cross, knowing what it was to be devastated and a "failure," yet offering himself in love for us.

- God of all light, you continue to send light into the world and into my life. May I recognize it, thank you for it, and participate in its work.

Monday 12th March
John 4:43–54

When the two days were over, he went from that place to Galilee (for Jesus himself had testified that a prophet has no honor in the prophet's own country). When he came to Galilee, the Galileans welcomed him, since they had seen all that he had done in Jerusalem at the festival; for they too had gone to the festival. Then he came again to Cana in Galilee where he had changed the water into wine. Now there was a royal official whose son lay ill in Capernaum. When he heard that Jesus had come from Judea to Galilee, he went and begged him to come down and heal his son, for he was at the point of death. Then Jesus said to him, "Unless you see signs and wonders you will not believe." The official said to him, "Sir, come down before my little boy dies." Jesus said to him, "Go; your son will live." The man believed the word that Jesus spoke to him and started on his way. As he was going down, his slaves met him and told him that his child was alive. So he asked them the hour when he began to recover, and they said to him, "Yesterday at one in the afternoon the fever left him." The father realized that this was the hour when Jesus had said to him, "Your son will live." So he himself believed, along with his whole household. Now this was the second sign that Jesus did after coming from Judea to Galilee.

- John structures his presentation of the public life of Jesus around seven "signs." The first is the turning of water into wine at Cana (Jn. 2:1–11). Today's reading describes the second. For John, a sign is not just an unusual external event but a mysterious happening that reveals God and leads to faith. The royal official, desperately trying to save his dying son, begs Jesus to heal him. When Jesus assures him that his son will live, "The man believed the word that Jesus spoke to him."

- This story also illustrates how Jesus does not discriminate when someone is in need. In the previous chapter, he reaches out to the Samaritan woman. Here he helps a Gentile. He has come as Savior of the world. In my personal world today, who might need to encounter Jesus?

Tuesday 13th March
John 5:1–16

After this there was a festival of the Jews, and Jesus went up to Jerusalem. Now in Jerusalem by the Sheep Gate there is a pool, called in Hebrew Beth-zatha, which has five porticoes. In these lay many invalids—blind, lame, and paralyzed. One man was there who had been ill for thirty-eight years. When Jesus saw him lying there and knew that he had been there a long time, he said to him, "Do you want to be made well?" The sick man answered him, "Sir, I have no one to put me into the pool when the water is stirred up; and while I am making my way, someone else steps down ahead of me." Jesus said to him, "Stand up, take your mat and walk." At once the man was made well, and he took up his mat and began to walk. // Now that day was a sabbath. So the Jews said to the man who had been cured, "It is the sabbath; it is not lawful for you to carry your mat." But he answered them, "The man who made me well said to me, 'Take up your mat and walk.'" They asked him, "Who is the man who said to you, 'Take it up and walk'?" Now the man who had been healed did not know who it was, for Jesus had disappeared in the crowd that was there. Later Jesus found him in the temple and said to him, "See, you have been made well! Do not sin any more, so that nothing worse happens to you." The man went away and told the Jews that it was Jesus who had made him well. Therefore the Jews started persecuting Jesus, because he was doing such things on the sabbath.

- The anonymous man lying by the pool called Bethzatha had waited thirty-eight years for healing. He might be described as "living with desire" all that time. Our prayers are not always answered immediately. We have to "live with desire." Remember T. S. Eliot's line: "But the faith and the love and the hope are all in the waiting."

- The opponents of Jesus criticize the man who had been cured—for carrying his mat on the Sabbath. We think of kindness as attractive; yet here a compassionate act by Jesus evokes hostility. Have you ever seen a person's goodness evoking an evil response?

Wednesday 14th March
John 5:17–30

But Jesus answered them, "My Father is still working, and I also am working." For this reason the Jews were seeking all the more to kill him, because he was not only breaking the sabbath, but was also calling God his own Father, thereby making himself equal to God. // Jesus said to them, "Very truly, I tell you, the Son can do nothing on his own, but only what he sees the Father doing; for whatever the Father does, the Son does likewise. The Father loves the Son and shows him all that he himself is doing; and he will show him greater works than these, so that you will be astonished. Indeed, just as the Father raises the dead and gives them life, so also the Son gives life to whomsoever he wishes. The Father judges no one but has given all judgement to the Son, so that all may honor the Son just as they honor the Father. Anyone who does not honor the Son does not honor the Father who sent him. Very truly, I tell you, anyone who hears my word and believes him who sent me has eternal life, and does not come under judgement, but has passed from death to life. Very truly,

I tell you, the hour is coming, and is now here, when the dead will hear the voice of the Son of God, and those who hear will live. For just as the Father has life in himself, so he has granted the Son also to have life in himself; and he has given him authority to execute judgement, because he is the Son of Man. Do not be astonished at this; for the hour is coming when all who are in their graves will hear his voice and will come out— those who have done good, to the resurrection of life, and those who have done evil, to the resurrection of condemnation. I can do nothing on my own. As I hear, I judge; and my judgement is just, because I seek to do not my own will but the will of him who sent me."

• The relationship between Jesus and his heavenly Father is the topic in this enigmatic passage. Jesus traces everything in his being and in his choices to their source in the Father. "I can do nothing on my own." He and his Father are intertwined in every way, so much so that they are one (Jn. 10:30).

• Note the striking statement: "My Father is still working, and I also am working." God is present among us, but this is not a passive presence. It is an active presence through which God is involved in the drama of our lives as a fellow-actor or partner.

Thursday 15th March
John 5:31–47

Jesus said, "If I testify about myself, my testimony is not true. There is an-other who testifies on my behalf, and I know that his testimony to me is true. You sent messengers to John, and he testified to the truth. Not that I accept such human testimony, but I say these things so that you may be saved. He was a burning and shining lamp, and you were willing to rejoice for a while in his light. But I have a testimony greater than John's. The works that the Father has given me to complete, the very works that I am doing, testify on my behalf that the Father has sent me. And the Father who sent me has himself testified on my behalf. You have never heard his voice or seen his form, and you do not have his word abiding in you, because you do not believe him whom he has sent. You search the scriptures because you think that in them you have eternal life; and it is they that testify on my behalf. Yet you refuse to come to me to have life. I do not accept glory from human beings. But I know that you do not have the love of God in you. I have come in my Father's name, and you do not accept me; if another comes in his own name, you will accept him. How can you believe when you accept glory from one another and do not seek the glory that comes from the one who alone is God? Do not think that I will accuse you before the Father; your accuser is Moses, on whom you have set your hope. If you believed Moses, you would believe me, for he wrote about me. But if you do not believe what he wrote, how will you believe what I say?"

- Who is Jesus? This is the core question being teased out in today's reading. The answer hinges on his relationship to God (whom he calls his Father). A secondary question is: Who (or what) bears testimony (witness) to Jesus? John indicates four witnesses: John the Baptist, the works of Jesus himself, the Father, and the Scriptures. Do you understand this style of argument?

- Who is Jesus? John approaches the question from a Jewish religious and cultural perspective. How would you answer the question today from within your own cultural terms of reference? How would you answer it out of your personal experience of knowing him?

Friday 16th March
John 7:1–2, 10, 25–30

After this Jesus went about in Galilee. He did not wish to go about in Judea because the Jews were looking for an opportunity to kill him. Now the Jewish festival of Booths was near. // But after his brothers had gone to the festival, then he also went, not publicly but as it were in secret. Now some of the people of Jerusalem were saying, "Is not this the man whom they are trying to kill? And here he is, speaking openly, but they say nothing to him! Can it be that the authorities really know that this is the Messiah? Yet we know where this man is from; but when the Messiah comes, no one will know where he is from." Then Jesus cried out as he was teaching in the temple, "You know me, and you know where I am from. I have not come on my own. But the one who sent me is true, and you do not know him. I know him, because I am from him, and he sent me." Then they tried to arrest him, but no one laid hands on him, because his hour had not yet come.

- The festival of Booths (or Tabernacles) commemorates the wandering of the Hebrew people in the desert, part of the first Exodus. Jesus' death and resurrection will constitute the second exodus.

- Jesus is claiming to be "from God" because he is sent. Note the number of times in John's Gospel that Jesus refers to God (or more usually his Father) as "the one who sent me." Is it possible to say that you and I are also sent because God is our Father too?

Saturday 17th March
John 7:40–53

When they heard these words, some in the crowd said, "This is really the prophet." Others said, "This is the Messiah." But some asked, "Surely the Messiah does not come from Galilee, does he? Has not the scripture said that the Messiah is descended from David and comes from Bethlehem, the village where David lived?" So there was a division in the crowd because of him. Some of them wanted to arrest him, but no one laid hands on him. // Then the temple police went back to the chief priests and Pharisees, who asked them, "Why did you not arrest him?" The police answered, "Never has anyone spoken like this!" Then the Pharisees replied, "Surely you have not been deceived too, have you? Has any one of the authorities or of the Pharisees believed in him? But this crowd, which does not know the law— they are accursed." Nicodemus, who had gone to Jesus before, and who was one of them, asked, "Our law does not judge people without first giving them a hearing to find out what they are doing, does it?" They replied, "Surely you are not also from Galilee, are you? Search and you will see that no prophet is to arise from Galilee." Then each of them went home.

- The Jewish religious leaders and experts in the Law cannot agree on who Jesus is. Notice the constant appeal to the Old Testament. We may be more convinced by what the temple police report: "Never has anyone spoken like this!" Jesus speaks with integrity, wisdom, and authority. This impresses these unsophisticated men. They recognize the goodness of Jesus, which was hidden from the religious leaders.

- Pope Francis teaches that we must listen to the poor and the marginalized because they have a special insight into the reality of the world and of God. Who, in my daily encounters, might have authentic insight into the reality of God?

The Fifth Week of Lent
March 18—March 24

Something to think and pray about each day this week:

Keeping Hope
Viktor Frankl, the famous psychiatrist and concentration-camp survivor, observed in his important book *Man's Search for Meaning* that only those who had a reason to persevere in the horrific experience of the camps survived; those who lost hope quickly died. Quoting Nietzsche, he believed that "those who have a 'why' to live, can bear with almost any 'how.'" For Frankl, sacrifice is tolerable when it is meaningful.

The Evangelists portray Jesus as facing his suffering with resolve, not ignoring its reality, but choosing to enter it with his "face like flint." All four use the language of Psalm 22, described as "a poem of the person abandoned by God" or "a prayer of an innocent person." They also borrow the language and themes of the suffering servant of God, found in Isaiah, including the text above. They describe Jesus as fulfilling what Isaiah had described as a person who, in the midst of the great exile of Israel in Babylon, was called "to raise up the tribes of Jacob and to restore the survivors of Israel" (Isaiah 49:6) in order that God's salvation might reach to the ends of the earth. Jesus is faithful to his death.

Recalling the way Jesus approached his death, Paul would later write of how he himself thought nothing of the sufferings he faced.

> For I am convinced that neither death, nor life, nor angels, nor rulers, nor things present, nor things to come, nor powers, nor height, nor depth, nor anything else in all creation, will be able to separate us from the love of God in Christ Jesus our Lord.
>
> —Romans 8:38–39

Following Jesus, and following Paul's understanding of what Jesus' sacrifice meant, our prayer is that we might live in fidelity to our God who loves us, with perfect readiness to go where he calls us, unafraid of the consequences of that call.

—Tim Muldoon, *The Ignatian Workout for Lent*

The Presence of God

Dear Jesus, today I call on you, but not to ask for anything. I'd like only to dwell in your presence. May my heart respond to your love.

Freedom

God my creator, you gave me life and the gift of freedom. Through your love I exist in this world. May I never take the gift of life for granted. May I always respect others' right to life.

Consciousness

I ask how I am today. Am I particularly tired, stressed, or anxious? If any of these characteristics apply, can I try to let go of the concerns that disturb me?

The Word

The word of God comes down to us through the Scriptures. May the Holy Spirit enlighten my mind and my heart to respond to the gospel teachings. (Please turn to the Scripture on the following pages. Inspiration points are there should you need them. When you are ready, return here to continue.)

Conversation

I begin to talk with Jesus about the Scripture I have just read. What part of it strikes a chord in me? Perhaps the words of a friend—or some story I have heard recently—will rise to the surface in my consciousness. If so, does the story throw light on what the Scripture passage may be saying to me?

Conclusion

Glory be to the Father, and to the Son, and to the Holy Spirit,
As it was in the beginning, is now and ever shall be,
World without end. Amen.

Sunday 18th March
Fifth Sunday of Lent
John 12:20–33

Now among those who went up to worship at the festival were some Greeks. They came to Philip, who was from Bethsaida in Galilee, and said to him, "Sir, we wish to see Jesus." Philip went and told Andrew; then Andrew and Philip went and told Jesus. Jesus answered them, "The hour has come for the Son of Man to be glorified. Very truly, I tell you, unless a grain of wheat falls into the earth and dies, it remains just a single grain; but if it dies, it bears much fruit. Those who love their life lose it, and those who hate their life in this world will keep it for eternal life. Whoever serves me must follow me, and where I am, there will my servant be also. Whoever serves me, the Father will honor. // 'Now my soul is troubled. And what should I say—'Father, save me from this hour'? No, it is for this reason that I have come to this hour. Father, glorify your name." Then a voice came from heaven, "I have glorified it, and I will glorify it again." The crowd standing there heard it and said that it was thunder. Others said, "An angel has spoken to him." Jesus answered, "This voice has come for your sake, not for mine. Now is the judgement of this world; now the ruler of this world will be driven out. And I, when I am lifted up from the earth, will draw all people to myself." He said this to indicate the kind of death he was to die.

- The humble wish of the Greeks is to see Jesus. Lord, that is my wish also. That is why I give this time to prayer. May I see you more clearly, love you more dearly, and follow you more nearly, as the ancient prayer puts it.

- Jesus, in this time of prayer I imagine you putting a grain of wheat into my hand. You and I talk about what it can mean. When I next eat bread, it will have a deeper significance for me. When I share in the Eucharist, I will try to be aware that it means your own life, which is blessed, broken, shared, and consumed for the life of the world.

Monday 19th March
Saint Joseph, Spouse of the Blessed Virgin Mary
Matthew 1:16, 18–21, 24

and Jacob the father of Joseph the husband of Mary, of whom Jesus was born, who is called the Messiah. Now the birth of Jesus the Messiah took place in this way. When his mother Mary had been engaged to Joseph, but before they lived together, she was found to be with child from the Holy Spirit. Her husband Joseph, being a righteous man and unwilling to expose her to public disgrace, planned to dismiss her quietly. But just when he had resolved to do this, an angel of the Lord appeared to him in a dream and said, "Joseph, son of David, do not be afraid to take Mary as your wife, for the child conceived in her is from the Holy Spirit. She will bear a son, and you are to name him Jesus, for he will save his people from their sins." When Joseph awoke from sleep, he did as the angel of the Lord commanded him; he took her as his wife.

- Matthew invites us to ponder the birth of Jesus from the perspective of Joseph, the husband of Mary. He finds himself in a moral dilemma when he learns of Mary's pregnancy, which had come about "before they lived together." He is a righteous man who wants to do what is best for everyone and what is in harmony with the will of God. An angel is sent to enlighten him.

- Not all the decisions we are faced with in life are clearly between right and wrong. We may have to operate in morally grey areas, or in so-called "no-win" situations (where we will be misunderstood no matter what choice we make). We need to tap into the experience of others and pray for the wisdom of God's Holy Spirit.

Tuesday 20th March
John 8:21–30

Again he said to them, "I am going away, and you will search for me, but you will die in your sin. Where I am going, you cannot come." Then the Jews said, "Is he going to kill himself? Is that what he means by saying, 'Where I am going, you cannot come'?" He said to them, "You are from below, I am from above; you are of this world, I am not of this world. I told you that you would die in your sins, for you will die in your sins unless you believe that I am he." They said to him, "Who are you?" Jesus said to them, "Why do I speak to you at all? I have much to say about you and much to condemn; but the one who sent me is true, and I declare to the world what I have heard from him." They did not understand that he was speaking to them about the Father. So Jesus said, "When you have lifted up the Son of Man, then you will realize that I am he, and that I do nothing on my own, but I speak these things as the Father instructed me. And the one who sent me is with me; he has not left me alone, for I always do what is pleasing to him." As he was saying these things, many believed in him.

- The discussion is quite heated. "You will die in your sins unless you believe that I am he." And further down: "When you have lifted up the Son of Man, then you will realize that I am he." Jesus hanging on the cross is the ultimate answer to the question "Who are you?"

- The readings of these days may need to be simplified when brought to prayer. You might take a single verse, or even a single phrase. For example, "The one who sent me is with me; he has not left me alone." Or sit quietly with the overall mystery of who Jesus is!

Wednesday 21st March
John 8:31–42

Then Jesus said to the Jews who had believed in him, "If you continue in my word, you are truly my disciples; and you will know the truth, and the truth will make you free." They answered him, "We are descendants of Abraham and have never been slaves to anyone. What do you mean by saying, 'You will be made free'?" // Jesus answered them, "Very truly, I tell you, everyone who commits sin is a slave to sin. The slave does not have a permanent place in the household; the Son has a place there forever. So if the Son makes you free, you will be free indeed. I know that you are descendants of Abraham; yet you look for an opportunity to kill me, because there is no place in you for my word. I declare what I have seen in the Father's presence; as for you, you should do what you have heard from the Father." // They answered him, "Abraham is our father." Jesus said to them, "If you were Abraham's children, you would be doing what Abraham did, but now you are trying to kill me, a man who has told you the truth that I heard from God. This is not what Abraham did. You are indeed doing what your father does." They said to him, "We are not illegitimate children; we have one father, God himself." Jesus said to them, "If God were your Father, you would love me, for I came from God and now I am here. I did not come on my own, but he sent me."

- "The truth will make you free." This is one of the most frequently quoted statements of Jesus. But what is the meaning of "truth" and what is the meaning of "free"? Jesus discusses these issues with his listeners. Such discussion continues to this day among believers and even unbelievers. But does the statement make sense to you experientially? Can you point to a situation where being faced with the truth freed you from some unfreedom, addiction, obsession, or inner darkness?

- John will write much about love later in his Gospel and in his letters. But his use of the word in this reading comes as a surprise, as if it is out of place. Had you noticed?

Thursday 22nd March
John 8:51–59

"Very truly, I tell you, whoever keeps my word will never see death." The Jews said to him, "Now we know that you have a demon. Abraham died, and so did the prophets; yet you say, 'Whoever keeps my word will never taste death.' Are you greater than our father Abraham, who died? The prophets also died. Who do you claim to be?" Jesus answered, "If I glorify myself, my glory is nothing. It is my Father who glorifies me, he of whom you say, 'He is our God,' though you do not know him. But I know him; if I were to say that I do not know him, I would be a liar like you. But I do know him and I keep his word. Your ancestor Abraham rejoiced that he would see my day; he saw it and was glad." Then the Jews said to him, "You are not yet fifty years old, and have you seen Abraham?" Jesus said to them, "Very truly, I tell you, before Abraham was, I am." So they picked up stones to throw at him, but Jesus hid himself and went out of the temple.

- "Who do you claim to be?" The discussion about the identity of Jesus continues. This relentless questioning shows how important the issue is—then and now. But instead of leading to a meeting of minds, Jesus' arguments provoke his enemies even further. "They picked up stones to throw at him." His life is now in danger. Can you understand this hostility to Jesus?

- Note yet another "I am" statement: "Before Abraham was, I am." Jesus claims both pre-existence and oneness with God.

Friday 23rd March

John 10:31–42

The Jews took up stones again to stone him. Jesus replied, "I have shown you many good works from the Father. For which of these are you going to stone me?" The Jews answered, "It is not for a good work that we are going to stone you, but for blasphemy, because you, though only a human being, are making yourself God." Jesus answered, "Is it not written in your law, 'I said, you are gods'? If those to whom the word of God came were called 'gods'—and the scripture cannot be annulled—can you say that the one whom the Father has sanctified and sent into the world is blaspheming because I said, 'I am God's Son'? If I am not doing the works of my Father, then do not believe me. But if I do them, even though you do not believe me, believe the works, so that you may know and understand that the Father is in me and I am in the Father." Then they tried to arrest him again, but he escaped from their hands. // He went away again across the Jordan to the place where John had been baptizing earlier, and he remained there. Many came to him, and they were saying, "John performed no sign, but everything that John said about this man was true." And many believed in him there.

- Another threat to stone Jesus is followed by another attempt to arrest him. In between, the debate rages on with the word "blasphemy" coming to the fore. Jesus is guilty of blasphemy because (his opponents say), "You, though only a human being, are making yourself God." This, of course, is the heart of the matter. Christian faith affirms that Jesus is fully human and fully divine.

- Jesus tries to get his listeners to pay attention to his works as well as to his words. His works also speak, communicate, witness, teach, reveal. Jesus can do these works only from the power and will of the Father. Can our own words and actions be traced so clearly back to the God who is our Father?

Saturday 24th March
John 11:45–56

Many of the Jews therefore, who had come with Mary and had seen what Jesus did, believed in him. But some of them went to the Pharisees and told them what he had done. So the chief priests and the Pharisees called a meeting of the council, and said, "What are we to do? This man is performing many signs. If we let him go on like this, everyone will believe in him, and the Romans will come and destroy both our holy place and our nation." But one of them, Caiaphas, who was high priest that year, said to them, "You know nothing at all! You do not understand that it is better for you to have one man die for the people than to have the whole nation destroyed." He did not say this on his own, but being high priest that year he prophesied that Jesus was about to die for the nation, and not for the nation only, but to gather into one the dispersed children of God. So from that day on they planned to put him to death. // Jesus therefore no longer walked about openly among the Jews, but went from there to a town called Ephraim in the region near the wilderness; and he remained there with the disciples. Now the Passover of the Jews was near, and many went up from the country to Jerusalem before the Passover to purify themselves. They were looking for Jesus and were asking one another as they stood in the temple, "What do you think? Surely he will not come to the festival, will he?"

- Caiaphas was a Sadducee—ruthless, political, determined to buttress the status quo and the privileges of his wealthy class. He used the argument of the powerful in every age: we must eliminate the awkward troublemaker in the name of the common good—meaning the comfort of those in power. But Caiaphas spoke more wisely than he knew. One man, Jesus, was to die for the people, and for you and me.

- Those appointed to be the community's spiritual leaders now plotted to kill Jesus. Is this shocking to you? Why, or why not? Have you known other leaders, spiritual or otherwise, who stooped to such evil?

Holy Week
March 25—March 31

Something to think and pray about each day this week:

That Little Lost Lamb

The Word of God pitched his tent among us, sinners who are in need of mercy. And we all must hasten to receive the grace he offers us. Instead, the Gospel of St. John continues, "his own people received him not" (1:11). We reject him too many times, we prefer to remain closed in our errors and the anxiety of our sins. But Jesus does not desist and never ceases to offer himself and his grace, which saves us! Jesus is patient; he knows how to wait, and he waits for us always. This is a message of hope, a message of salvation, ancient and ever new. And we are called to witness with joy to this message of the Gospel of life, to the Gospel of light, of hope, and of love. For Jesus' message is this: life, light, hope, and love.

Jesus is all mercy. Jesus is all love: he is God made man. Each one of us is that little lost lamb, the coin that was mislaid; each one of us is that son who has squandered his freedom on false idols, illusions of happiness, and has lost everything. But God does not forget us; the Father never abandons us. He is a patient father, always waiting for us! He respects our freedom, but he remains faithful forever. And when we come back to him, he welcomes us like children into his house, for he never ceases, not for one instant, to wait for us with love. And his heart rejoices over every child who returns. He is celebrating because he is joy. God has this joy, when one of us sinners goes to him and asks his forgiveness.

—Pope Francis, *The Joy of Discipleship*

The Presence of God
God is with me, but even more astounding, God is within me.
Let me dwell for a moment on God's life-giving presence
in my body, in my mind, in my heart,
as I sit here, right now.

Freedom
Lord, may I never take the gift of freedom for granted. You gave me the
great blessing of freedom of spirit. Fill my spirit with your peace and joy.

Consciousness
I remind myself that I am in the presence of God, who is my strength in
times of weakness and my comforter in times of sorrow.

The Word
I take my time to read the word of God slowly, a few times, allowing myself to dwell on anything that strikes me. (Please turn to the Scripture on
the following pages. Inspiration points are there should you need them.
When you are ready, return here to continue.)

Conversation
Jesus, you always welcomed little children when you walked on this earth.
Teach me to have a childlike trust in you. Teach me to live in the knowl-
edge that you will never abandon me.

Conclusion
Glory be to the Father, and to the Son, and to the Holy Spirit,
As it was in the beginning, is now and ever shall be,
World without end. Amen.

Sunday 25th March
Palm Sunday of the Passion of the Lord
Mark 15:1–39

As soon as it was morning, the chief priests held a consultation with the elders and scribes and the whole council. They bound Jesus, led him away, and handed him over to Pilate. Pilate asked him, "Are you the King of the Jews?" He answered him, "You say so." Then the chief priests accused him of many things. Pilate asked him again, "Have you no answer? See how many charges they bring against you." But Jesus made no further reply, so that Pilate was amazed. // Now at the festival he used to release a prisoner for them, anyone for whom they asked. Now a man called Barabbas was in prison with the rebels who had committed murder during the insurrection. So the crowd came and began to ask Pilate to do for them according to his custom. Then he answered them, "Do you want me to release for you the King of the Jews?" For he realized that it was out of jealousy that the chief priests had handed him over. But the chief priests stirred up the crowd to have him release Barabbas for them instead. Pilate spoke to them again, "Then what do you wish me to do with the man you call the King of the Jews?" They shouted back, "Crucify him!" Pilate asked them, "Why, what evil has he done?" But they shouted all the more, "Crucify him!" So Pilate, wishing to satisfy the crowd, released Barabbas for them; and after flogging Jesus, he handed him over to be crucified. // Then the soldiers led him into the courtyard of the palace (that is, the governor's headquarters); and they called together the whole cohort. And they clothed him in a purple cloak; and after twisting some thorns into a crown, they put it on him. And they began saluting him, "Hail, King of the Jews!" They struck his head with a reed, spat upon him, and knelt down in homage to him. After mocking him, they stripped him of the purple cloak and put his own clothes on him. Then they led him out to crucify him. // They compelled a passer-by, who was coming in from the country, to carry his cross; it was Simon of Cyrene, the father of Alexander and Rufus. Then they brought Jesus to the place called Golgotha (which means the place of a skull). And they offered him wine mixed with myrrh; but he did not take it. And they crucified him, and divided his clothes among them, casting lots to decide what each should take. // It was nine o'clock in the morning when they crucified him. The inscription of the charge against him read, "The King of the Jews." And with him they crucified two bandits, one on his right and one on his left. Those who passed by derided him, shaking their heads and saying, "Aha! You who would destroy the temple and build it in three days, save yourself, and come down from the cross!" In the same way the chief priests, along with the scribes, were also mocking him among themselves and saying, "He saved others; he cannot save himself. Let the Messiah, the King of Israel, come down from the cross now, so that we may see and believe." Those who were crucified with him also taunted him. // When it was noon, darkness came over the whole land until three in the afternoon. At three o'clock Jesus cried out with a loud voice, "Eloi, Eloi, lema sabachthani?" which means, "My God, my God, why have you forsaken me?" When some of the bystanders heard it, they said, "Listen, he is calling for Elijah." And someone ran, filled a sponge with sour wine, put it on a stick, and gave it to him to drink, saying, "Wait, let us see whether Elijah will come to take him down." Then Jesus gave a loud cry and breathed his last. And the curtain of the temple was torn in two, from top to bottom. Now when the centurion, who stood facing him, saw that in this way he breathed his last, he said, "Truly this man was God's Son!"

- Where would I be in this drama? Which person in the crowd? What would I think of all I witnessed? How would my heart respond?

- Lord, help me walk with you on this dark journey. Teach me how to share in your pain but also in your faith.

Monday 26th March
Monday of Holy Week
John 12:1–11

Six days before the Passover Jesus came to Bethany, the home of Lazarus, whom he had raised from the dead. There they gave a dinner for him. Martha served, and Lazarus was one of those at the table with him. Mary took a pound of costly perfume made of pure nard, anointed Jesus' feet, and wiped them with her hair. The house was filled with the fragrance of the perfume. But Judas Iscariot, one of his disciples (the one who was about to betray him), said, 'Why was this perfume not sold for three hundred denarii and the money given to the poor?' (He said this not because he cared about the poor, but because he was a thief; he kept the common purse and used to steal what was put into it.) Jesus said, "Leave her alone. She bought it so that she might keep it for the day of my burial. You always have the poor with you, but you do not always have me." // When the great crowd of the Jews learned that he was there, they came not only because of Jesus but also to see Lazarus, whom he had raised from the dead. So the chief priests planned to put Lazarus to death as well, since it was on account of him that many of the Jews were deserting and were believing in Jesus.

- The home of Martha and Mary in Bethany was always a place of welcome and refuge for Jesus. With his life increasingly under threat he chooses to enjoy a meal there with his friends. But Mary's action of anointing his feet with costly perfume causes friction. Judas, who was also present, objects to such extravagance. Jesus defends Mary and links her action with his coming death and burial.

- Whose side are you on? Perhaps you can see some validity in what Judas says. Yet it is Mary who continues to be admired for her loving and uninhibited gesture.

Tuesday 27th March
Tuesday of Holy Week
John 13:21–33, 36–38

After saying this Jesus was troubled in spirit, and declared, "Very truly, I tell you, one of you will betray me." The disciples looked at one another, uncertain of whom he was speaking. One of his disciples—the one whom Jesus loved—was reclining next to him; Simon Peter therefore motioned to him to ask Jesus of whom he was speaking. So while reclining next to Jesus, he asked him, "Lord, who is it?" Jesus answered, "It is the one to whom I give this piece of bread when I have dipped it in the dish." So when he had dipped the piece of bread, he gave it to Judas son of Simon Iscariot. After he received the piece of bread, Satan entered into him. Jesus said to him, "Do quickly what you are going to do." Now no one at the table knew why he said this to him. Some thought that, because Judas had the common purse, Jesus was telling him, "Buy what we need for the festival"; or, that he should give something to the poor. So, after receiving the piece of bread, he immediately went out. And it was night. // When he had gone out, Jesus said, "Now the Son of Man has been glorified, and

God has been glorified in him. If God has been glorified in him, God will also glorify him in himself and will glorify him at once. Little children, I am with you only a little longer. You will look for me; and as I said to the Jews so now I say to you, 'Where I am going, you cannot come.'" // Simon Peter said to him, "Lord, where are you going?" Jesus answered, "Where I am going, you cannot follow me now; but you will follow afterwards." Peter said to him, "Lord, why can I not follow you now? I will lay down my life for you." Jesus answered, "Will you lay down your life for me? Very truly, I tell you, before the cock crows, you will have denied me three times."

- Imagine yourself reclining at the table during the Last Supper. Are you picking up the tensions among the other participants? Do you notice how Jesus is "troubled in spirit"? Have you sensed his inner turmoil as one of his friends is plotting to betray him? Let the drama of the scene draw you into it. What are your predominant feelings? Speak freely to Jesus about the whole situation and your reactions to it.

- Toward the end of the reading we see Peter boasting and blustering and making a fool of himself. Jesus reads the human heart and knows Peter. Far from laying down his life for Jesus, Peter will soon be denying (three times!) that he ever knew him. What would you say to Peter if you were there?

Wednesday 28th March
Wednesday of Holy Week
Matthew 26:14–25

Then one of the twelve, who was called Judas Iscariot, went to the chief priests and said, "What will you give me if I betray him to you?" They paid him thirty pieces of silver. And from that moment he began to look for an opportunity to betray him. // On the first day of Unleavened Bread the disciples came to Jesus, saying, "Where do you want us to make the preparations for you to eat the Passover?" He said, "Go into the city to a certain man, and say to him, 'The Teacher says, My time is near; I will keep the Passover at your house with my disciples.'" So the disciples did as Jesus had directed them, and they prepared the Passover meal. // When it was evening, he took his place with the twelve; and while they were eating, he said, "Truly I tell you, one of you will betray me." And they became greatly distressed and began to say to him one after another, "Surely not I, Lord?" He answered, "The one who has dipped his hand into the bowl with me will betray me. The Son of Man goes as it is written of him, but woe to that one by whom the Son of Man is betrayed! It would have been better for that one not to have been born." Judas, who betrayed him, said, "Surely not I, Rabbi?" He replied, "You have said so."

• In some places this day is known as Spy Wednesday. Judas is the "spy" or sly, sneaky person who secretly approaches the chief priests with the intention of betraying Jesus to them. Like all such spies he is looking for a reward and agrees on thirty pieces of silver. The naming of the price is meant to shock us. Is this all that the life of the Son of Man is worth?

• Jesus uses only words to persuade Judas not to carry out his pact with the chief priests. He takes no other measures that might prevent his arrest. Does this surprise you? Can you understand it?

Thursday 29th March
Thursday of Holy Week (Holy Thursday)
John 13:1–15

Now before the festival of the Passover, Jesus knew that his hour had come to depart from this world and go to the Father. Having loved his own who were in the world, he loved them to the end. The devil had already put it into the heart of Judas son of Simon Iscariot to betray him. And during supper Jesus, knowing that the Father had given all things into his hands, and that he had come from God and was going to God, got up from the table, took off his outer robe, and tied a towel around himself. Then he poured water into a basin and began to wash the disciples' feet and to wipe them with the towel that was tied around him. He came to Simon Peter, who said to him, "Lord, are you going to wash my feet?" Jesus answered, "You do not know now what I am doing, but later you will understand." Peter said to him, "You will never wash my feet." Jesus answered, "Unless I wash you, you have no share with me." Simon Peter said to him, "Lord, not my feet only but also my hands and my head!" Jesus said to him, "One who has bathed does not need to wash, except for the feet, but is entirely clean. And you are clean, though not all of you." For he knew who was to betray him; for this reason he said, "Not all of you are clean." // After he had washed their feet, had put on his robe, and had returned to the table, he said to them, "Do you know what I have done to you? You call me Teacher and Lord—and you are right, for that is what I am. So if I, your Lord and Teacher, have washed your feet, you also ought to wash one another's feet. For I have set you an example, that you also should do as I have done to you."

- John introduces this story with great solemnity. He takes care to specify precisely the point in Jesus' life when he decides to wash his disciples' feet. Afterwards, Jesus explains the meaning of what he has done. He holds it up as an example for the apostles to follow. They are to express love within their community with humility and in practical ways. Note that this service is to be mutual: "to wash one another's feet." What are you called to do in your life circumstances?

- There is no description of the institution of the Eucharist in John's Gospel. Commentators see the washing of the feet as taking its place. Do you grasp the common values that underlie both events?

Friday 30th March
Friday of the Passion of the Lord (Good Friday)
John 18:1—19:42

After Jesus had spoken these words, he went out with his disciples across the Kidron valley to a place where there was a garden, which he and his disciples entered. Now Judas, who betrayed him, also knew the place, because Jesus often met there with his disciples. So Judas brought a detachment of soldiers together with police from the chief priests and the Pharisees, and they came there with lanterns and torches and weapons. Then Jesus, knowing all that was to happen to him, came forward and asked them, "Whom are you looking for?" They answered, "Jesus of Nazareth." Jesus replied, "I am he." Judas, who betrayed him, was standing with them. When Jesus said to them, "I am he," they stepped back and fell to the ground. Again he asked them, "Whom are you looking for?" And they said, "Jesus of Nazareth." Jesus answered, "I told you that I am he. So if you are looking for me, let these men go." This was to fulfill the word that he had spoken, "I did not lose a single one of those whom you gave me." Then Simon Peter, who had a sword, drew it, struck the high priest's slave, and cut off his right ear. The slave's name was

Malchus. Jesus said to Peter, "Put your sword back into its sheath. Am I not to drink the cup that the Father has given me?" // So the soldiers, their officer, and the Jewish police arrested Jesus and bound him. First they took him to Annas, who was the father-in-law of Caiaphas, the high priest that year. Caiaphas was the one who had advised the Jews that it was better to have one person die for the people. // Simon Peter and another disciple followed Jesus. Since that disciple was known to the high priest, he went with Jesus into the courtyard of the high priest, but Peter was standing outside at the gate. So the other disciple, who was known to the high priest, went out, spoke to the woman who guarded the gate, and brought Peter in. The woman said to Peter, "You are not also one of this man's disciples, are you?" He said, "I am not." Now the slaves and the police had made a charcoal fire because it was cold, and they were standing around it and warming themselves. Peter also was standing with them and warming himself. // Then the high priest questioned Jesus about his disciples and about his teaching. Jesus answered, "I have spoken openly to the world; I have always taught in synagogues and in the temple, where all the Jews come together. I have said nothing in secret. Why do you ask me? Ask those who heard what I said to them; they know what I said." When he had said this, one of the police standing nearby struck Jesus on the face, saying, "Is that how you answer the high priest?" Jesus answered, "If I have spoken wrongly, testify to the wrong. But if I have spoken rightly, why do you strike me?" Then Annas sent him bound to Caiaphas the high priest. // Now Simon Peter was standing and warming himself. They asked him, "You are not also one of his disciples, are you?" He denied it and said, "I am not." One of the slaves of the high priest, a relative of the man whose ear Peter had cut off, asked, "Did I not see you in the garden with him?" Again Peter denied it, and at that moment the cock crowed. // Then they took Jesus from Caiaphas to Pilate's headquarters. It was early in the morning. They themselves did not enter the headquarters, so as to avoid ritual defilement and to be able to eat the Passover. So Pilate went out to them and said, "What accusation do you bring against this man?" They answered, "If this man were not a criminal, we would not have handed him over to you." Pilate said to them, "Take him yourselves and judge him according to your law." The Jews replied, "We are not permitted to put anyone to death." (This was to fulfill what Jesus had said when he indicated the kind of death he was to die.) // Then Pilate entered the headquarters again, summoned Jesus, and asked him, "Are you the King of the Jews?" Jesus answered, "Do you ask this on your own, or did others tell you about me?" Pilate replied, "I am not a Jew, am I? Your own nation and the chief priests have handed you over to me. What have you done?" Jesus answered, "My kingdom is not from this world. If my kingdom were from this world, my followers would be fighting to keep me from being handed over to the Jews. But as it is, my kingdom is not from here." Pilate asked him, "So you are a king?" Jesus answered, "You say that I am a king. For this I was born, and for this I came into the world, to testify to the truth. Everyone who belongs to the truth listens to my voice." Pilate asked him, "What is truth?" // After he had said this, he went out to the Jews again and told them, "I find no case against him. But you have a custom that I release someone for you at the Passover. Do you want me to release for you the King of the Jews?" They shouted in reply, "Not this man, but Barabbas!" Now Barabbas was a bandit. // Then Pilate took Jesus and had him flogged. And the soldiers wove a crown of thorns and put it on his head, and they dressed him in a purple robe. They kept coming up to him, saying, "Hail, King of the Jews!" and striking him on the face. Pilate went out again and said to them, "Look, I am bringing him out to you to let you know that I find no case against him." So Jesus came out, wearing the crown of thorns and the purple robe. Pilate said to them, "Here is the man!" When the chief priests and the police saw him, they shouted, "Crucify him! Crucify him!" Pilate said to them, "Take him yourselves and crucify him; I find no case against him." The Jews answered him, "We have a law, and according to that law he ought to die because he has claimed to be the Son of God." // Now when Pilate heard this, he was more afraid than ever. He entered his headquarters again and asked Jesus, "Where are you from?" But Jesus gave him no answer. Pilate therefore said to him, "Do you refuse to speak to me? Do you not know that I have power to release you, and power to crucify you?" Jesus answered him, "You would have no power over me unless it had been given you from above; therefore the one who handed me over to you is guilty of a greater sin." From then on Pilate tried to release him, but the Jews cried out, "If you release this man, you are no friend of the emperor. Everyone who claims to be a king sets himself against the emperor." // When Pilate heard these words, he brought Jesus outside and sat on the judge's bench at a place called The Stone Pavement, or in Hebrew Gabbatha. Now it was the day of Preparation for the Passover; and it was about noon. He said to the Jews, "Here is your King!" They cried out, "Away with him! Away with him! Crucify him!" Pilate asked them, "Shall I crucify your King?" The chief priests answered, "We have no king but the emperor." Then he handed him over to them to be crucified. // So they took Jesus; and carrying the cross by himself, he went out to what is called The Place of the Skull, which in Hebrew is called Golgotha. There they crucified him, and with him two others, one on either side, with Jesus between them. Pilate also had an inscription written and put on the cross. It read, "Jesus of Nazareth, the King of the Jews." Many of the Jews read this inscription, because the place where Jesus was crucified was near the city; and it was written in Hebrew, in Latin, and in Greek. Then the chief priests of the Jews said to Pilate, "Do not write, 'The King of the Jews,' but, 'This man said, I am King of the Jews.'" Pilate answered, "What I have written I have written." When the soldiers had crucified Jesus, they took his clothes and divided them into four parts, one for each soldier. They also took his tunic; now the tunic was seamless, woven in one piece from the top. So they said to one another, "Let us not tear it, but cast lots for it to see who will get it." This was to fulfill what the scripture says,

"They divided my clothes among themselves,
    and for my clothing they cast lots."

And that is what the soldiers did.

Meanwhile, standing near the cross of Jesus were his mother, and his mother's sister, Mary the wife of Clopas, and Mary Magdalene. When Jesus saw his mother and the disciple whom he loved standing beside her, he said to his mother, "Woman, here is your son." Then he said to the disciple, "Here is your mother." And from that hour the disciple took her into his own home. // After this, when Jesus knew that all was now finished, he said (in order to fulfill the scripture), "I am thirsty." A jar full of sour wine was standing there. So they put a sponge full of the wine on a branch of hyssop and held it to his mouth. When Jesus had received the wine, he said, "It is finished." Then he bowed his head and gave up his spirit. // Since it was the day of Preparation, the Jews did not want the bodies left on the cross during the sabbath, especially because that sabbath was a day of great solemnity. So they asked Pilate to have the legs of the crucified men broken and the bodies removed. Then the soldiers came and broke the legs of the first and of the other who had been crucified with him. But when they came to Jesus and saw that he was already dead, they did not break his legs. Instead, one of the soldiers pierced his side with a spear, and at once blood and water came out. (He who saw this has testified so that you also may believe. His testimony is true, and he knows that he tells the truth.) These things occurred so that the scripture might be fulfilled, "None of his bones shall be broken." And again another passage of scripture says, "They will look on the one whom they have pierced." // After these things, Joseph of Arimathea, who was a disciple of Jesus, though a secret one because of his fear of the Jews, asked Pilate to let him take away the body of Jesus. Pilate gave him permission; so he came and removed his body. Nicodemus, who had at first come to Jesus by night, also came, bringing a mixture of myrrh and aloes, weighing about a hundred pounds. They took the body of Jesus and wrapped it with the spices in linen cloths, according to the burial custom of the Jews. Now there was a garden in the place where he was crucified, and in the garden there was a new tomb in which no one had ever been laid. And so, because it was the Jewish day of Preparation, and the tomb was nearby, they laid Jesus there.

- Good Friday puts the cross before me and challenges me not to look away. If I have followed Jesus' footsteps to Calvary, I do not have to fear because I, like him, am confident in God's enduring presence.

- Wherever there is suffering or pain, I seek the face of Jesus. I ask him for the strength I need to be a sign of hope wherever there is despair, to be a presence of love wherever it is most needed.

Saturday 31st March
Holy Saturday
Mark 16:1–7

When the sabbath was over, Mary Magdalene, and Mary the mother of James, and Salome bought spices, so that they might go and anoint him. And very early on the first day of the week, when the sun had risen, they went to the tomb. They had been saying to one another, "Who will roll away the stone for us from the entrance to the tomb?" When they looked up, they saw that the stone, which was very large, had already been rolled back. As they entered the tomb, they saw a young man, dressed in a white robe, sitting on the right side; and they were alarmed. But he said to them, "Do not be alarmed; you are looking for Jesus of Nazareth, who was crucified. He has been raised; he is not here. Look, there is the place they laid him. But go, tell his disciples and Peter that he is going ahead of you to Galilee; there you will see him, just as he told you."

• Angels could have come to the women in their homes, couldn't they? But they allowed them to make the sorrowful walk to the tomb. They needed to see for themselves that it was empty. They had to experience the surprise, the shock, then the alarm when the angel appeared to them. God does not eliminate our need for learning and perceiving, step-by-step.

• No sooner have they understood that Jesus has been raised than they are given the crucial task of taking this news to the disciples. We see the love and bravery of these women, who did not run from the scene and panic but stood their ground and listened to God's message. Lord, may I develop this kind of sturdy faith in you.

Octave of Easter
April 1—April 7

Something to think and pray about each day this week:

The Moments That Surprise
Vulnerability opens us to God's surprises. Mary Magdalene was surprised when Christ called her name. Peter and his fellow fisherman were surprised by the sudden pull in their casted nets. Thomas was surprised by the solidness of the person in front of him. The men walking the road to Emmaus were surprised by their guest at table, later noticing the longing within themselves: "Were not our hearts burning within us on the road?" We too recognize the Resurrected Jesus in these moments of surprise—in a familiar voice calling us by name, in unexpected abundance, in a concrete experience of God's presence, in the breaking of the bread. These surprises are moments of recognition—when we know the Risen God is in our midst and that Easter is not a one-time event. The wait is over and daybreak comes. Joy surprises, and everywhere resurrection is happening.

—Elizabeth Eiland Figueroa on *dotMagis*, the blog of
IgnatianSpirituality.com
http://www.ignatianspirituality.com/21204/waiting-for-daybreak

The Presence of God

Dear Lord, as I come to you today, fill my heart, my whole being, with the wonder of your presence. Help me remain receptive to you as I put aside the cares of this world. Fill my mind with your peace.

Freedom

Lord, grant me the grace to be free from the excesses of this life. Let me not get caught up with the desire for wealth. Keep my heart and mind free to love and serve you.

Consciousness

I exist in a web of relationships: links to nature, people, God.
I trace out these links, giving thanks for the life that flows through them.
Some links are twisted or broken; I may feel regret, anger, disappointment.
I pray for the gift of acceptance and forgiveness.

The Word

God speaks to each of us individually. I listen attentively, to hear what he is saying to me. Read the text a few times, then listen. (Please turn to the Scripture on the following pages. Inspiration points are there should you need them. When you are ready, return here to continue.)

Conversation

Jesus, you speak to me through the words of the Gospels. May I respond to your call today. Teach me to recognize your hand at work in my daily living.

Conclusion

I thank God for these moments we have spent together and for any insights I have been given concerning the text.

Sunday 1st April
Easter Sunday of the Resurrection of the Lord
Luke 24:13–35

Now on that same day two of them were going to a village called Emmaus, about seven miles from Jerusalem, and talking with each other about all these things that had happened. While they were talking and discussing, Jesus himself came near and went with them, but their eyes were kept from recognizing him. And he said to them, "What are you discussing with each other while you walk along?" They stood still, looking sad. Then one of them, whose name was Cleopas, answered him, "Are you the only stranger in Jerusalem who does not know the things that have taken place there in these days?" He asked them, "What things?" They replied, "The things about Jesus of Nazareth, who was a prophet mighty in deed and word before God and all the people, and how our chief priests and leaders handed him over to be condemned to death and crucified him. But we had hoped that he was the one to redeem Israel. Yes, and besides all this, it is now the third day since these things took place. Moreover, some women of our group astounded us. They were at the tomb early this morning, and when they did not find his body there, they came back and told us that they had indeed seen a vision of angels who said that he was alive. Some of those who were with us went to the tomb and found it just as the women had said; but they did not see him." Then he said to them, "Oh, how foolish you are, and how slow of heart to believe all that the prophets have declared! Was it not necessary that the Messiah should suffer these things and then enter into his glory?" Then beginning with Moses and all the prophets, he interpreted to them the things about himself in all the scriptures. // As they came near the village to which they were going, he walked ahead as if he were going on. But they urged him strongly, saying, "Stay with us, because it is almost evening and the day is now nearly over." So he went in to stay with them. When he was at the table with them, he took bread, blessed and broke it, and gave it to them. Then their eyes were opened, and they recognized him; and he vanished from their sight. They said to each other, "Were not our hearts burning within us while he was talking to us on the road, while he was opening the scriptures to us?" That same hour they got up and returned to Jerusalem; and they found the eleven and their companions gathered together. They were saying, "The Lord has risen indeed, and he has appeared to Simon!" Then they told what had happened on the road, and how he had been made known to them in the breaking of the bread.

- Sit at table with the disciples and Jesus in the inn at Emmaus. Notice the eucharistic overtones of what Jesus does with the bread. Each time we attend Mass do we recognize him in the breaking of the bread?

- Are we like the two disciples in wanting to share their experience of the risen Lord? Even though it was night, they headed back to Jerusalem to share this news. Lord, I confess that I don't feel such urgency. But I am willing.

Monday 2nd April
Matthew 28:8–15

So they left the tomb quickly with fear and great joy, and ran to tell his disciples. Suddenly Jesus met them and said, "Greetings!" And they came to him, took hold of his feet, and worshipped him. Then Jesus said to them, "Do not be afraid; go and tell my brothers to go to Galilee; there they will see me." // While they were going, some of the guard went into the city and told the chief priests everything that had happened. After the priests had assembled with the elders, they devised a plan to give a large sum of money to the soldiers, telling them, "You must say, 'His disciples came by night and stole him away while we were asleep.' If this comes to the governor's ears, we will satisfy him and keep you out of trouble." So they took the money and did as they were directed. And this story is still told among the Jews to this day."

- In Matthew's account, two of the women disciples are the first to receive the message of the angel (telling them that Jesus is risen), the first to meet him in person, and the first to announce this good news (gospel) to the male disciples.

- The remainder of the reading is about the cover-up orchestrated by the chief priests and elders. Bribery buys the silence of the soldiers, and further bribery is promised to make sure the governor does not cause trouble. We are familiar with this pattern of corruption, are we not? But Jesus is still risen! Alleluia!

Tuesday 3rd April
John 20:11–18

But Mary stood weeping outside the tomb. As she wept, she bent over to look into the tomb; and she saw two angels in white, sitting where the body of Jesus had been lying, one at the head and the other at the feet. They said to her, "Woman, why are you weeping?" She said to them, "They have taken away my Lord, and I do not know where they have laid him." When she had said this, she turned around and saw Jesus standing there, but she did not know that it was Jesus. Jesus said to her, "Woman, why are you weeping? Whom are you looking for?" Supposing him to be the gardener, she said to him, "Sir, if you have carried him away, tell me where you have laid him, and I will take him away." Jesus said to her, "Mary!" She turned and said to him in Hebrew, "Rabbouni!" (which means Teacher). Jesus said to her, "Do not hold on to me, because I have not yet ascended to the Father. But go to my brothers and say to them, 'I am ascending to my Father and your Father, to my God and your God.'" Mary Magdalene went and announced to the disciples, "I have seen the Lord"; and she told them that he had said these things to her.

• How well we come to know Mary Magdalene in this scene! Grief-stricken at the loss of her beloved Jesus, she stands disconsolate and disoriented at the empty tomb. See how Jesus turns her heartache into joy, her misery into delight, simply by calling her by name. Her dear friend lives! And more, he has a mission to entrust to her. She is to tell the other disciples: "I have seen the Lord." This is the testimony we, too, are called to give to the world.

• What does the risen Jesus entrust to me? And how will I recognize him?

Wednesday 4th April
Luke 24:13–35

Now on that same day two of them were going to a village called Emmaus, about seven miles from Jerusalem, and talking with each other about all these things that had happened. While they were talking and discussing, Jesus himself came near and went with them, but their eyes were kept from recognizing him. And he said to them, "What are you discussing with each other while you walk along?" They stood still, looking sad.

Then one of them, whose name was Cleopas, answered him, "Are you the only stranger in Jerusalem who does not know the things that have taken place there in these days?" He asked them, "What things?" They replied, "The things about Jesus of Nazareth, who was a prophet mighty in deed and word before God and all the people, and how our chief priests and leaders handed him over to be condemned to death and crucified him. But we had hoped that he was the one to redeem Israel. Yes, and besides all this, it is now the third day since these things took place. Moreover, some women of our group astounded us. They were at the tomb early this morning, and when they did not find his body there, they came back and told us that they had indeed seen a vision of angels who said that he was alive. Some of those who were with us went to the tomb and found it just as the women had said; but they did not see him." Then he said to them, "Oh, how foolish you are, and how slow of heart to believe all that the prophets have declared! Was it not necessary that the Messiah should suffer these things and then enter into his glory?" Then beginning with Moses and all the prophets, he interpreted to them the things about himself in all the scriptures. // As they came near the village to which they were going, he walked ahead as if he were going on. But they urged him strongly, saying, "Stay with us, because it is almost evening and the day is now nearly over." So he went in to stay with them. When he was at the table with them, he took bread, blessed and broke it, and gave it to them. Then their eyes were opened, and they recognized him; and he vanished from their sight. They said to each other, "Were not our hearts burning within us while he was talking to us on the road, while he was opening the scriptures to us?" That same hour they got up and returned to Jerusalem; and they found the eleven and their companions gathered together. They were saying, "The Lord has risen indeed, and he has appeared to Simon!" Then they told what had happened on the road, and how he had been made known to them in the breaking of the bread.

- Join the two disciples on their journey from Jerusalem to Emmaus. Sense their disappointment, despondency, and disorientation. Listen as Jesus explains the meaning of the Scriptures to them. Be aware how their hearts are burning within them. What a change of mood! From desolation to consolation! Is Jesus warming your heart? Are you seeing anything in a new light?

- Sit at table with the disciples and Jesus in the inn at Emmaus. Notice the eucharistic overtones of what Jesus does with the bread. Each time we attend Mass, do we recognize him in the breaking of the bread? Are we like the two disciples in wanting to share their experience of the risen Lord?

Thursday 5th April
Luke 24:35–48

Then they told what had happened on the road, and how he had been made known to them in the breaking of the bread. While they were talking about this, Jesus himself stood among them and said to them, "Peace be with you." They were startled and terrified, and thought that they were seeing a ghost. He said to them, "Why are you frightened, and why do doubts arise in your hearts? Look at my hands and my feet; see that it is I myself. Touch me and see; for a ghost does not have flesh and bones as you see that I have." And when he had said this, he showed them his hands and his feet. While in their joy they were disbelieving and still wondering, he said to them, "Have you anything here to eat?" They gave him a piece of broiled fish, and he took it and ate in their presence. Then he said to them, "These are my words that I spoke to you while I was still with you—that everything written about me in the law of Moses, the prophets, and the psalms must be fulfilled." Then he opened their minds to understand the scriptures, and he said to them, "Thus it is written, that the Messiah is to suffer and to rise from the dead on the third day, and that repentance and forgiveness of sins is to be proclaimed in his name to all nations, beginning from Jerusalem. You are witnesses of these things."

- Luke wants to affirm that the risen Christ is not a ghost or a pure spirit. There is still a physicality about him even though his body is now transformed. Hence Luke presents the disciples as not just looking but also touching and Jesus as not only speaking but also eating. Yet the precise nature of the risen body must remain a mystery.

- "You are witnesses to these things." All through the Resurrection stories people come to faith by meeting Jesus, and at the same time they become witnesses to others. How do you witness to those around you: family, workmates, friends?

Friday 6th April

John 21:1–14

After these things Jesus showed himself again to the disciples by the Sea of Tiberias; and he showed himself in this way. Gathered there together were Simon Peter, Thomas called the Twin, Nathanael of Cana in Galilee, the sons of Zebedee, and two others of his disciples. Simon Peter said to them, "I am going fishing." They said to him, "We will go with you." They went out and got into the boat, but that night they caught nothing. // Just after daybreak, Jesus stood on the beach; but the disciples did not know that it was Jesus. Jesus said to them, "Children, you have no fish, have you?" They answered him, "No." He said to them, "Cast the net to the right side of the boat, and you will find some." So they cast it, and now they were not able to haul it in because there were so many fish. That disciple whom Jesus loved said to Peter, "It is the Lord!" When Simon Peter heard that it was the Lord, he put on some clothes, for he was naked, and jumped into the lake. But the other disciples came in the boat, dragging the net full of fish, for they were not far from the land, only about a hundred yards off. // When they had gone ashore, they saw a charcoal fire there, with fish on it, and bread. Jesus said to them, "Bring some of the fish that you have just caught." So Simon Peter went aboard and hauled the net ashore, full of large fish, a hundred and fifty-three of them; and though there were so many, the net was not torn. Jesus said to them, "Come and have breakfast." Now none of the disciples dared to ask him, "Who are you?" because they knew it was the Lord. Jesus came and took the bread and gave it to them, and did the same with the fish. This was now the third time that Jesus appeared to the disciples after he was raised from the dead."

- Peter is lost, floundering. He feels that he is a failure at what he usually does well. Can I identify with him sometimes? But Peter is open to another voice, which he dimly recognizes, but not quite. He does what is suggested to him, and wonderful results follow.

- So it can be for me, if I am open to being surprised. Lord, let me accept you today as a God of good surprises.

Saturday 7th April
Mark 16:9–15

Now after Jesus rose, early on the first day of the week, he appeared first to Mary Magdalene, from whom he had cast out seven demons. She went out and told those who had been with him, while they were mourning and weeping. But when they heard that he was alive and had been seen by her, they would not believe it. After this he appeared in another form to two of them, as they were walking into the country. And they went back and told the rest, but they did not believe them. Later he appeared to the eleven themselves as they were sitting at the table; and he upbraided them for their lack of faith and stubbornness, because they had not believed those who saw him after he had risen. And he said to them, "Go into all the world and proclaim the good news to the whole creation."

- The disciples are slow to believe in Jesus' Resurrection. They are stubborn, mourning and weeping, stuck in a gray world. Perhaps I often feel that way? But Jesus does not despair of his followers. He gives them the extraordinary commission to bring good news to the whole of creation!

- Pope Francis echoes that call: every Christian is to be an evangelizer, to bring good news to those around them. This leaves no space for sulking, self-absorption, or doubting. This means I am able to do as Jesus asks. He does the hard work, if I am willing.

The Second Week of Easter
April 8—April 14

Something to think and pray about each day this week:

Rereading Everything on the Basis of the Cross

After the death of the Master, the disciples had scattered, their faith been utterly shaken. Everything seemed over, all their certainties had crumbled and their hopes had died. But now that message of the women, incredible as it was, came to them like a ray of light in the darkness. The news spread: Jesus is risen, just as he said. And then there was his command to go to Galilee; the women had heard it twice, first from the angel and then from Jesus himself: "Let them go to Galilee; there they will see me." "Do not fear" and "Go to Galilee."

Galilee is the place where they were first called, where everything began! The apostles were to return there, to the place where they were originally called. Jesus had walked along the shores of the lake as the fishermen were casting their nets. He had called them, and they left everything and followed him (see Matt. 4:18–22).

To return to Galilee means to reread everything on the basis of the cross and its victory, fearlessly: "do not be afraid." To reread everything—Jesus' preaching, his miracles, the new community, the excitement and the defections, even the betrayal—to reread everything starting from the end, which is a new beginning, from this supreme act of love.

—Pope Francis, *The Joy of Discipleship*

The Presence of God
Dear Jesus, I come to you today longing for your presence. I desire to love you as you love me. May nothing ever separate me from you.

Freedom
Lord grant me the grace to have freedom of the spirit. Cleanse my heart and soul so that I may live joyously in your love.

Consciousness
Where am I with God? With others?
Do I have something to be grateful for? Then I give thanks.
Is there something I am sorry for? Then I ask forgiveness.

The Word
The word of God comes down to us through the Scriptures. May the Holy Spirit enlighten my mind and my heart to respond to the gospel teachings. (Please turn to the Scripture on the following pages. Inspiration points are there should you need them. When you are ready, return here to continue.)

Conversation
How has God's word moved me? Has it left me cold?
Has it consoled me or moved me to act in a new way?
I imagine Jesus standing or sitting beside me;
I turn and share my feelings with him

Conclusion
I thank God for these moments we have spent together and for any insights I have been given concerning the text.

Sunday 8th April
Second Sunday of Easter (or Sunday of Divine Mercy)
John 20:19–31

When it was evening on that day, the first day of the week, and the doors of the house where the disciples had met were locked for fear of the Jews, Jesus came and stood among them and said, "Peace be with you." After he said this, he showed them his hands and his side. Then the disciples rejoiced when they saw the Lord. Jesus said to them again, "Peace be with you. As the Father has sent me, so I send you." When he had said this, he breathed on them and said to them, "Receive the Holy Spirit. If you forgive the sins of any, they are forgiven them; if you retain the sins of any, they are retained." // But Thomas (who was called the Twin), one of the twelve, was not with them when Jesus came. So the other disciples told him, "We have seen the Lord." But he said to them, "Unless I see the mark of the nails in his hands, and put my finger in the mark of the nails and my hand in his side, I will not believe." A week later his disciples were again in the house, and Thomas was with them. Although the doors were shut, Jesus came and stood among them and said, "Peace be with you." Then he said to Thomas, "Put your finger here and see my hands. Reach out your hand and put it in my side. Do not doubt but believe." Thomas answered him, "My Lord and my God!" Jesus said to him, "Have you believed because you have seen me? Blessed are those who have not seen and yet have come to believe." // Now Jesus did many other signs in the presence of his disciples, which are not written in this book. But these are written so that you may come to believe that Jesus is the Messiah, the Son of God, and that through believing you may have life in his name.

- Here we are shown twice how Jesus breaks into the lives of his friends. Can he break in on me? Where am I in these scenes? Am I hesitant like Thomas? Am I looking for some sign before committing myself to the fact that I am living in a new world, the world of the Resurrection?

- I let Jesus whisper to me, "You will be blessed if you decide to believe!" To believe in him is to give my heart to him, not just my head. It is not too demanding to do this, because he has already given his heart to me.

Monday 9th April
The Annunciation of the Lord
Luke 1:26–38

In the sixth month the angel Gabriel was sent by God to a town in Galilee called Nazareth, to a virgin engaged to a man whose name was Joseph, of the house of David. The virgin's name was Mary. And he came to her and said, "Greetings, favored one! The Lord is with you." But she was much perplexed by his words and pondered what sort of greeting this might be. The angel said to her, "Do not be afraid, Mary, for you have found favor with God. And now, you will conceive in your womb and bear a son, and you will name him Jesus. He will be great, and will be called the Son of the Most High, and the Lord God will give to him the throne of his ancestor David. He will reign over the house of Jacob forever, and of his kingdom there will be no end." Mary said to the angel, "How can this be, since I am a virgin?" The angel said to her, "The Holy Spirit will come upon you, and the power of the Most High will overshadow you; therefore the child to be born will be holy; he will be called Son of God. And now, your relative Elizabeth in her old age has also conceived a son; and this is the sixth month for her who was said to be barren. For nothing will be impossible with God." Then Mary said, "Here am I, the servant of the Lord; let it be with me according to your word." Then the angel departed from her.

- This scene is an image of what true prayer is about. God comes to visit me through a messenger: a line from Scripture, an event, a memory. I entertain God! God takes the initiative and greets me, surprisingly, as "the favored one." What does it feel like to be in God's favor?

- God has something in mind for me to do; like Mary, I am to bear good news to others, and the Holy Spirit will help me. God waits for my response. If I say Yes! the work of God in our world will be brought forward. Like her, I dare to say, "Here am I, the servant of the Lord; let it be with me according to your word." It is all so simple and yet so awesome.

Tuesday 10th April
John 3:7–15

"Jesus said, 'Do not be astonished that I said to you, 'You must be born from above.' The wind blows where it chooses, and you hear the sound of it, but you do not know where it comes from or where it goes. So it is with everyone who is born of the Spirit." Nicodemus said to him, "How can these things be?" Jesus answered him, "Are you a teacher of Israel, and yet you do not understand these things? Very truly, I tell you, we speak of what we know and testify to what we have seen; yet you do not receive our testimony. If I have told you about earthly things and you do not believe, how can you believe if I tell you about heavenly things? No one has ascended into heaven except the one who descended from heaven, the Son of Man. And just as Moses lifted up the serpent in the wilderness, so must the Son of Man be lifted up, that whoever believes in him may have eternal life."

- Like Nicodemus, I am puzzled about being "born again." I ask Jesus to explain. He tells me that he wants me to present myself in the world in a new way: I am to start over.

- Jesus speaks of the Spirit being at work, bringing about inner birth. He wants me to live a Spirit-filled life. When have I sensed the Spirit "blowing" through my day, my thoughts, my senses?

Wednesday 11th April
John 3:16–21

"For God so loved the world that he gave his only Son, so that everyone who believes in him may not perish but may have eternal life. Indeed, God did not send the Son into the world to condemn the world, but in order that the world might be saved through him. Those who believe in him are not condemned; but those who do not believe are condemned already, because they have not believed in the name of the only Son of God. And this is the judgment, that the light has come into the world, and people loved darkness rather than light because their deeds were evil. For all who do evil hate the light and do not come to the light, so that their deeds may not be exposed. But those who do what is true come to the light, so that it may be clearly seen that their deeds have been done in God."

- It has been said that if all the Gospels had been lost early on, except the first sentence above, that would be enough for us. Once we know that God truly loves the world, we have hope. Today, I will meditate on "For God so loved the world . . ."

- God is hard at work to save us—from evil and failure and ruin and darkness. God's plan is to bring us all into eternal life. Pope Francis puts it daringly: "When everything is said and done, we are infinitely loved" (*The Joy of the Gospel*, 6). That can be my mantra for today and every day.

Thursday 12th April
John 3:31–36

The one who comes from above is above all; the one who is of the earth belongs to the earth and speaks about earthly things. The one who comes from heaven is above all. He testifies to what he has seen and heard, yet no one accepts his testimony. Whoever has accepted his testimony has certified this, that God is true. He whom God has sent speaks the words of God, for he gives the Spirit without measure. The Father loves the Son and has placed all things in his hands. Whoever believes in the Son has eternal life; whoever disobeys the Son will not see life, but must endure God's wrath.

- Lord, when I look at you, I feel so earthbound. I am stuck in the mud, busy about my little anxieties and desires. Raise me up; keep reminding me that you want me to be with you in that divine dimension that you inhabit.

- All things are in your hands, Lord, including me. Help me believe more deeply in you and your promise of eternal life. Let me be like you and speak the words of God to others.

Friday 13th April
John 6:1–15

After this Jesus went to the other side of the Sea of Galilee, also called the Sea of Tiberias. A large crowd kept following him, because they saw the signs that he was doing for the sick. Jesus went up the mountain and sat down there with his disciples. Now the Passover, the festival of the Jews, was near. When he looked up and saw a large crowd coming towards him,

Jesus said to Philip, "Where are we to buy bread for these people to eat?" He said this to test him, for he himself knew what he was going to do. Philip answered him, "Six months' wages would not buy enough bread for each of them to get a little." One of his disciples, Andrew, Simon Peter's brother, said to him, "There is a boy here who has five barley loaves and two fish. But what are they among so many people?" Jesus said, "Make the people sit down." Now there was a great deal of grass in the place; so they sat down, about five thousand in all. Then Jesus took the loaves, and when he had given thanks, he distributed them to those who were seated; so also the fish, as much as they wanted. When they were satisfied, he told his disciples, "Gather up the fragments left over, so that nothing may be lost." So they gathered them up, and from the fragments of the five barley loaves, left by those who had eaten, they filled twelve baskets. When the people saw the sign that he had done, they began to say, "This is indeed the prophet who is to come into the world." When Jesus realized that they were about to come and take him by force to make him king, he withdrew again to the mountain by himself.

- This scene provides a revelation of the sort of person God is. Our resources are never enough, but God has limitless resources, enough for us to do what God wants done.

- Jesus reveals the God of abundance, but notice that the focus is on the poor and the needy, not on making rich people richer. Jesus needs my help in caring for those at the bottom of the human pyramid. This is the theme of Pope Francis' encyclical, *Laudato Si*. May I develop the spiritual habit of seeing abundance, not scarcity, in God's economy.

Saturday 14th April
John 6:16–21

When evening came, his disciples went down to the sea, got into a boat, and started across the sea to Capernaum. It was now dark, and Jesus had not yet come to them. The sea became rough because a strong wind was blowing. When they had rowed about three or four miles, they saw Jesus walking on the sea and coming near the boat, and they were terrified. But he said to them, "It is I; do not be afraid." Then they wanted to take him into the boat, and immediately the boat reached the land toward which they were going.

- Here we see a characteristic of Jesus: he keeps his disciples in view, not only when things are going well, but when conditions are stormy. Lord, help me trust that you will never let me out of your sight and that you watch over the Christian community as it labors along.

- Today I can take as my mantra your promise, "It is I; do not be afraid."

The Third Week of Easter
April 15—April 21

Something to think and pray about each day this week:

Forgiveness Means God's Joy
The Gospel of Luke 15 contains three parables of mercy: the lost sheep, the lost coin, and then the longest of them, characteristic of St. Luke, the parable of the father of two sons, the "prodigal" son and the son who believes he is "righteous," who believes he is saintly. All three of these parables speak of the joy of God. God is joyful. This is interesting: God is joyful! And what is the joy of God? The joy of God is forgiving. . . . The joy of a shepherd who finds his little lamb; the joy of a woman who finds her coin; it is the joy of a father welcoming home the son who was lost, who was as though dead and has come back to life, who has come home. Here is the entire Gospel—here! The whole Gospel, all of Christianity, is here. But make sure that it is not sentiment, a matter of simply being a "do-gooder." On the contrary, mercy is the true force that can save humanity and the world from the cancer that is sin, moral evil, and spiritual evil. Only love fills . . . the negative chasms that evil opens in hearts and in history. Only love can do this, and this is God's joy.

—Pope Francis, *The Joy of Discipleship*

The Presence of God
As I sit here, the beating of my heart,
the ebb and flow of my breathing, the movements of my mind
are all signs of God's ongoing creation of me.
I pause for a moment and become aware
of this presence of God within me.

Freedom
I will ask God's help
to be free from my own preoccupations,
to be open to God in this time of prayer,
to come to know, love, and serve God more.

Consciousness
At this moment, Lord, I turn my thoughts to you.
I will leave aside my chores and preoccupations.
I will take rest and refreshment in your presence.

The Word
Now I turn to the Scripture set out for me this day. I read slowly over the
words and see if any sentence or sentiment appeals to me. (Please turn to
the Scripture on the following pages. Inspiration points are there should
you need them. When you are ready, return here to continue.)

Conversation
Begin to talk to Jesus about the Scripture you have just read. What part
of it strikes a chord in you? Perhaps the words of a friend—or some story
you have heard recently—will slowly rise to the surface of your consciousness. If so, does the story throw light on what the Scripture passage may
be saying to you?

Conclusion
Glory be to the Father, and to the Son, and to the Holy Spirit,
As it was in the beginning, is now and ever shall be,
World without end. Amen.

Sunday 15th April
Third Sunday of Easter
Luke 24:35–48

Then they told what had happened on the road, and how he had been made known to them in the breaking of the bread. While they were talking about this, Jesus himself stood among them and said to them, "Peace be with you." They were startled and terrified, and thought that they were seeing a ghost. He said to them, "Why are you frightened, and why do doubts arise in your hearts? Look at my hands and my feet; see that it is I myself. Touch me and see; for a ghost does not have flesh and bones as you see that I have." And when he had said this, he showed them his hands and his feet. While in their joy they were disbelieving and still wondering, he said to them, "Have you anything here to eat?" They gave him a piece of broiled fish, and he took it and ate in their presence. Then he said to them, "These are my words that I spoke to you while I was still with you—that everything written about me in the law of Moses, the prophets, and the psalms must be fulfilled." Then he opened their minds to understand the scriptures, and he said to them, "Thus it is written, that the Messiah is to suffer and to rise from the dead on the third day, and that repentance and forgiveness of sins is to be proclaimed in his name to all nations, beginning from Jerusalem. You are witnesses of these things."

- "These are my words that I spoke to you while I was still with you." Jesus has already spoken many words to me. But do I remember? Do I take them to heart?

- Jesus wants repentance and forgiveness of sins to be proclaimed—this is the astounding, world-changing news. Today I will ponder how to communicate to others the transformative power of repentance and forgiveness.

Monday 16th April
John 6:22–29

The next day the crowd that had stayed on the other side of the sea saw that there had been only one boat there. They also saw that Jesus had not got into the boat with his disciples, but that his disciples had gone away alone. Then some boats from Tiberias came near the place where they had eaten the bread after the Lord had given thanks. So when the crowd saw that neither Jesus nor his disciples were there, they themselves got into the boats and went to Capernaum looking for Jesus. // When they found him on the other side of the sea, they said to him, "Rabbi, when did you come here?" Jesus answered them, "Very truly, I tell you, you are looking for me, not because you saw signs, but because you ate your fill of the loaves. Do not work for the food that perishes, but for the food that endures for eternal life, which the Son of Man will give you. For it is on him that God the Father has set his seal." Then they said to him, "What must we do to perform the works of God?" Jesus answered them, "This is the work of God, that you believe in him whom he has sent."

- I notice the energy of the crowds: they go to great lengths to find Jesus. Do I make a similar effort to meet him? Do I give quality time to my prayer? Often I sit down to pray and simply wait for something to happen. But he is there before me, so let me engage with him, chat with him, and ask his advice and help.

- The crowds look for Jesus where he was the day before, but he has moved on. Each day I must try to meet him where he is. Day by day, may I notice the disturbing freshness of the Christ's presence.

Tuesday 17th April
John 6:30–35

So they said to Jesus, "What sign are you going to give us then, so that we may see it and believe you? What work are you performing? Our ancestors ate the manna in the wilderness; as it is written, 'He gave them bread from heaven to eat.'" Then Jesus said to them, "Very truly, I tell you, it was not Moses who gave you the bread from heaven, but it is my Father who gives you the true bread from heaven. For the bread of God is that which comes down from heaven and gives life to the world." They said to him, "Sir, give us this bread always." Jesus said to them, "I am the bread of life. Whoever comes to me will never be hungry, and whoever believes in me will never be thirsty."

- The word *bread* comes up six times in this short passage. What does bread mean for me? I love freshly baked bread: its taste, texture and smell. Do I truly sense that my need for Jesus is as immediate as my need for daily food?

- The people keep looking for a sign. But Jesus points them to himself. Lord, adjust my vision. I don't want to be gazing all around, looking for signs when you are right here with me.

Wednesday 18th April
John 6:35–40

Jesus said to them, "I am the bread of life. Whoever comes to me will never be hungry, and whoever believes in me will never be thirsty. But I said to you that you have seen me and yet do not believe. Everything that the Father gives me will come to me, and anyone who comes to me I will never drive away; for I have come down from heaven, not to do my own will, but the will of him who sent me. And this is the will of him who sent me, that I should lose nothing of all that he has given me, but raise it up on the last day. This is indeed the will of my Father, that all who see the Son and believe in him may have eternal life; and I will raise them up on the last day."

- Jesus, you shower me here with an abundance of promises. You are the bread of life for us: you will meet all our deepest needs. What needs? We hunger and thirst for happiness and joy; we want to be welcomed by the Father; we want to live eternally. And all we have to do is to give ourselves over to you for our needs to be satisfied. You are faithful to your promises, because promises are the language of love. Thank you!

- You will not drive anyone way who comes to you, Lord—you said this yourself. Yet I sometimes live as if I'm expecting you to send me away. Renew my faith in your enduring love.

Thursday 19th April
John 6:44–51

Jesus said, "No one can come to me unless drawn by the Father who sent me; and I will raise that person up on the last day. It is written in the prophets, 'And they shall all be taught by God.' Everyone who has heard and learned from the Father comes to me. Not that anyone has seen the Father except the one who is from God; he has seen the Father. Very truly, I tell you, whoever believes has eternal life. I am the bread of life. Your ancestors ate the manna in the wilderness, and they died. This is the bread that comes down from heaven, so that one may eat of it and not die. I am the living bread that came down from heaven. Whoever eats of this bread will live forever; and the bread that I will give for the life of the world is my flesh."

- The Father is drawing me always toward his Son: that is why I am now at prayer! I watch flower bulbs growing: they are drawn by the warmth of the sun. I watch children learning: they are drawn by the love of knowledge and truth. I watch people who have fallen in love: each is being drawn by the goodness of the other.

- I can also grow in sensitivity to the drawing of God in the depths of my heart. God is out ahead of me, drawing me forward into ever fuller development and deeper dimensions of loving. I am so grateful that I don't do this spiritual life on my own.

Friday 20th April
John 6:52–59

The Jews then disputed among themselves, saying, "How can this man give us his flesh to eat?" So Jesus said to them, "Very truly, I tell you, unless you eat the flesh of the Son of Man and drink his blood, you have no life in you. Those who eat my flesh and drink my blood have eternal life, and I will raise them up on the last day; for my flesh is true food and my blood is true drink. Those who eat my flesh and drink my blood abide in me, and I in them. Just as the living Father sent me, and I live because of the Father, so whoever eats me will live because of me. This is the bread that came down from heaven, not like that which your ancestors ate, and they died. But the one who eats this bread will live forever." He said these things while he was teaching in the synagogue at Capernaum.

- Jesus, when you talk about us eating your flesh and drinking your blood, people can be shocked. But you are trying to convey something of what happens when a divine person is given over to a tiny human being like me. You use graphic images to hint at the fact that you love me completely, that you are given over to me fully, and that your friendship with me is infinitely deep. Help me to respond to your love, however inadequately. Help me to love you with heart, soul, body, strength, and mind.

- It's as simple as this: I need you, Jesus, if I am to live. You are my source, my strength, my nourishment. Remind me that my truest hunger is for life with you.

Saturday 21st April
John 6:60–69

When many of his disciples heard it, they said, "This teaching is difficult; who can accept it?" But Jesus, being aware that his disciples were complaining about it, said to them, "Does this offend you? Then what if you were to see the Son of Man ascending to where he was before? It is the spirit that gives life; the flesh is useless. The words that I have spoken to you are spirit and life. But among you there are some who do not believe." For Jesus knew from the first who were the ones that did not believe, and who was the one that would betray him. And he said, "For this reason I have told you that no one can come to me unless it is granted by the Father." // Because of this many of his disciples turned back and no longer went about with him. So Jesus asked the twelve, "Do you also wish to go away?" Simon Peter answered him, "Lord, to whom can we go? You have the words of eternal life. We have come to believe and know that you are the Holy One of God."

- Lord, how deeply do I desire this transforming relationship you offer me? You want to raise me to the level of "spirit and life." Saint Irenaeus long ago said, "The glory of God is the human person fully alive." I know that I'm only half alive at best, so here and now I ask you to work on me so that I become more like you.

- Jesus, you are fully alive as a human being, and this is because you are totally open to God. Make that happen to me, whatever it takes! Take me by the hand, hold me tight, and bring me along with you, so I shall become like you.

The Fourth Week of Easter
April 22—April 28

Something to think and pray about each day this week:

Invited to Involvement

Jesus is not a lone missionary; he does not want to fulfill his mission alone but involves his disciples. In addition to the twelve apostles he calls another seventy-two and sends them to the villages, two by two, to proclaim that the Kingdom of God is close at hand. This is very beautiful! Jesus does not want to act alone; he came to bring the love of God into the world, and he wants to spread it in the style of communion, in the style of brotherhood. That is why he immediately forms a community of disciples, which is a missionary community. He trains them straight away for the mission, to go forth.

The Gospel of Luke tells us that those seventy-two came back from their mission full of joy because they had experienced the power of Christ's name over evil. Jesus says it: to these disciples he gives the power to defeat the evil one. But he adds, "Do not rejoice in this, that the spirits are subject to you; but rejoice that your names are written in heaven" (Luke 10:20). We should not boast as if we were the protagonists: there is only one protagonist, the Lord! The Lord's grace is the protagonist. He is the one hero. And our joy is just this: to be his disciples, his friends. May Our Lady help us to be good agents of the Gospel.

—Pope Francis, *The Joy of Discipleship*

The Presence of God

"Be still and know that I am God!" Lord, your words lead us to the calmness and greatness of your presence.

Freedom

God is not foreign to my freedom. The Spirit breathes life into my most intimate desires, gently nudging me toward all that is good. I ask for the grace to let myself be enfolded by the Spirit.

Consciousness

Where do I sense hope, encouragement, and growth in my life? By looking back over the past few months, I may be able to see which activities and occasions have produced rich fruit. If I do notice such areas, I will determine to give those areas both time and space in the future.

The Word

The word of God comes down to us through the Scriptures. May the Holy Spirit enlighten my mind and my heart to respond to the gospel teachings. (Please turn to the Scripture on the following pages. Inspiration points are there should you need them. When you are ready, return here to continue.)

Conversation

What is stirring in me as I pray? Am I consoled, troubled, left cold? I imagine Jesus standing or sitting at my side, and I share my feelings with him.

Conclusion

Glory be to the Father, and to the Son, and to the Holy Spirit,
As it was in the beginning, is now and ever shall be,
World without end. Amen.

Sunday 22nd April
Fourth Sunday of Easter
John 10:11–18

"I am the good shepherd. The good shepherd lays down his life for the sheep. The hired hand, who is not the shepherd and does not own the sheep, sees the wolf coming and leaves the sheep and runs away—and the wolf snatches them and scatters them. The hired hand runs away because a hired hand does not care for the sheep. I am the good shepherd. I know my own and my own know me, just as the Father knows me and I know the Father. And I lay down my life for the sheep. I have other sheep that do not belong to this fold. I must bring them also, and they will listen to my voice. So there will be one flock, one shepherd. For this reason the Father loves me, because I lay down my life in order to take it up again. No one takes it from me, but I lay it down of my own accord. I have power to lay it down, and I have power to take it up again. I have received this command from my Father."

- Sunday reminds us that we do not come to God alone; our worship draws us into community and identifies us as sheep of the Good Shepherd. Being thought of as "sheep" does not demean us, but rescues us from thinking too much of ourselves. Jesus calls us to humility and trust, cautioning us against those who work only for what they get and warning against whatever might snatch or scatter us.

- The shepherd keeps the sheep in view, regarding them and seeing beyond them. I ask God for the humility I need, that I might listen for the voice of the Good Shepherd, allowing him to lead me, and trusting that he is leading others too—even if it is in ways I don't understand.

Monday 23rd April
John 10:1–10

"Very truly, I tell you, anyone who does not enter the sheepfold by the gate but climbs in by another way is a thief and a bandit. The one who enters by the gate is the shepherd of the sheep. The gatekeeper opens the gate for him, and the sheep hear his voice. He calls his own sheep by name and leads them out. When he has brought out all his own, he goes ahead of them, and the sheep follow him because they know his voice. They will not follow a stranger, but they will run from him because they do not know the voice of strangers." Jesus used this figure of speech with them, but they did not understand what he was saying to them. // So again Jesus said to them, "Very truly, I tell you, I am the gate for the sheep. All who came before me are thieves and bandits; but the sheep did not listen to them. I am the gate. Whoever enters by me will be saved, and will come in and go out and find pasture. The thief comes only to steal and kill and destroy. I came that they may have life, and have it abundantly."

- A good way to start my prayer is to settle down and become quiet, and then listen as Jesus calls me by my name. Jesus is very personal. Think of his meeting with Mary of Magdala near the tomb on the first Easter Sunday and how softly he speaks the word "Mary!"

- He loves me as he loved her, and he speaks my name with overflowing tenderness. My name in fact is written on the palms of his hands (See Isaiah 49:16). I can imagine myself opening his hands and discovering that it's true! There I am, in print!

Tuesday 24th April
John 10:22–30

At that time the festival of the Dedication took place in Jerusalem. It was winter, and Jesus was walking in the temple, in the portico of Solomon. So the Jews gathered round him and said to him, "How long will you keep us in suspense? If you are the Messiah, tell us plainly." Jesus answered, "I have told you, and you do not believe. The works that I do in my Father's name testify to me; but you do not believe, because you do not belong to my sheep. My sheep hear my voice, and I know them, and they follow me. I give them eternal life, and they will never perish. No one will snatch them out of my hand. What my Father has given me is greater than all else, and no one can snatch it out of the Father's hand. The Father and I are one."

- If my prayer and my Christian life are dull and lifeless, is it because I "do not believe" all that Jesus has told me about his love for me? We Christians should be the happiest of people, no matter what our problems. Our future is fully secure and totally attractive. There are no terms and conditions.

- No one is able to snatch me from God's care—no one. Today, may I have confidence in this one, simple truth.

Wednesday 25th April
Mark 16:15–20

And he said to them, "Go into all the world and proclaim the good news to the whole creation. The one who believes and is baptized will be saved; but the one who does not believe will be condemned. And these signs will accompany those who believe: by using my name they will cast out demons; they will speak in new tongues; they will pick up snakes in their hands, and if they drink any deadly thing, it will not hurt them; they will lay their hands on the sick, and they will recover." // So then the Lord Jesus, after he had spoken to them, was taken up into heaven and sat down at the right hand of God. And they went out and proclaimed the good news everywhere, while the Lord worked with them and confirmed the message by the signs that accompanied it.

- Pope Francis is calling us today to obey the Lord's command given two thousand years ago. We are to work out together how to share the good news. We cannot bury or hoard the gift we have been given, because everyone needs to hear the good news that they are loved. We are to be "the good news in the present tense."

- God is determined to bring us all into the final community of love, which is gathering day by day. So, Lord, let me listen to you as you say "Go!" and let me find creative ways to be good news to those around me.

Thursday 26th April
John 13:16–20

"Very truly, I tell you, servants are not greater than their master, nor are messengers greater than the one who sent them. If you know these things, you are blessed if you do them. I am not speaking of all of you; I know whom I have chosen. But it is to fulfill the scripture, 'The one who ate my bread has lifted his heel against me.' I tell you this now, before it occurs, so that when it does occur, you may believe that I am he. Very truly, I tell you, whoever receives one whom I send receives me; and whoever receives me receives him who sent me."

- If I were asked "Who are you, deep down?" would I think to say that I am God's servant, God's messenger? I am someone sent on an errand by the Lord, and he accompanies me and identifies with me as I do it.

Whatever small thing I can do to serve the growth of the kingdom of God, I do it in companionship with him.

- Jesuits call themselves "companions of Jesus," but anyone else can, too, if they are trying to be available to God's call.

Friday 27th April
John 14:1–6

Jesus said to the disciples, "Do not let your hearts be troubled. Believe in God, believe also in me. In my Father's house there are many dwelling places. If it were not so, would I have told you that I go to prepare a place for you? And if I go and prepare a place for you, I will come again and will take you to myself, so that where I am, there you may be also. And you know the way to the place where I am going." Thomas said to him, "Lord, we do not know where you are going. How can we know the way?" Jesus said to him, "I am the way, and the truth, and the life. No one comes to the Father except through me."

- Dear Jesus, I invite you into my heart-space now. Let me be quiet and listen while you speak the words of this passage to me. They form one of the most consoling statements of your good news. They reveal such love and appreciation of me. They put all my troubles into second place. My future is with you.

- Jesus makes clear that "the way" is life with him. It is no formula. It isn't even a religious system or a philosophy or a doctrine. If I am confused about all the "ways" pointed out to me by society, culture, sometimes even other Christians, I can go back to this: stay in communion with Jesus.

Saturday 28th April
John 14:7–14

"If you know me, you will know my Father also. From now on you do know him and have seen him." Philip said to him, "Lord, show us the Father, and we will be satisfied." Jesus said to him, "Have I been with you all this time, Philip, and you still do not know me? Whoever has seen me has seen the Father. How can you say, 'Show us the Father'? Do you not believe that I am in the Father and the Father is in me? The words that I say to you I do not speak on my own; but the Father who dwells in me does his works. Believe me that I am in the Father and the Father is in me; but if you do not, then believe me because of the works themselves. Very truly, I tell you, the one who believes in me will also do the works that I do and, in fact, will do greater works than these, because I am going to the Father. I will do whatever you ask in my name, so that the Father may be glorified in the Son. If in my name you ask me for anything, I will do it."

- Some years ago, the theologian Hans Urs von Balthasar wrote a little book called, *Does Jesus Know Us? Do We Know Him?* Jesus, you know me in the way that lifetime partners know one another, only so much better. Yours is a knowledge born of limitless love. But do I know you? Am I passionate about you? Do you mean much to me?

- I pray the thirteenth-century prayer, which was refreshed in the musical *Godspell* in 1971, "Dear Lord, three things I pray: to see you more clearly, love you more dearly, and follow you more nearly, day by day." Then I shall know you in the scriptural meaning of that word.

The Fifth Week of Easter
April 29—May 5

Something to think and pray about each day this week:

Beauty Everywhere
Now that it's firmly Spring, I find myself thinking immediately of the beauty of God's creation—not just natural beauty, but also all the beautiful things that humanity offers. I have friends who, no matter their ages or circumstance, bring beauty into my life. Architecture, secular and sacred, speaks loudly to me, but so do art and music. God's beauty is everywhere—in an old man holding his granddaughter's hand as they prepare to cross the street, in the tender ministrations of a nurse as she bathes a patient, in a woman rushing to a second job to keep her family afloat. Why can't I see this all the time?
—Paul Brian Campbell, SJ, on his blog *People for Others*

The Presence of God

"Come to me, all you who are weary and are carrying heavy burdens, and I will give you rest." Here I am, Lord. I come to seek your presence. I long for your healing power.

Freedom

By God's grace I was born to live in freedom. Free to enjoy the pleasures he created for me. Dear Lord, grant that I may live as you intended, with complete confidence in your loving care.

Consciousness

Knowing that God loves me unconditionally, I look honestly over the past day, its events, and my feelings. Do I have something to be grateful for? Then I give thanks. Is there something I am sorry for? Then I ask forgiveness.

The Word

God speaks to each of us individually. I listen attentively, to hear what he is saying to me. Read the text a few times, then listen. (Please turn to the Scripture on the following pages. Inspiration points are there should you need them. When you are ready, return here to continue.)

Conversation

I know with certainty that there were times when you carried me, Lord. There were times when it was through your strength that I got through the dark times in my life.

Conclusion

Glory be to the Father, and to the Son, and to the Holy Spirit,
As it was in the beginning, is now and ever shall be,
World without end. Amen.

Sunday 29th April
Fifth Sunday of Easter
John 15:1–8

"I am the true vine, and my Father is the vinegrower. He removes every branch in me that bears no fruit. Every branch that bears fruit he prunes to make it bear more fruit. You have already been cleansed by the word that I have spoken to you. Abide in me as I abide in you. Just as the branch cannot bear fruit by itself unless it abides in the vine, neither can you unless you abide in me. I am the vine, you are the branches. Those who abide in me and I in them bear much fruit, because apart from me you can do nothing. Whoever does not abide in me is thrown away like a branch and withers; such branches are gathered, thrown into the fire, and burned. If you abide in me, and my words abide in you, ask for whatever you wish, and it will be done for you. My Father is glorified by this, that you bear much fruit and become my disciples."

• Dear Jesus, you seem to love that little word *abide*. You use it eight times here! Let me love it too. Your abiding is steady; you are constantly at home with me. You don't drift off or grow bored, as I do. Teach me this art of abiding.

• I need to learn that I don't have to be always on the go. Grapes mature simply by being on the vine; they don't have to work to blossom and ripen. The same is true for me. Simply being with you is enough.

Monday 30th April
John 14:21–26

Jesus said, "They who have my commandments and keep them are those who love me; and those who love me will be loved by my Father, and I will love them and reveal myself to them." Judas (not Iscariot) said to him, "Lord, how is it that you will reveal yourself to us, and not to the world?" Jesus answered him, "Those who love me will keep my word, and my Father will love them, and we will come to them and make our home with them. Whoever does not love me does not keep my words; and the word that you hear is not mine, but is from the Father who sent me. I have said these things to you while I am still with you. But the Advocate, the Holy Spirit, whom the Father will send in my name, will teach you everything, and remind you of all that I have said to you."

- The Holy Spirit, the ally and spirit of Jesus, remains with me through my life, keeping the words of Jesus in my mind, helping me deepen my understanding of them as I apply them to the constantly changing situations I face.

- This is how you work with me, Lord. The Holy Spirit does not whisper new tidings in my ear but rather reminds me of you, of your life, and of your words, so that gradually I put on Christ. I learn only what I already know.

Tuesday 1st May
Matthew 13:54–58

Jesus came to his hometown and began to teach the people in their synagogue, so that they were astounded and said, "Where did this man get this wisdom and these deeds of power? Is not this the carpenter's son? Is not his mother called Mary? And are not his brothers James and Joseph and Simon and Judas? And are not all his sisters with us? Where then did this man get all this?" And they took offense at him. But Jesus said to them, "Prophets are not without honor except in their own country and in their own house." And he did not do many deeds of power there, because of their unbelief.

- Jesus was rejected by his own people, who were astonished by his wisdom and power. They couldn't accept this ordinary man—one of their own, whose family attended their synagogue—as their teacher. Though he spoke the truth they chose not to listen.

- I pray for wisdom and enlightenment so that I may listen to and reflect on the teachings of Jesus with renewed insight and wisdom, seeing their relevance to my walk of faith with him.

Wednesday 2nd May
John 15:1–8

"I am the true vine, and my Father is the vinegrower. He removes every branch in me that bears no fruit. Every branch that bears fruit he prunes to make it bear more fruit. You have already been cleansed by the word that I have spoken to you. Abide in me as I abide in you. Just as the branch cannot bear fruit by itself unless it abides in the vine, neither can you unless you abide in me. I am the vine, you are the branches. Those who abide in me and I in them bear much fruit, because apart from me you can do nothing. Whoever does not abide in me is thrown away like a branch and withers; such branches are gathered, thrown into the fire, and burned. If you abide in me, and my words abide in you, ask for whatever you wish, and it will be done for you. My Father is glorified by this, that you bear much fruit and become my disciples."

- Dear Jesus, you seem to love that little word *abide*. You use it eight times here! Help me love it too. Your abiding is steady: you are constantly at home with me. You don't drift off or grow bored, as I do. Teach me this art of abiding.

- God who created me, may I remember each day that I glorify you by abiding in Jesus, bearing good fruit in my life.

Thursday 3rd May
John 14:6–14

Jesus said to him, "I am the way, and the truth, and the life. No one comes to the Father except through me. If you know me, you will know my Father also. From now on you do know him and have seen him." // Philip said to him, "Lord, show us the Father, and we will be satisfied." Jesus said to him, "Have I been with you all this time, Philip, and you still do not know me? Whoever has seen me has seen the Father. How can you say, 'Show us the Father' Do you not believe that I am in the Father and the Father is in me? The words that I say to you I do not speak on my own; but the Father who dwells in me does his works. Believe me that I am in the Father and the Father is in me; but if you do not, then believe me because of the works themselves. Very truly, I tell you, the one who believes in me will also do the works that I do and, in fact, will do greater works than these, because I am going to the Father. I will do whatever you ask in my name, so that the Father may be glorified in the Son. If in my name you ask me for anything, I will do it."

- Philip is one of the lesser-known apostles. Slow of understanding, he elicits a gentle but somewhat exasperated rebuke from Jesus at the Last Supper: "Philip, have I been with you for so long a time and you still do not know me?" Philip was there from the beginning; according to John's Gospel, he was the fourth apostle Jesus chose. Whereas Andrew and John saw and followed Jesus, and Peter was brought to him by

Andrew, Jesus "found Philip and said to him, 'Follow me.'" Can I hear that call in my own life?

- Jesus sees not with human eyes but with the eyes of the Spirit. He looks not at outward appearances but at the heart. Lord, grant that I may look at my brothers and sisters with your eyes, as equally valuable and deeply lovable members of your earthly family.

Friday 4th May
John 15:12–17

"This is my commandment, that you love one another as I have loved you. No one has greater love than this, to lay down one's life for one's friends. You are my friends if you do what I command you. I do not call you servants any longer, because the servant does not know what the master is doing; but I have called you friends, because I have made known to you everything that I have heard from my Father. You did not choose me but I chose you. And I appointed you to go and bear fruit, fruit that will last, so that the Father will give you whatever you ask him in my name. I am giving you these commands so that you may love one another."

- The more I become aware that I am infinitely loved, the more I am able to share that reservoir of love with people who need it. I must not wait for the other person to love me, just as God does not await my love but initiates the relationship.

- "I call you friend!" I let the Lord breathe that precious word across the space between us. I let him say it over and over again until it penetrates the thick crust of my disbelief.

Saturday 5th May
John 15:18–21

Jesus said to his disciples, "If the world hates you, be aware that it hated me before it hated you. If you belonged to the world, the world would love you as its own. Because you do not belong to the world, but I have chosen you out of the world—therefore the world hates you. Remember the word that I said to you, 'Servants are not greater than their master.' If they persecuted me, they will persecute you; if they kept my word, they will keep yours also. But they will do all these things to you on account of my name, because they do not know him who sent me."

- Lord, could I bear to be hated? Perhaps, but only if I keep in mind that I am not alone; you are with me.

- Witnessing to love means standing for justice, and the unjust will not like it. Standing for truth will infuriate those who live by lies. I won't look for trouble, but if it comes, let me not run away. Your kingdom is a kingdom of justice and truth. At the end of my life, I will be glad to have contributed what I could to its growth, and those I stood by will intercede for me.

The Sixth Week of Easter
May 6—May 12

Something to think and pray about each day this week:

This Is the Time
In the spring, it is my job to envision fruitfulness
and commit to it. It is my task to breathe in the air
and perceive the earth and ripe, vulnerable seed,
to grasp the possibility.
In spring my work is to imagine
and to dig and dig and feel and listen and smell and taste.
It is time to learn my desires and put them to work.
Spring is the time to test my strength and stretch my thoughts,
to raise my arms, open my heart,
invite sunlight, wind, downpour, silence, night,
to participate, then, in the world waking up.

—Watch a video version of this reflection by Vinita Hampton Wright
http://www.ignatianspirituality.com/18718/the-tasks-of-spring

The Presence of God

"Be still and know that I am God!" Lord, your words lead us to the calmness and greatness of your presence.

Freedom

Leave me here / freely all alone In cell where never sunlight shone / Should no one ever speak to me. / This golden silence makes me free!

—Part of a poem by Bl. Titus Brandsma, written while he was a prisoner at Dachau concentration camp

Consciousness

Knowing that God loves me unconditionally, I can afford to be honest about how I am.

How has the day been, and how do I feel now? I share my feelings openly with the Lord.

The Word

I take my time to read the word of God slowly, a few times, allowing myself to dwell on anything that strikes me. (Please turn to the Scripture on the following pages. Inspiration points are there should you need them. When you are ready, return here to continue.)

Conversation

Sometimes I wonder what I might say if I were to meet you in person, Lord.

I think I might say "Thank you" because you are always there for me.

Conclusion

I thank God for these moments we have spent together and for any insights I have been given concerning the text.

Sunday 6th May
Sixth Sunday of Easter
John 15:9–17

Jesus said to his disciples, "As the Father has loved me, so I have loved you; abide in my love. If you keep my commandments, you will abide in my love, just as I have kept my Father's commandments and abide in his love. I have said these things to you so that my joy may be in you, and that your joy may be complete. // "This is my commandment, that you love one another as I have loved you. No one has greater love than this, to lay down one's life for one's friends. You are my friends if you do what I command you. I do not call you servants any longer, because the servant does not know what the master is doing; but I have called you friends, because I have made known to you everything that I have heard from my Father. You did not choose me but I chose you. And I appointed you to go and bear fruit, fruit that will last, so that the Father will give you whatever you ask him in my name. I am giving you these commands so that you may love one another."

- Joy is not an obvious emotion to associate with keeping God's commandments! Yet, by keeping the greatest of all the commandments, we will give and receive that love that the Jesuit, Teilhard de Chardin, described as "the most universal, the most tremendous and the most mystical of cosmic forces. Love is the primal and universal psychic energy. Love is a sacred reserve of energy; it is like the blood of spiritual evolution."

- With Teilhard, I pray "Glorious Christ, you whose divine influence is active at the very heart of matter, and at the dazzling center where the innumerable fibers of the multiple meet: you whose power is as implacable as the world and as warm as life . . . you whose hands imprison the stars; you are the first and the last, the living and the dead and the risen again; it is to you to whom our being cries out a desire as vast as the universe: in truth you are our Lord and our God! Amen."

Monday 7th May
John 15:26—16:4

Jesus said to the disciples, "When the Advocate comes, whom I will send to you from the Father, the Spirit of truth who comes from the Father, he will testify on my behalf. You also are to testify because you have been with me from the beginning. I have said these things to you to keep you from stumbling. They will put you out of the synagogues. Indeed, an hour is coming when those who kill you will think that by doing so they are offering worship to God. And they will do this because they have not known the Father or me. But I have said these things to you so that when their hour comes you may remember that I told you about them. I did not say these things to you from the beginning, because I was with you."

- The disciples could testify to Jesus because they had lived and worked alongside him. In this passage, Jesus promises to send them the Advocate after he has gone. We can bear witness to Jesus because the testimony of his disciples has been handed down to us. And the Spirit of God, whom he gave to the disciples, is given to us too.

- The Spirit is described by St. Paul as "[one] who consoles us in all our affliction, so that we may be able to console those who are in any affliction with the consolation with which we ourselves are consoled by God." Holy Spirit, move through my life to pass along the comfort you have brought to me.

Tuesday 8th May

John 16:5–11

Jesus said, "Now I am going to him who sent me; yet none of you asks me, 'Where are you going?' But because I have said these things to you, sorrow has filled your hearts. Nevertheless, I tell you the truth: it is to your advantage that I go away, for if I do not go away, the Advocate will not come to you; but if I go, I will send him to you. And when he comes, he will prove the world wrong about sin and righteousness and judgement: about sin, because they do not believe in me; about righteousness, because I am going to the Father and you will see me no longer; about judgement, because the ruler of this world has been condemned."

- These words of Jesus at the Last Supper reflect some of the heavy sorrow of that meal, darkened by the disciples' awareness that they were losing Jesus. What he says to them applies to us also: Jesus remains with us through his spirit, the Paraclete dwelling in us and linking us to the Father as he linked Jesus to the Father.

- In my various sorrows, Lord, I sometimes forget that the Advocate is with me. Encourage my memory and strengthen my faith.

Wednesday 9th May
John 16:12–15

Jesus said, "I still have many things to say to you, but you cannot bear them now. When the Spirit of truth comes, he will guide you into all the truth; for he will not speak on his own, but will speak whatever he hears, and he will declare to you the things that are to come. He will glorify me, because he will take what is mine and declare it to you. All that the Father has is mine. For this reason I said that he will take what is mine and declare it to you."

- The mystery of the Trinity is at the heart of this passage. Pope Francis reminds us that "everything, in Christian life, revolves around the mystery of the Trinity and is fulfilled in this infinite mystery. Let us look, therefore, to keep high the 'tone' of our life, reminding ourselves to what end, for what glory we exist, work, struggle, suffer; and to which immense prize we are called."

- Saint Augustine summed up the heart of the Church's belief in the mystery of the Father, Son, and Holy Spirit by simply stating, "If you see charity, you see the Trinity." Lord, please open my eyes to the work of the Trinity in my life.

Thursday 10th May
The Ascension of the Lord
Mark 16:15–20

And he said to them, "Go into all the world and proclaim the good news to the whole creation. The one who believes and is baptized will be saved; but the one who does not believe will be condemned. And these signs will accompany those who believe: by using my name they will cast out demons; they will speak in new tongues; they will pick up snakes in their hands, and if they drink any deadly thing, it will not hurt them; they will lay their hands on the sick, and they will recover." // So then the Lord Jesus, after he had spoken to them, was taken up into heaven and sat down at the right hand of God. And they went out and proclaimed the good news everywhere, while the Lord worked with them and confirmed the message by the signs that accompanied it.

- What do we proclaim? The good news. To whom? The whole of creation. And what is the good news? Is it a bundle of complicated doctrine that pulls us into arguments with people? Holy Spirit, show me the simplicity and beauty of the good news.

- Jesus says that, in his name, miraculous things will happen. How do I feel about this part of his message in these verses? Am I comfortable—or not—with the idea of wonders still happening today?

Friday 11th May
John 16:20–23

"Very truly, I tell you, you will weep and mourn, but the world will rejoice; you will have pain, but your pain will turn into joy. When a woman is in labor, she has pain, because her hour has come. But when her child is born, she no longer remembers the anguish because of the joy of having brought a human being into the world. So you have pain now; but I will see you again, and your hearts will rejoice, and no one will take your joy from you. On that day you will ask nothing of me. Very truly, I tell you, if you ask anything of the Father in my name, he will give it to you."

- In the four Gospels, the emphasis on Christ's Passion and crucifixion almost overwhelms the Resurrection narrative. Church teaching often suggests that we find God through suffering, but far less frequently that we find God through joy. Yet Jesus himself never saw suffering as an end in itself—he endured the Cross "for the sake of the joy that was set before him." At the Last Supper, he urged his disciples to abide in his love, "that my joy may be in you, and that your joy may be complete."

- According to Teilhard de Chardin, joy is the infallible sign of the presence of God. Lord, may your joy be abundant in our hearts!

Saturday 12th May
John 16:23–28

Jesus said to his disciples, "Very truly, I tell you, if you ask anything of the Father in my name, he will give it to you. Until now you have not asked for anything in my name. Ask and you will receive, so that your joy may be complete. I have said these things to you in figures of speech. The hour is coming when I will no longer speak to you in figures, but will tell you plainly of the Father. On that day you will ask in my name. I do not say to you that I will ask the Father on your behalf; for the Father himself loves you, because you have loved me and have believed that I came from God. I came from the Father and have come into the world; again, I am leaving the world and am going to the Father."

- As Christ died on the cross, the veil of the temple in Jerusalem was rent in two. It was a highly symbolic event. The veil was the barrier that separated the Holy of holies from the rest of the temple, preventing the people from entering God's presence. Now, the way into God's presence has been opened forever by Christ's death. In prayer, we can directly approach God in Jesus' name.

- We need not worry about what we will say or what language we will use. What matters is that we pray. Inspired by God, the prophet Isaiah wrote, "Before they call I will answer; while they are yet speaking, I will hear." Do I truly believe that God is working ahead of my prayers and desires?

The Seventh Week of Easter
May 13—May 19

Something to think and pray about each day this week:

Have I Tasted the Fresh Spring Air?
As I sat on the patio the other night, I slowed down a little to consider why I love it out there so much. I often notice the changing colors of the blooming flowers, the lush green of the grass, and the beautiful blue sky with birds and clouds that work collaboratively to offer their admirers an ever-changing canvas. To a lesser extent, I also notice the sounds on the patio: the birds' changing melodies, neighborhood children playing exuberantly, lawn mowers hard at work. I admit, however, that I usually stop short of appreciating the scene beyond those two aspects. How often do I venture off the patio to feel the grass through my fingers and toes? How often do I close my eyes and inhale deeply the smells of this little retreat of mine? Have I ever tasted the fresh spring air?
Slow down. Feel the world around you. Taste it. Smell it. There is grace to be found in all of it.

—Cara Callbeck on *dotMagis*, the blog of *IgnatianSpirituality.com*
http://www.ignatianspirituality.com/21852/
composition-of-place-on-my-patio

The Presence of God

"Come to me, all you who are weary and are carrying heavy burdens, and I will give you rest." Here I am, Lord. I come to seek your presence. I long for your healing power.

Freedom

By God's grace I was born to live in freedom. Free to enjoy the pleasures he created for me. Dear Lord, grant that I may live as you intended, with complete confidence in your loving care.

Consciousness

Knowing that God loves me unconditionally, I look honestly over the past day, its events, and my feelings. Do I have something to be grateful for? Then I give thanks. Is there something I am sorry for? Then I ask forgiveness.

The Word

God speaks to each of us individually. I listen attentively, to hear what he is saying to me. Read the text a few times, then listen. (Please turn to the Scripture on the following pages. Inspiration points are there should you need them. When you are ready, return here to continue.)

Conversation

I know with certainty that there were times when you carried me, Lord. There were times when it was through your strength that I got through the dark times in my life.

Conclusion

Glory be to the Father, and to the Son, and to the Holy Spirit,
As it was in the beginning, is now and ever shall be,
World without end. Amen.

Sunday 13th May
Seventh Sunday of Easter
John 17:11–19

Jesus said to the disciples, "And now I am no longer in the world, but they are in the world, and I am coming to you. Holy Father, protect them in your name that you have given me, so that they may be one, as we are one. While I was with them, I protected them in your name that you have given me. I guarded them, and not one of them was lost except the one destined to be lost, so that the scripture might be fulfilled. But now I am coming to you, and I speak these things in the world so that they may have my joy made complete in themselves. I have given them your word, and the world has hated them because they do not belong to the world, just as I do not belong to the world. I am not asking you to take them out of the world, but I ask you to protect them from the evil one. They do not belong to the world, just as I do not belong to the world. Sanctify them in the truth; your word is truth. As you have sent me into the world, so I have sent them into the world. And for their sakes I sanctify myself, so that they also may be sanctified in truth."

- The earth may belong to us, but we must not belong to it: we must not be possessed by worldly cares. With Pope Francis, we pray that Jesus "may free us from being Christians without hope, who live as if the Lord were not risen, as if our problems were the center of our lives."

- Jesus prays that we be protected from the "evil one." Pope Francis points out that the Spirit "does not remove evil with a magic wand;" instead "he pours into us the vitality of life, which is not the absence of problems, but the certainty of being loved and always forgiven by Christ, who for us has conquered sin, death and fear." The reality of the risen Christ is that, from now on, nothing and no one will ever be able to separate us from his love.

Monday 14th May
John 15:9–17

Jesus said to his disciples, "As the Father has loved me, so I have loved you; abide in my love. If you keep my commandments, you will abide in my love, just as I have kept my Father's commandments and abide in his love. I have said these things to you so that my joy may be in you, and that your joy may be complete. // "This is my commandment, that you love one another as I have loved you. No one has greater love than this, to lay down one's life for one's friends. You are my friends if you do what I command you. I do not call you servants any longer, because the servant does not know what the master is doing; but I have called you friends, because I have made known to you everything that I have heard from my Father. You did not choose me but I chose you. And I appointed you to go and bear fruit, fruit that will last, so that the Father will give you whatever you ask him in my name. I am giving you these commands so that you may love one another."

- Jesus gives us knowledge, spiritual information, so that our joy may be full. He is always bringing to us joy, life, peace, faith. Have I received any of these from him today?

- It would have been entirely appropriate for Jesus' followers to call him master—this is what disciples called the one who taught them. But Jesus takes the relationship beyond master-student, certainly beyond master-slave. Can I get my mind around the fact that Jesus—God of the universe—wants my friendship?

Tuesday 15th May
John 17:1–11

After Jesus had spoken these words, he looked up to heaven and said, "Father, the hour has come; glorify your Son so that the Son may glorify you, since you have given him authority over all people, to give eternal life to all whom you have given him. And this is eternal life, that they may know you, the only true God, and Jesus Christ whom you have sent. I glorified you on earth by finishing the work that you gave me to do. So now, Father, glorify me in your own presence with the glory that I had in your presence before the world existed. // "I have made your name known to those whom you gave me from the world. They were yours, and you gave them to me, and they have kept your word. Now they know that everything you have given me is from you; for the words that you gave to me I have given to them, and they have received them and know in truth that I came from you; and they have believed that you sent me. I am asking on their behalf; I am not asking on behalf of the world, but on behalf of those whom you gave me, because they are yours. All mine are yours, and yours are mine; and I have been glorified in them. And now I am no longer in the world, but they are in the world, and I am coming to you. Holy Father, protect them in your name that you have given me, so that they may be one, as we are one."

- As long as we have breath left in our bodies, we have work to do on earth to glorify God. We can never begin this work too early, or too late. What work does the Lord call on me to do today?

- Audacious though it may seem, the words in this passage prompt me to pray that the Lord of the universe may be glorified in me.

Wednesday 16th May
John 17:11–19

Jesus said to the disciples, "And now I am no longer in the world, but they are in the world, and I am coming to you. Holy Father, protect them in your name that you have given me, so that they may be one, as we are one. While I was with them, I protected them in your name that you have given me. I guarded them, and not one of them was lost except the one destined to be lost, so that the scripture might be fulfilled. But now I am coming to you, and I speak these things in the world so that they may have my joy made complete in themselves. I have given them your word, and the world has hated them because they do not belong to the world, just as I do not belong to the world. I am not asking you to take them out of the world, but I ask you to protect them from the evil one. They do not belong to the world, just as I do not belong to the world. Sanctify them in the truth; your word is truth. As you have sent me into the world, so I have sent them into the world. And for their sakes I sanctify myself, so that they also may be sanctified in truth."

- "I speak these things in the world so that they may have my joy made complete in themselves." Joy is not an emotion that springs from simple comfort or pleasure. Joy is an attitude that floods us when we understand the truth of God's love for us and Jesus' friendship with us. Lord, help me look not simply for a "good day" but for the good that flows from my life when I walk in the confidence of your love and friendship.

- Jesus says that God's word is truth. It has the power to sanctify us, to make us holy and put us in communion with God. When we listen to God's word proclaimed in church or even shared in a small-group discussion, might we remember that this word refines us and shapes us? When we tell the truth, even a small truth, or when we sift out falsehood through careful listening and reason, we join in God's ongoing work of making us holy—making us whole. We can make others whole, too. Jesus knew the power of God's truth telling. May I remember this great gift.

Thursday 17th May
John 17:20–26

"I ask not only on behalf of these, but also on behalf of those who will believe in me through their word, that they may all be one. As you, Father, are in me and I am in you, may they also be in us, so that the world may believe that you have sent me. The glory that you have given me I have given them, so that they may be one, as we are one, I in them and you in me, that they may become completely one, so that the world may know that you have sent me and have loved them even as you have loved me. Father, I desire that those also, whom you have given me, may be with me where I am, to see my glory, which you have given me because you loved me before the foundation of the world. // "Righteous Father, the world does not know you, but I know you; and these know that you have sent me. I made your name known to them, and I will make it known, so that the love with which you have loved me may be in them, and I in them."

- Jesus' prayer that "all may be one" can be misinterpreted. This oneness is something much greater and deeper than uniformity, than people professing the same faith and observing the same religious practices. This is a oneness in which love is given and received, a love that embraces difference. Jesus and the Father, while being one, remain distinct from each other. The disciples, while being one with Jesus, retain their own identity and individuality.

- Lord, help me understand that in love there is difference, but not division.

Friday 18th May
John 21:15–19

When they had finished breakfast, Jesus said to Simon Peter, "Simon son of John, do you love me more than these?" He said to him, "Yes, Lord;

you know that I love you." Jesus said to him, "Feed my lambs." A second time he said to him, "Simon son of John, do you love me?" He said to him, "Yes, Lord; you know that I love you." Jesus said to him, "Tend my sheep." He said to him the third time, "Simon son of John, do you love me?" Peter felt hurt because he said to him the third time, "Do you love me?" And he said to him, "Lord, you know everything; you know that I love you." Jesus said to him, "Feed my sheep. Very truly, I tell you, when you were younger, you used to fasten your own belt and to go wherever you wished. But when you grow old, you will stretch out your hands, and someone else will fasten a belt around you and take you where you do not wish to go." (He said this to indicate the kind of death by which he would glorify God.) After this he said to him, "Follow me."

• Jesus' question, asked three times, echoes the three times Peter denied Christ. It may be hard to forgive, but it can be harder to accept forgiveness. The ability to believe we are forgiven is crucial to our spiritual growth. This was the defining difference between Peter and Judas. Vacillating Peter went from the shame of his threefold denial of Christ to become the rock on which Christ's church was founded. Judas could not contemplate the possibility of forgiveness. He, who had heard Christ say that one must forgive seventy times seven, could not bring himself to ask Christ to forgive him. Instead, he died in despair.

• Lord, may I never cease asking for forgiveness. If we must be prepared to forgive limitlessly, then we must also be ready to ask for forgiveness—and believe we are forgiven—until the moment we die.

Saturday 19th May
John 21:20–25

Peter turned and saw the disciple whom Jesus loved following them; he was the one who had reclined next to Jesus at the supper and had said, "Lord, who is it that is going to betray you?" When Peter saw him, he said to Jesus, "Lord, what about him?" Jesus said to him, "If it is my will that he remain until I come, what is that to you? Follow me!" So the rumor spread in the community that this disciple would not die. Yet Jesus did not say to him that he would not die, but, "If it is my will that he remain until I come, what is that to you?" // This is the disciple who is testifying to these things and has written them, and we know that his testimony is true. But there are also many other things that Jesus did; if every one of them were written down, I suppose that the world itself could not contain the books that would be written.

- "What about him?" asked Peter. Is there a hint here of sibling rivalry or jealous curiosity? There is a reproach in Jesus' comment: "What is that to you?"

- Lord, will I ever outgrow this sense of rivalry, comparing myself to others in this family of faith? Let your love flow through me in an unselfish way.

The Seventh Week of Ordinary Time
May 20—May 26

Something to think and pray about each day this week:

A Time of Astonishment

A fundamental element of Pentecost is astonishment. Our God is a God of astonishment; this we know. No one expected anything more from the disciples: after Jesus' death they were a small, insignificant group of defeated orphans of their Master. There occurred instead an unexpected event that astounded: the people were astonished because each of them heard the disciples speaking in their own tongues, telling of the great works of God (cf. Acts 2:6–7, 11). The Church born at Pentecost is an astounding community because, with the force of her arrival from God, a new message is proclaimed—the resurrection of Christ—with a new language, the universal one of love. A new proclamation: Christ lives, he is risen. A new language: the language of love. The disciples are adorned with power from above and speak with courage. Only minutes before, they all were cowardly, but now they speak with courage and candor, with the freedom of the Holy Spirit.

Thus the Church is called into being forever, capable of astounding while proclaiming to all that Jesus Christ has conquered death, that God's arms are always open, that his patience is always there awaiting us in order to heal us, to forgive us. The risen Jesus bestowed his Spirit on the Church for this very mission.

Take note: if the Church is alive, she must always surprise. It is incumbent upon the living Church to astound. A Church that is unable to astound is a Church that is weak, sick, dying, and that needs admission to the intensive care unit as soon as possible!

—Pope Francis, *Walking with Jesus*

The Presence of God

"I am standing at the door, knocking" says the Lord. What a wonderful privilege that the Lord of all creation desires to come to me. I welcome his presence.

Freedom

Everything has the potential to draw forth from me a fuller love and life. Yet my desires are often fixed, caught, on illusions of fulfillment. I ask that God, through my Freedom, may orchestrate my desires in a vibrant loving melody rich in harmony.

Consciousness

To be conscious about something is to be aware of it.
Dear Lord, help me to remember that you gave me life.
Thank you for the gift of life.
Teach me to slow down, to be still and enjoy the pleasures created for me. To be aware of the beauty that surrounds me: the marvel of mountains, the calmness of lakes, the fragility of a flower petal. I need to remember that all these things come from you.

The Word

I read the word of God slowly, a few times over, and I listen to what God is saying to me. (Please turn to the Scripture on the following pages. Inspiration points are there should you need them. When you are ready, return here to continue.)

Conversation

What feelings are rising in me as I pray and reflect on God's word? I imagine Jesus himself sitting or standing near me, and I open my heart to him.

Conclusion

I thank God for these moments we have spent together and for any insights I have been given concerning the text.

Sunday 20th May
Pentecost Sunday
John 20:19–23

When it was evening on that day, the first day of the week, and the doors of the house where the disciples had met were locked for fear of the Jews, Jesus came and stood among them and said, "Peace be with you." After he said this, he showed them his hands and his side. Then the disciples rejoiced when they saw the Lord. Jesus said to them again, "Peace be with you. As the Father has sent me, so I send you." When he had said this, he breathed on them and said to them, "Receive the Holy Spirit. If you forgive the sins of any, they are forgiven them; if you retain the sins of any, they are retained."

• The disciples are baptized in the Holy Spirit. This is a new birth and a new baptism. The regenerative power of the Spirit makes it possible for us to become children of God. With this new birth, we become a new creation, formed by the same Spirit of God that moved over the world in the opening lines of Genesis, when "the earth was a formless void and darkness covered the face of the deep."

• What is it that blinds me to the reality of what I read about Pentecost? What makes me refuse to acknowledge that it can happen to me just as it did to the apostles? That, within my unworthy self, there is a temple in which the Spirit adores without ceasing? Lord, is it a fear that, by accepting your greatness at the center of myself, great things will be asked of me? Is it possible that, in my desire to avoid pain, I also deprive myself of experiencing joy?

Monday 21st May
Mark 9:14–29

When they came to the disciples, they saw a great crowd around them, and some scribes arguing with them. When the whole crowd saw him, they were immediately overcome with awe, and they ran forward to greet him. He asked them, "What are you arguing about with them?" Someone from the crowd answered him, "Teacher, I brought you my son; he has a spirit that makes him unable to speak; and whenever it seizes him, it dashes him down; and he foams and grinds his teeth and becomes rigid; and I asked your disciples to cast it out, but they could not do so." He answered them, "You faithless generation, how much longer must I be among you? How much longer must I put up with you? Bring him to me." And they brought the boy to him. When the spirit saw him, immediately it threw the boy into convulsions, and he fell on the ground and rolled about, foaming at the mouth. Jesus asked the father, "How long has this been happening to him?" And he said, "From childhood. It has often cast him into the fire and into the water, to destroy him; but if you are able to do anything, have pity on us and help us." Jesus said to him, "If you are able!—All things can be done for the one who believes." Immediately the father of the child cried out, "I believe; help my unbelief!" When Jesus saw that a crowd came running together, he rebuked the unclean spirit, saying to it, "You spirit that keeps this boy from speaking and hearing, I command you, come out of him, and never enter him again!" After crying out and convulsing him terribly, it came out, and the boy was like a corpse, so that most of them said, "He is dead." But Jesus took him by the hand and lifted him up, and he was able to stand. When he had entered the house, his disciples asked him privately, "Why could we not cast it out?" He said to them, "This kind can come out only through prayer."

- The desperate father in this passage should be a source of great encouragement to all of us who struggle with our faith. He called on Jesus with the shreds of what belief he possessed, and gave us that mighty prayer: "I believe; help my unbelief!" Jesus responded instantly. If Jesus were to ask me "Do you believe?" what would I answer?

- Karl Rahner, the Jesuit theologian, writes, "In the midst of our lives, of our freedom and our struggles, we have to make a radical, absolute decision. And we never know when lightening will strike us out of the blue. It may be when we least expect to be asked whether we have the absolute faith and trust to say yes."

Tuesday 22nd May
Mark 9:30–37

They went on from there and passed through Galilee. Jesus did not want anyone to know it; for he was teaching his disciples, saying to them, "The Son of Man is to be betrayed into human hands, and they will kill him, and three days after being killed, he will rise again." But they did not understand what he was saying and were afraid to ask him. Then they came to Capernaum; and when he was in the house he asked them, "What were you arguing about on the way?" But they were silent, for on the way they had argued with one another who was the greatest. He sat down, called the twelve, and said to them, "Whoever wants to be first must be last of all and servant of all." Then he took a little child and put it among them; and taking it in his arms, he said to them, "Whoever welcomes one such child in my name welcomes me, and whoever welcomes me welcomes not me but the one who sent me."

• The tenderness of Jesus' love for children is immense. In every adult, there is an inner child: vulnerable, sensitive, playful, open. Before the world cast its film of familiarity, boredom, and cynicism, the child in us was full of wonder. It is only through wonder that that we can experience the glory and the greatness of God.

• Many of the great saints retained that capacity for wonder, a delight in creator and creation, an enduring youthfulness. The great Dominican mystic, Meister Eckhardt, joyfully claimed that "my soul is as young as when I was created, aye, much younger. And I tell you, I should be ashamed were she not younger tomorrow than today." God my creator, I am willing to be that childlike. I do want to know wonder again.

Wednesday 23rd May
Mark 9:38–40

John said to him, "Teacher, we saw someone casting out demons in your name, and we tried to stop him, because he was not following us." But Jesus said, "Do not stop him; for no one who does a deed of power in my name will be able soon afterward to speak evil of me. Whoever is not against us is for us."

• Once having known Jesus, there should be no halfway house. We can embrace him or resist him. We cannot say yes and no at the same time. As Saint. Paul says, "For in him every one of God's promises is a 'Yes.' For this reason it is through him that we say the 'Amen,' to the glory of God." What do I say this day?

• How often do we watch with suspicion people of faith who are not of our "group"? Perhaps their beliefs vary from ours, or their vocabulary seems strange to us. Jesus' response here in Mark 9 reveals God's openness to anyone who believes. I pray to be more accepting of others and their faith practices.

Thursday 24th May
Mark 9:41–50

Jesus said to his disciples, "For truly I tell you, whoever gives you a cup of water to drink because you bear the name of Christ will by no means lose the reward. If any of you put a stumbling block before one of these little ones who believe in me, it would be better for you if a great millstone were hung around your neck and you were thrown into the sea. If your hand causes you to stumble, cut it off; it is better for you to enter life maimed than to have two hands and to go to hell, to the unquenchable fire. And if your foot causes you to stumble, cut it off; it is better for you to enter life lame than to have two feet and to be thrown into hell. And if your eye causes you to stumble, tear it out; it is better for you to enter the kingdom of God with one eye than to have two eyes and to be thrown into hell, where their worm never dies, and the fire is never quenched. For everyone will be salted with fire. Salt is good; but if salt has lost its saltiness, how can you season it? Have salt in yourselves, and be at peace with one another."

- As a Christian, I bear the name of Christ. I strive to think and feel and act as he might. I pray that today, and every day, I may see with his eyes, listen with his ears, speak with his words, and touch with his hands.

- As Christians, we are the salt of the earth. Salt has always been used to preserve, to cleanse, to add flavor, and to purify. Salt in the Old Testament was the symbol of an unbreakable covenant. May we never break faith with you, Lord.

Friday 25th May
Mark 10:1–12

He left that place and went to the region of Judea and beyond the Jordan. And crowds again gathered around him; and, as was his custom, he again taught them. Some Pharisees came, and to test him they asked, "Is it lawful for a man to divorce his wife?" He answered them, "What did Moses command you?" They said, "Moses allowed a man to write a certificate of dismissal and to divorce her." But Jesus said to them, "Because of your hardness of heart he wrote this commandment for you. But from the beginning of creation, 'God made them male and female. For this reason a man shall leave his father and mother and be joined to his wife, and the two shall become one flesh.' So they are no longer two, but one flesh. Therefore what God has joined together, let no one separate." // Then in the house the disciples asked him again about this matter. He said to them, "Whoever divorces his wife and marries another commits adultery against her; and if she divorces her husband and marries another, she commits adultery."

- Jesus sets out the ideal for marriage. He reminds us of what it is meant to be, even though, perhaps through no fault of our own, we may fail to live up to it. God is always present lovingly to the spouses, even if through human weakness they must part.

- Jesus denounces any hardness of heart that can bring about divorce. Spouses must not treat each other as worthless property to be discarded. They are called instead to a life of mutual respect and interdependence. Today, I pray for married people I know, that they will receive the grace to remain loving toward each other and not allow their hearts to become hard.

Saturday 26th May
Mark 10:13–16

People were bringing little children to Jesus in order that he might touch them; and the disciples spoke sternly to them. But when Jesus saw this, he was indignant and said to them, "Let the little children come to me; do not stop them; for it is to such as these that the kingdom of God belongs. Truly I tell you, whoever does not receive the kingdom of God as a little child will never enter it." And he took them up in his arms, laid his hands on them, and blessed them.

- It is the child in us who can truly be open to God's constant invitation to be born again, to be part of the creation, which is itself constantly being recreated. It is the child in us who can thrill to a sense of closeness to the source of all creation. Without a sense of wonder, our praise of God will be sterile. I want the fresh hope of a child!

- It is the child in us who can most truly live in a state of becoming, always open to growth and change. It is the child in us who can sense the perfection and stability of eternity, where there is neither time nor space, neither before nor after but, in Meister Eckhart's words, "everything present in one new, fresh-springing now where millenniums last no longer than the twinkling of an eye."

The Eighth Week of Ordinary Time
May 27—June 2

Something to think and pray about each day this week:

Unexpected Conversations
God and I have many unexpected conversations in daily life, especially at the grocery store. God comes to me in the lobby, the produce aisle, over by frozen foods, and last week, in the parking lot. I was returning to my car, trying to ignore the gray, bleak day—another in a long line of chilly non-spring days. With the season weeks behind schedule, everyone wants spring and the warmth, flowers, and promise of new life it brings.

As I pushed my cart across the parking lot, I was startled to see the car next to me. Nestled at the windshield was a large bouquet of flowers. Flowers! Beautiful spring blooms tied with a bright blue ribbon. There they were, just waiting for owner to return to the car and discover them.

Who were they from? Who were they for? I drove home imagining the joy that someone had planning, buying the bouquet, and leaving it. Was the giver waiting a few rows of cars away to watch the reaction? Was there a note with it, of apology or perhaps a declaration of love? I could picture the joy and sense of being loved that the driver would feel to return to the car on this cold and overcast day and find a spring surprise.

I am always looking for a more direct communication with God, like a phone call or a letter saying how loved I am or what I should do with a problem. I got home wishing that God sent flowers and realized that, of course, he does. They are in the grocery store, on the windshield, and now even peeking out from the ground in our gardens.

—Maureen McCann Waldron on *dotMagis*,
the blog of *IgnatianSpirituality.com*
http://www.ignatianspirituality.com/16217/
the-flowers-appear-on-the-earth

The Presence of God

"Be still and know that I am God!" Lord, your words lead us to the calmness and greatness of your presence.

Freedom

God is not foreign to my freedom. The Spirit breathes life into my most intimate desires, gently nudging me toward all that is good. I ask for the grace to let myself be enfolded by the Spirit.

Consciousness

Where do I sense hope, encouragement, and growth in my life? By looking back over the past few months, I may be able to see which activities and occasions have produced rich fruit. If I do notice such areas, I will determine to give those areas both time and space in the future.

The Word

The word of God comes down to us through the Scriptures. May the Holy Spirit enlighten my mind and my heart to respond to the gospel teachings. (Please turn to the Scripture on the following pages. Inspiration points are there should you need them. When you are ready, return here to continue.)

Conversation

What is stirring in me as I pray? Am I consoled, troubled, left cold? I imagine Jesus standing or sitting at my side, and I share my feelings with him.

Conclusion

Glory be to the Father, and to the Son, and to the Holy Spirit,
As it was in the beginning, is now and ever shall be,
World without end. Amen.

Sunday 27th May
The Most Holy Trinity
Matthew 28:16–20

Now the eleven disciples went to Galilee, to the mountain to which Jesus had directed them. When they saw him, they worshiped him; but some doubted. And Jesus came and said to them, "All authority in heaven and on earth has been given to me. Go therefore and make disciples of all nations, baptizing them in the name of the Father and of the Son and of the Holy Spirit, and teaching them to obey everything that I have commanded you. And remember, I am with you always, to the end of the age."

- Lord, you terrify me with this command: Go and teach all nations. You were talking to eleven men without education, money, or influence, in a despised province of the Roman Empire. But they obeyed you, because they knew you were with them. And today Christians are the largest body of believers on this planet. Today's preaching is different. We are educated, sometimes too well. It is harder than ever to make our voice heard. Yet, through us, your word goes out potentially to all nations, and you are still with us.

- How do we make disciples now? How do we reach all nations? In what ways do I teach others to follow Jesus?

Monday 28th May
Mark 10:17–27

As Jesus was setting out on a journey, a man ran up and knelt before him, and asked him, "Good Teacher, what must I do to inherit eternal life?" Jesus said to him, "Why do you call me good? No one is good but God alone. You know the commandments: 'You shall not murder; You shall not commit adultery; You shall not steal; You shall not bear false witness; You shall not defraud; Honor your father and mother.'" He said to him, "Teacher, I have kept all these since my youth." Jesus, looking at him, loved him and said, "You lack one thing; go, sell what you own, and give the money to the poor, and you will have treasure in heaven; then come, follow me." When he heard this, he was shocked and went away grieving, for he had many possessions. // Then Jesus looked around and said to his disciples, "How hard it will be for those who have wealth to enter the kingdom of God!" And the disciples were perplexed at these words. But

Jesus said to them again, "Children, how hard it is to enter the kingdom of God! It is easier for a camel to go through the eye of a needle than for someone who is rich to enter the kingdom of God." They were greatly astounded and said to one another, "Then who can be saved?" Jesus looked at them and said, "For mortals it is impossible, but not for God; for God all things are possible."

- Jesus does not invite us to mediocrity. He asks everything, but he asks it with great love. The young man has clearly been leading a respectable life, but it is not enough. Imagine being in this man's shoes. How would you react to what Jesus asks? What does this reaction tell you about your spiritual life?

- In the closing words of the passage, Jesus makes it clear that our efforts can never put us in possession of eternal life. What we cannot do, Christ has done for us, and does in us. We pray for the grace to reject what stands between us and him, and we surrender ourselves to him, so that eternal life will enter us here on earth.

Tuesday 29th May
Mark 10:28–31

Peter began to say to Jesus, "Look, we have left everything and followed you." Jesus said, "Truly I tell you, there is no one who has left house or brothers or sisters or mother or father or children or fields, for my sake and for the sake of the good news, who will not receive a hundredfold now in this age—houses, brothers and sisters, mothers and children, and fields with persecutions—and in the age to come eternal life. But many who are first will be last, and the last will be first."

- Jesus announces radical change in relationships. His followers are to be part of an immense family. This huge community will not be without its trials, but the reward will be joy in this world and everlasting life hereafter. The early Christians lived out this vision, in a community where everything was shared, and where all belonged.

- In the final sentence, all perceived wisdom is overturned. We are called to look upon the world with Jesus' eyes—not as a world of haves and have-nots, but a world of those who give and those who do not. Among which group do I find myself?

Wednesday 30th May
Mark 10:32–45

They were on the road, going up to Jerusalem, and Jesus was walking ahead of them; they were amazed, and those who followed were afraid. He took the twelve aside again and began to tell them what was to happen to him, saying, "See, we are going up to Jerusalem, and the Son of Man will be handed over to the chief priests and the scribes, and they will condemn him to death; then they will hand him over to the Gentiles; they will mock him, and spit upon him, and flog him, and kill him; and after three days he will rise again." // James and John, the sons of Zebedee, came forward to him and said to him, "Teacher, we want you to do for us whatever we ask of you." And he said to them, "What is it you want me to do for you?" And they said to him, "Grant us to sit, one at your right hand and one at your left, in your glory." But Jesus said to them, "You do not know what you are asking. Are you able to drink the cup that I drink, or be baptized with the baptism that I am baptized with?" They replied, "We are able." Then Jesus said to them, "The cup that I drink you will drink; and with the baptism with which I am baptized, you will be baptized; but to sit at my right hand or at my left is not mine to grant, but it is for those for whom it has been prepared." // When the ten heard this, they began to be angry with James and John. So Jesus called them and said to them, "You know that among the Gentiles those whom they recognize as their rulers lord it over them, and their great ones are tyrants over them. But it is not so among you; but whoever wishes to become great among you must be your servant, and whoever wishes to be first among you must be slave of all. For the Son of Man came not to be served but to serve, and to give his life a ransom for many."

- Jesus is on his way to Jerusalem. Priest and victim, he is heading for the gruesome altar of Calvary. The disciples by now seem to have grasped the idea that Jesus will rise after three days, but their aspirations remain rooted in a different world. In Jesus' kingship, authority is empowerment of others, not control over them. It is won though sacrifice of self. That the disciples finally came to know this is evidenced by the fact that James, one of the questioners in this passage, went on to become the first apostle to be martyred.

- How would I answer Jesus if he asked me, "Are you able to drink the cup that I drink?"

Thursday 31st May
The Visitation of the Blessed Virgin Mary
Luke 1:39–56

In those days Mary set out and went with haste to a Judean town in the hill country, where she entered the house of Zechariah and greeted Elizabeth. When Elizabeth heard Mary's greeting, the child leapt in her womb. And Elizabeth was filled with the Holy Spirit and exclaimed with a loud cry, "Blessed are you among women, and blessed is the fruit of your womb. And why has this happened to me, that the mother of my Lord comes to me? For as soon as I heard the sound of your greeting, the child in my womb leapt for joy. And blessed is she who believed that there would be a fulfillment of what was spoken to her by the Lord."

And Mary said,
    "My soul magnifies the Lord,
        and my spirit rejoices in God my Savior,
    for he has looked with favor on the lowliness of his servant.
        Surely, from now on all generations will call me blessed;
    for the Mighty One has done great things for me,
        and holy is his name.
    His mercy is for those who fear him
        from generation to generation.
    He has shown strength with his arm;
        he has scattered the proud in the thoughts of their hearts.
    He has brought down the powerful from their thrones,
        and lifted up the lowly;
    he has filled the hungry with good things,
        and sent the rich away empty.
    He has helped his servant Israel,
        in remembrance of his mercy,
    according to the promise he made to our ancestors,
        to Abraham and to his descendants forever."

And Mary remained with her for about three months and then returned to her home.

- There is no false humility in Mary's tremendous prayer, only the true humility of knowing that all that is accomplished in her is being accomplished by God, "for the Mighty One has done great things for me." Mary makes no effort to minimize this greatness. She accepts it—fully, joyfully, and expectantly. Her great song of praise is a glorious expression of Mary's hope.

• I ask you, Lord, to give me Mary's confidence and generosity of spirit. I ask not just to listen to your voice and do your will, but also to do it joyfully and fearlessly. I want to answer your call with an exultant *Yes!* secure in the knowledge that as I move into the unknown, my journey will be made radiant by your transfiguring presence, and that, as the psalmist foretold, "your hand shall lead me, and your right hand shall hold me fast."

Friday 1st June
Mark 11:11–26

Then he entered Jerusalem and went into the temple; and when he had looked around at everything, as it was already late, he went out to Bethany with the twelve. On the following day, when they came from Bethany, he was hungry. Seeing in the distance a fig tree in leaf, he went to see whether perhaps he would find anything on it. When he came to it, he found nothing but leaves, for it was not the season for figs. He said to it, "May no one ever eat fruit from you again." And his disciples heard it. // Then they came to Jerusalem. And he entered the temple and began to drive out those who were selling and those who were buying in the temple, and he overturned the tables of the money changers and the seats of those who sold doves; and he would not allow anyone to carry anything through the temple. He was teaching and saying, "Is it not written,

'My house shall be called a house of prayer for all the nations'?
But you have made it a den of robbers."

And when the chief priests and the scribes heard it, they kept looking for a way to kill him; for they were afraid of him, because the whole crowd was spellbound by his teaching. And when evening came, Jesus and his disciples went out of the city. // In the morning as they passed by, they saw the fig tree withered away to its roots. Then Peter remembered and said to him, "Rabbi, look! The fig tree that you cursed has withered." Jesus answered them, "Have faith in God. Truly I tell you, if you say to this mountain, 'Be taken up and thrown into the sea,' and if you do not doubt in your heart, but believe that what you say will come to pass, it will be done for you. So I tell you, whatever you ask for in prayer, believe that you have received it, and it will be yours. Whenever you stand praying, forgive, if you have anything against anyone; so that your Father in heaven may also forgive you your trespasses."

- Jesus is on his way to the temple to carry out the act that will hasten his crucifixion. The incident of the fig tree (which is, in the Old Testament, a symbol of the nation of Israel) is closely connected to the cleansing of the temple. Jesus is condemning a religion that does not bear fruit. What fruit will I bear today?

- C.S. Lewis wrote, "To be a Christian means to forgive the inexcusable because God has forgiven the inexcusable in you." Whom have I forgiven lately?

Saturday 2nd June
Mark 11:27–33

Again they came to Jerusalem. As he was walking in the temple, the chief priests, the scribes, and the elders came to him and said, "By what authority are you doing these things? Who gave you this authority to do them?" Jesus said to them, "I will ask you one question; answer me, and I will tell you by what authority I do these things. Did the baptism of John come from heaven, or was it of human origin? Answer me." They argued with one another, "If we say, 'From heaven,' he will say, 'Why then did you not believe him?' But shall we say, 'Of human origin'?"—they were afraid of the crowd, for all regarded John as truly a prophet. So they answered Jesus, "We do not know." And Jesus said to them, "Neither will I tell you by what authority I am doing these things."

- The opponents of Jesus question the source of his authority. They fear it may undermine their own power. Jesus knew that answering the Pharisees' question would lead only to further debate.

- Have there been situations in which I willfully refused to see the presence and activity of God? I pray that I will be alert to his voice in all my encounters today.

The Ninth Week of Ordinary Time
June 3—June 9

Something to think and pray about each day this week:

Forgiveness as Spiritual Practice

Even when we understand that forgiveness is essential to our health and happiness, it's still a challenge to forgive. My friend Rachael admits that, even after accepting an apology, she often continues to hold onto the injury and negative feelings.

"It is very difficult for me to forgive, and I'm not happy or proud about that," Rachael says. "I completely believe that forgiveness is the best way to go. But apparently, my head knows things my heart cannot accomplish."

Rachael understands forgiveness as a spiritual practice: "We're supposed to forgive one another 'seventy times seven,' and that is just the beginning of how much God forgives us. We need to offer that soul-clearing forgiveness to others."

You know how difficult feats look simple when professionals perform them? Think of Olympic figure skaters leaping and gliding over the ice, or Yo-Yo Ma playing the cello. They're so graceful, so joyful. But what we never see is how many times the skaters have fallen or how many times a much less experienced Yo-Yo Ma messed up.

Like so many spiritual practices, we have to work at forgiveness to get better at it.

—Jennifer Grant, *Wholehearted Living*

The Presence of God
As I sit here, the beating of my heart,
the ebb and flow of my breathing, the movements of my mind
are all signs of God's ongoing creation of me.
I pause for a moment and become aware
of this presence of God within me.

Freedom
I will ask God's help
to be free from my own preoccupations,
to be open to God in this time of prayer,
to come to know, love, and serve God more.

Consciousness
At this moment, Lord, I turn my thoughts to you.
I will leave aside my chores and preoccupations.
I will take rest and refreshment in your presence.

The Word
Now I turn to the Scripture set out for me this day. I read slowly over the words and see if any sentence or sentiment appeals to me. (Please turn to the Scripture on the following pages. Inspiration points are there should you need them. When you are ready, return here to continue.)

Conversation
Begin to talk to Jesus about the Scripture you have just read. What part of it strikes a chord in you? Perhaps the words of a friend—or some story you have heard recently—will slowly rise to the surface of your consciousness. If so, does the story throw light on what the Scripture passage may be saying to you?

Conclusion
Glory be to the Father, and to the Son, and to the Holy Spirit,
As it was in the beginning, is now and ever shall be,
World without end. Amen.

Sunday 3rd June
The Most Holy Body and Blood of Christ
Mark 14:12–16, 22–26

On the first day of Unleavened Bread, when the Passover lamb is sacrificed, his disciples said to him, "Where do you want us to go and make the preparations for you to eat the Passover?" So he sent two of his disciples, saying to them, "Go into the city, and a man carrying a jar of water will meet you; follow him, and wherever he enters, say to the owner of the house, 'The Teacher asks, Where is my guest room where I may eat the Passover with my disciples?' He will show you a large room upstairs, furnished and ready. Make preparations for us there." So the disciples set out and went to the city, and found everything as he had told them; and they prepared the Passover meal. // While they were eating, he took a loaf of bread, and after blessing it he broke it, gave it to them, and said, "Take; this is my body." Then he took a cup, and after giving thanks he gave it to them, and all of them drank from it. He said to them, "This is my blood of the covenant, which is poured out for many. Truly I tell you, I will never again drink of the fruit of the vine until that day when I drink it new in the kingdom of God." When they had sung the hymn, they went out to the Mount of Olives.

- Today's feast of Corpus Christi is a revisiting of the liturgy of Holy Thursday with an emphasis on the institution of the Eucharist. We are reminded of the Jewish context of the Last Supper (Passover meal, sacrificial lamb). The terms "my body" and "my blood of the covenant" both express the total self-giving of Jesus for us. The Last Supper is the prologue to the Passion.

- Do I appreciate the "bread from heaven" that Jesus offers us?

Monday 4th June
Mark 12:1–12

Then Jesus began to speak to them in parables. "A man planted a vineyard, put a fence around it, dug a pit for the wine press, and built a watch-tower; then he leased it to tenants and went to another country. When the season came, he sent a slave to the tenants to collect from them his share of the produce of the vineyard. But they seized him, and beat him, and sent him away empty-handed. And again he sent another slave to them;

this one they beat over the head and insulted. Then he sent another, and that one they killed. And so it was with many others; some they beat, and others they killed. He had still one other, a beloved son. Finally he sent him to them, saying, 'They will respect my son.' But those tenants said to one another, 'This is the heir; come, let us kill him, and the inheritance will be ours.' So they seized him, killed him, and threw him out of the vineyard. What then will the owner of the vineyard do? He will come and destroy the tenants and give the vineyard to others. Have you not read this scripture:

> 'The stone that the builders rejected
>   has become the cornerstone;
> this was the Lord's doing,
>   and it is amazing in our eyes.'"

When they realized that he had told this parable against them, they wanted to arrest him, but they feared the crowd. So they left him and went away.

- The parable of the vineyard demonstrates how God gives us everything we need to produce rich fruit; he doesn't stand over us but trusts us to cultivate our vineyard ourselves. However, the time will come when we have to give a reckoning of the harvest we have gathered. I pray that I will be ready for that day.

- Jesus is the stone prophesied by Isaiah; he is the cornerstone, but the builders have rejected him. I may follow Jesus, but I must know that others will reject the one I trust, the one on whom I build my life. Have I ever felt others' rejection of my faith?

Tuesday 5th June
Mark 12:13–17

Then they sent to Jesus some Pharisees and some Herodians to trap him in what he said. And they came and said to him, "Teacher, we know that you are sincere, and show deference to no one; for you do not regard people with partiality, but teach the way of God in accordance with truth. Is it lawful to pay taxes to the emperor, or not? Should we pay them, or should we not?" But knowing their hypocrisy, he said to them, "Why are you putting me to the test? Bring me a denarius and let me see it." And they brought one. Then he said to them, "Whose head is this, and whose title?" They answered, "The emperor's." Jesus said to them, "Give to the emperor the things that are the emperor's, and to God the things that are God's." And they were utterly amazed at him.

- The hypocrisy of the Pharisees and Herodians does not lie in the question they are asking (this is fair and relevant) but in their motivation for asking it. They want to trick Jesus. When have I used seemingly honest questions to distract the discussion from a point I find uncomfortable? Do I ever argue with Jesus so that I can avoid some action he wants in my life?

- How do I understand the final statement of Jesus in the circumstances of my own life and times?

Wednesday 6th June
Mark 12:18–27

Some Sadducees, who say there is no resurrection, came to Jesus and asked him a question, saying, "Teacher, Moses wrote for us that if a man's brother dies, leaving a wife but no child, the man shall marry the widow and raise up children for his brother. There were seven brothers; the first married and, when he died, left no children; and the second married her and died, leaving no children; and the third likewise; none of the seven left children. Last of all the woman herself died. In the resurrection whose wife will she be? For the seven had married her." // Jesus said to them, "Is not this the reason you are wrong, that you know neither the scriptures nor the power of God? For when they rise from the dead, they neither marry nor are given in marriage, but are like angels in heaven. And as for the dead being raised, have you not read in the book of Moses, in the story about the bush, how God said to him, 'I am the God of Abraham, the God of Isaac, and the God of Jacob'? He is God not of the dead, but of the living; you are quite wrong."

- God is not of the dead, but of the living. Our world is so concerned with competition and the violence it generates that it needs to hear this wonderful message. Yet, religious people seem to waste so much time arguing about details, while the life-giving message is neglected. May my life show that God has come to give us life, and life in abundance.

- Do I sometimes find myself closing my heart to others in God's name, because I am a Christian? Lord Jesus, save me from such blasphemy and hypocrisy.

Thursday 7th June
Mark 12:28–34

One of the scribes came near and heard them disputing with one another, and seeing that he answered them well, he asked him, "Which commandment is the first of all?" Jesus answered, "The first is, 'Hear, O Israel: the Lord our God, the Lord is one; you shall love the Lord your God with all your heart, and with all your soul, and with all your mind, and with all your strength.' The second is this, 'You shall love your neighbor as yourself.' There is no other commandment greater than these." Then the scribe said to him, "You are right, Teacher; you have truly said that 'he is one, and besides him there is no other'; and 'to love him with all the heart, and with all the understanding, and with all the strength', and 'to love one's neighbor as oneself'—this is much more important than all whole burnt offerings and sacrifices." When Jesus saw that he answered wisely, he said to him, "You are not far from the kingdom of God." After that no one dared to ask him any question.

- I, too, often ask myself, what is the first commandment of all? Which is the most important of my many obligations? Today, like the scribe, I ask Jesus to enlighten me with the answer to this vital question. I allow myself to be impressed by Jesus' clear answer: love. It is the most important thing I can ever do; it includes all my duties and all the commandments.

- Jesus tells me to love others as I love myself. Do I feel called to love myself as I am? Or do I feel guilty when I try to do so, feeling that I am being selfish? Jesus seems to imply the contrary; I will not be able to love others unless I love myself.

Friday 8th June
The Most Sacred Heart of Jesus
John 19:31–37

Since it was the day of Preparation, the Jews did not want the bodies left on the cross during the sabbath, especially because that sabbath was a day of great solemnity. So they asked Pilate to have the legs of the crucified men broken and the bodies removed. Then the soldiers came and broke the legs of the first and of the other who had been crucified with him. But when they came to Jesus and saw that he was already dead, they did not break his legs. Instead, one of the soldiers pierced his side with a spear, and at once blood and water came out. (He who saw this has testified so that you also may believe. His testimony is true, and he knows that he tells the truth.) These things occurred so that the scripture might be fulfilled, "None of his bones shall be broken." And again another passage of scripture says, "They will look on the one whom they have pierced."

- It is necessary to recognize the scriptural roots of devotion to the Sacred Heart. Otherwise an unhelpful sentimentality can creep in. The symbolism of the piercing of Jesus' side is a sound basis for the devotion. Enter this familiar scene on Calvary and "look on the one they have pierced." See the blood and water flowing from his pierced side. Some interpret this as representing the Eucharist and baptism. What does it represent for me?

- How is the Sacred Heart communicating his love for me today? Have I any response?

Saturday 9th June
The Immaculate Heart of the Blessed Virgin Mary
Luke 2:41–51

Now every year his parents went to Jerusalem for the festival of the Passover. And when he was twelve years old, they went up as usual for the festival. When the festival was ended and they started to return, the boy Jesus stayed behind in Jerusalem, but his parents did not know it. Assuming that he was in the group of travelers, they went a day's journey. Then they started to look for him among their relatives and friends. When they did not find him, they returned to Jerusalem to search for him. After three days they found him in the temple, sitting among the teachers, listening to them and asking them questions. And all who heard him were amazed at his understanding and his answers. When his parents saw him they were astonished; and his mother said to him, "Child, why have you treated us like this? Look, your father and I have been searching for you in great anxiety." He said to them, "Why were you searching for me? Did you not know that I must be in my Father's house?" But they did not understand what he said to them. Then he went down with them and came to Nazareth, and was obedient to them. His mother treasured all these things in her heart.

- Like every other mother, Mary was the person who had the greatest influence on her son's heart. She taught him how to love, share, pray, and be compassionate. She was the first to speak to him about God, and in her he could see these values come alive. Mary, shape and teach my heart to be as close to the heart of Jesus as your own heart was!

- The Gospel says very openly that Mary and Joseph did not understand their son's reply. This is true for the parents of many teenagers! Mary, help parents to keep believing in their children; sustain them in their struggle to love unconditionally.

The Tenth Week of Ordinary Time
June 10—June 16

Something to think and pray about each day this week:

What We Expect

A few years ago, a book was published about Mother Teresa. This collection of her writings describes how alienated she felt from God during all her years of service. Many people were shocked by this. How could someone who seemed to be so deeply religious and obedient to God say such things?

The only way to answer that is to ask if you've ever been in love with someone desperately. Your world revolves around this person and you want your beloved to respond to you in a certain way, but this person never does. Now, this person could love you just as much as you love, but because he or she never responds to you in the way you expect, you feel isolated, alone, vacant. Loneliness wraps its dark wings around you, and you feel as if you're going to die. This can happen between lovers, husbands and wives, parents and children.

This can happen between you and God.

Many people say you shouldn't have expectations in your spiritual life. I don't believe this. Moses had expectations—so did Jonah, so did Paul, so did Jesus. We should expect God to answer us, but we have to acquiesce *to the way* he responds.

He will respond, but watch out what you wish for, because once you get him started, you can't shut him up.

—Gary Jansen, *The 15-Minute Prayer Solution*

The Presence of God

At any time of the day or night we can call on Jesus.
He is always waiting, listening for our call.
What a wonderful blessing.
No phone needed, no emails, just a whisper.

Freedom

If God were trying to tell me something, would I know?
If God were reassuring me or challenging me, would I notice?
I ask for the grace to be free of my own preoccupations
and open to what God may be saying to me.

Consciousness

Help me, Lord, become more conscious of your presence. Teach me to recognize your presence in others. Fill my heart with gratitude for the times your love has been shown to me through the care of others.

The Word

In this expectant state of mind, please turn to the text for the day with confidence. Believe that the Holy Spirit is present and may reveal whatever the passage has to say to you. Read reflectively, listening with a third ear to what may be going on in your heart. (Please turn to the Scripture on the following pages. Inspiration points are there should you need them. When you are ready, return here to continue.)

Conversation

Conversation requires talking and listening.
As I talk to Jesus, may I also learn to pause and listen.
I picture the gentleness in his eyes and the love in his smile.
I can be totally honest with Jesus as I tell him my worries and cares.
I will open my heart to Jesus as I tell him my fears and doubts.
I will ask him to help me place myself fully in his care, knowing that he always desires good for me.

Conclusion

I thank God for these moments we have spent together and for any insights I have been given concerning the text.

Sunday 10th June
Tenth Sunday in Ordinary Time
Mark 3:20–35

And the crowd came together again, so that they could not even eat. When his family heard it, they went out to restrain him, for people were saying, "He has gone out of his mind." And the scribes who came down from Jerusalem said, "He has Beelzebul, and by the ruler of the demons he casts out demons." And he called them to him, and spoke to them in parables, "How can Satan cast out Satan? If a kingdom is divided against itself, that kingdom cannot stand. And if a house is divided against itself, that house will not be able to stand. And if Satan has risen up against himself and is divided, he cannot stand, but his end has come. But no one can enter a strong man's house and plunder his property without first tying up the strong man; then indeed the house can be plundered. // "Truly I tell you, people will be forgiven for their sins and whatever blasphemies they utter; but whoever blasphemes against the Holy Spirit can never have forgiveness, but is guilty of an eternal sin"—for they had said, "He has an unclean spirit." // Then his mother and his brothers came; and standing outside, they sent to him and called him. A crowd was sitting around him; and they said to him, "Your mother and your brothers and sisters are outside, asking for you." And he replied, "Who are my mother and my brothers?" And looking at those who sat around him, he said, "Here are my mother and my brothers! Whoever does the will of God is my brother and sister and mother."

- When we follow our spiritual path, sometimes our closest companions are not those in our own family—or even our oldest friends. Lord, help me let go of those who choose not to come with me as I walk with you.

- Jesus words probably upset expectations in a culture that was so family- and tribe-centered. He was not criticizing his family, but expanding the definition of who his family was. Who is my expanded family, the one that includes those in God's family?

Monday 11th June
Matthew 5:1–12

When Jesus saw the crowds, he went up the mountain; and after he sat down, his disciples came to him. Then he began to speak, and taught them, saying:

"Blessed are the poor in spirit, for theirs is the kingdom of heaven.

"Blessed are those who mourn, for they will be comforted.

"Blessed are the meek, for they will inherit the earth.

"Blessed are those who hunger and thirst for righteousness, for they will be filled.

"Blessed are the merciful, for they will receive mercy.

"Blessed are the pure in heart, for they will see God.

"Blessed are the peacemakers, for they will be called children of God.

"Blessed are those who are persecuted for righteousness' sake, for theirs is the kingdom of heaven.

"Blessed are you when people revile you and persecute you and utter all kinds of evil against you falsely on my account. Rejoice and be glad, for your reward is great in heaven, for in the same way they persecuted the prophets who were before you."

- Like the second Moses, Jesus goes up the mountain to give his new Law. It is a law of the heart, based not on fear or prohibitions but on a heart wide open, ready to embrace the paradoxes of life and to live it to the full. It is based on a call to happiness and blessedness. I can best understand the Beatitudes by contemplating Jesus and the way he lived: openly and courageously.

- The Beatitudes always strike a chord deep in my heart. Today I will stay with the one that speaks to me most, either because I feel called to that particular attitude or because it represents my present struggle. I ask Jesus for his blessing, and for the grace that I might be a blessing to others.

Tuesday 12th June
Matthew 5:13–16

Jesus said to the crowds, "You are the salt of the earth; but if salt has lost its taste, how can its saltiness be restored? It is no longer good for anything, but is thrown out and trampled under foot. You are the light of the world. A city built on a hill cannot be hid. No one after lighting a lamp puts it under the bushel basket, but on the lampstand, and it gives light to all in the house. In the same way, let your light shine before others, so that they may see your good works and give glory to your Father in heaven."

- Jesus seems recklessly confident of our potential: he calls us to be the salt and light of the world, without whose witness the world will be a different place. Yet, we are too ready to dismiss the influence our actions can have on others. But the life of the Beatitudes gives flavor to our life together, and being a follower of Christ is not an individualistic choice but one that involves others.

- I give glory to the Father in heaven for the witness of someone I know whose life impresses me. I ask for grace to throw light on the path of others so that they too may give glory to the Father.

Wednesday 13th June
Matthew 5:17–19

"Do not think that I have come to abolish the law or the prophets; I have come not to abolish but to fulfill. For truly I tell you, until heaven and earth pass away, not one letter, not one stroke of a letter, will pass from the law until all is accomplished. Therefore, whoever breaks one of the least of these commandments, and teaches others to do the same, will be called least in the kingdom of heaven; but whoever does them and teaches them will be called great in the kingdom of heaven."

- The relationship between the Old Testament and the novelty brought by Jesus was one of the main issues the gospel had to face. Here Jesus insists on the continuity between the law and himself. Yet, by affirming that he is bringing the law to its perfection, he is claiming special powers for himself, divine powers. This is the real difference: Jesus is God himself.

- The perfection that Jesus brings to the law is in its spirit and not in the individual observances: the law is fulfilled by love. Love becomes the greatest commandment of all in the spirit of freedom, the freedom of the children of God. I ask myself what is my manner of fulfilling the law and teaching it to others. I ask the Father for his pardon. I also ask him to give me his spirit of universal love and filial freedom.

Thursday 14th June
Matthew 5:20–26

"For I tell you, unless your righteousness exceeds that of the scribes and Pharisees, you will never enter the kingdom of heaven. You have heard that it was said to those of ancient times, 'You shall not murder'; and 'whoever murders shall be liable to judgement.' But I say to you that if you are angry with a brother or sister, you will be liable to judgement; and if you insult a brother or sister, you will be liable to the council; and if you say, 'You fool', you will be liable to the hell of fire. So when you are offering your gift at the altar, if you remember that your brother or sister has something against you, leave your gift there before the altar and go; first be reconciled to your brother or sister, and then come and offer your gift. Come to terms quickly with your accuser while you are on the way to court with him, or your accuser may hand you over to the judge, and the judge to the guard, and you will be thrown into prison. Truly I tell you, you will never get out until you have paid the last penny."

- Jesus starts by showing what he means by bringing the law to its perfection. The new standard is higher than the old, because it deals with our heart and not with the mere external action. It is not enough *not* to murder your brother; you owe him respect.

- Taking part in the liturgy makes sense only if we enjoy good relationships with others; it makes no sense for me to offer my sacrifice when I have problems with my brother. My worship is not a substitute for good behavior or a guarantee against the divine judgement; rather, it is an expression of what lies in my heart and of my desire to be more loving.

Friday 15th June
Matthew 5:27–32

Jesus said to the crowds, "You have heard that it was said, 'You shall not commit adultery.' But I say to you that everyone who looks at a woman with lust has already committed adultery with her in his heart. If your right eye causes you to sin, tear it out and throw it away; it is better for you to lose one of your members than for your whole body to be thrown into hell. And if your right hand causes you to sin, cut it off and throw it away; it is better for you to lose one of your members than for your whole body to go into hell. It was also said, 'Whoever divorces his wife, let him give her a certificate of divorce.' But I say to you that anyone who divorces his wife, except on the ground of unchastity, causes her to commit adultery; and whoever marries a divorced woman commits adultery."

- This is not an easy text to deal with, especially in our times, when relationships are so fragile and divorce so widespread. Experts differ in their interpretation: was Jesus expressing a precept or an ideal, as he does in the other paragraphs? What is the meaning of "except on the ground of unchastity"? It is certainly not within the scope of these notes to arrive at conclusions on this obscure point. But it must be obvious to even the casual reader that Jesus upholds the ideal of marriage as indissoluble.

- The Sermon on the Mount looks at our heart, from which our actions proceed as fruits from a tree. In this perspective, personal integrity always comes first, even if it comes at very high personal cost. Lord, help me be your disciple, whatever the cost.

Saturday 16th June
Matthew 5:33–37

Jesus said to the crowds, "Again, you have heard that it was said to those of ancient times, 'You shall not swear falsely, but carry out the vows you have made to the Lord.' But I say to you, Do not swear at all, either by heaven, for it is the throne of God, or by the earth, for it is his footstool, or by Jerusalem, for it is the city of the great King. And do not swear by your head, for you cannot make one hair white or black. Let your word be 'Yes, Yes' or 'No, No'; anything more than this comes from the evil one."

- Jesus is again insisting that his standards go beyond just being reasonable. Today the reading describes the level of integrity that is expected of the disciples of Jesus, both as individuals and as members of institutions. He lived before the age of spin, and he calls for "Yes, yes, No, no." The society he is proposing—the kingdom—is to be built on trust in such a way that we do not need to use oaths to believe each other.

- Am I true to myself? How important is truth in my relationships with others? Do I hold integrity in high esteem in my understanding of public life? How truthful am I before myself and before God? I look at Jesus and see the model of total integrity and honesty.

Eleventh Week of Ordinary Time
June 17—June 23

Something to think and pray about each day this week:

Lulled by Prayer

In centering prayer, you choose one word with sacred significance—*peace, faith, joy, Spirit, God, Jesus*—and focus your attention on that particular word, repeating it to yourself until, through the grace of God, you begin to experience an internal shift. On that day, my word was *love*.

As I sat down on the always-crowded 5:36 p.m. eastbound train to Long Island, snug between a sweaty guy with a hairnet and a woman who texted her BFF every thirty seconds, I started focusing on love, repeating it to myself. As the train lurched out of the station, my mind started to wander a bit—I was focusing on love, but then other things would enter my mind: worries, work, family, stop signs, light bulbs, the Yankees, and Pez dispensers. Then my mind shifted back to love.

Love. God. Love. Christ. Love. Mother Teresa. The word *love* in graffiti on a wall in Queens, New York. This homeless woman I passed on the street every day on my way to work. *Love. Resurrection. Love. God. Love.* Soon I experienced a tiny movement of the heart and I fell into a steady rhythm, and everything around me started to fall away. I couldn't feel the heat of sweaty dude next to me, and I no longer heard texting girl next to me chewing her gum like a horse. All the noise in the train vanished, and I was lulled into this state where love was the primary focus.

—Gary Jansen, *The 15-Minute Prayer Solution*

The Presence of God
Dear Jesus, as I call on you today, I realize that often I come asking for favors. Today I'd like just to be in your presence. Draw my heart in response to your love.

Freedom
It is so easy to get caught up
with the trappings of wealth in this life.
Grant, O Lord, that I may be free
from greed and selfishness.
Remind me that the best things in life are free:
Love, laughter, caring, and sharing.

Consciousness
How am I really feeling? Lighthearted? Heavyhearted? I may be very much at peace, happy to be here.
Equally, I may be frustrated, worried, or angry.
I acknowledge how I really am. It is the real me whom the Lord loves.

The Word
Lord Jesus, you became human to communicate with me.
You walked and worked on this earth.
You endured the heat and struggled with the cold.
All your time on this earth was spent in caring for humanity.
You healed the sick, you raised the dead.
Most important of all, you saved me from death.
(Please turn to the Scripture on the following pages. Inspiration points are there should you need them. When you are ready, return here to continue.)

Conversation
Do I notice myself reacting as I pray with the word of God? Do I feel challenged, comforted, angry? Imagining Jesus sitting or standing by me, I speak out my feelings, as one trusted friend to another.

Conclusion
Glory be to the Father, and to the Son, and to the Holy Spirit,
As it was in the beginning, is now and ever shall be,
World without end. Amen.

Sunday 17th June
Eleventh Sunday in Ordinary Time
Mark 4:26–34

Jesus said to the crowd, "The kingdom of God is as if someone would scatter seed on the ground, and would sleep and rise night and day, and the seed would sprout and grow, he does not know how. The earth produces of itself, first the stalk, then the head, then the full grain in the head. But when the grain is ripe, at once he goes in with his sickle, because the harvest has come." // He also said, "With what can we compare the kingdom of God, or what parable will we use for it? It is like a mustard seed, which, when sown upon the ground, is the smallest of all the seeds on earth; yet when it is sown it grows up and becomes the greatest of all shrubs, and puts forth large branches, so that the birds of the air can make nests in its shade." // With many such parables he spoke the word to them, as they were able to hear it; he did not speak to them except in parables, but he explained everything in private to his disciples.

- Jesus uses natural occurrences in our world to describe the kingdom of God. This kingdom does not float down, some alien form from outer space. It happens within the processes and daily actions we know well. Open my eyes, Lord, to see the kingdom as it grows in my life.

- Notice that the person scatters seed but then goes to sleep. The next day, it's clear that the seed has sprouted during the night. God gives us work to do, but the outcome is God's. We can do our work, and then rest easy.

Monday 18th June
Matthew 5:38–42

Jesus said to the crowds, "You have heard that it was said, 'An eye for an eye and a tooth for a tooth.' But I say to you, Do not resist an evildoer. But if anyone strikes you on the right cheek, turn the other also; and if anyone wants to sue you and take your coat, give your cloak as well; and if anyone forces you to go one mile, go also the second mile. Give to everyone who begs from you, and do not refuse anyone who wants to borrow from you."

- For many good Christians, this is one of the most difficult and paradoxical passages of the whole Gospel. On the one hand, we know that retribution will not get us anywhere, except to an ever deeper spiral of violence. Yet, how can we stop evil if we do as Jesus tells us and "not resist the evildoer?" Is it possible to turn the other cheek when we are attacked?

- Jesus is telling us that evil is overcome—and the evildoer's life changes—when we resist evil not with retribution but with the power of love and of goodness. It is the logic of the Resurrection, whereby the definitive victory was achieved when Jesus loved his friends to the end, to the point of giving up his life, though he was blameless. I ask the Father to give me the spirit of Jesus, his readiness to walk the extra mile and turn the other cheek.

Tuesday 19th June
Matthew 5:43–48

Jesus said to the disciples, "You have heard that it was said, 'You shall love your neighbor and hate your enemy.' But I say to you, Love your enemies and pray for those who persecute you, so that you may be children of your Father in heaven; for he makes his sun rise on the evil and on the good, and sends rain on the righteous and on the unrighteous. For if you love those who love you, what reward do you have? Do not even the tax collectors do the same? And if you greet only your brothers and sisters, what more are you doing than others? Do not even the Gentiles do the same? Be perfect, therefore, as your heavenly Father is perfect."

- I can spend today's prayer time doing what Jesus is telling me to do; I will pray for those who make my life difficult. I bring them to mind, one by one, and I ask the merciful Father to purify my heart of anger and help me look on them with more understanding and compassion.
- I dwell on that phrase that strikes me most in today's reading, and I ask for the grace to try to be like my Father in his mercy.

Wednesday 20th June
Matthew 6:1–6, 16–18

"Beware of practicing your piety before others in order to be seen by them; for then you have no reward from your Father in heaven. So whenever you give alms, do not sound a trumpet before you, as the hypocrites do in the synagogues and in the streets, so that they may be praised by others. Truly I tell you, they have received their reward. But when you give alms, do not let your left hand know what your right hand is doing, so that your alms may be done in secret; and your Father who sees in secret will reward you. And whenever you pray, do not be like the hypocrites; for they love to stand and pray in the synagogues and at the street corners, so that they may be seen by others. Truly I tell you, they have received their reward. But whenever you pray, go into your room and shut the door and pray to your Father who is in secret; and your Father who sees in secret will reward you. And whenever you fast, do not look dismal, like the hypocrites, for they disfigure their faces so as to show others that they are fasting. Truly I tell you, they have received their reward. But when you fast, put oil on your head and wash your face, so that your fasting may be seen not by others but by your Father who is in secret; and your Father who sees in secret will reward you."

• Praying, almsgiving, and fasting were the three actions expected of a pious Jew in Jesus' time. As he has already said, Jesus did not come to destroy the law but to bring it to perfection and to raise it to a higher level. He insists that we not perform these good actions to be seen and praised by others, but rather, we should do them "in secret," for the Father who sees our hearts will reward us.

• Our consumerist culture puts great store on outward signs. Often we catch ourselves being influenced by the widely-publicized actions of celebrities, even though we know that some of these actions are artificial hype. Jesus' words remain a real challenge to me, and I let them shine a light on my actions and choices. I ask for the purity of heart described in the Beatitudes, and I ask pardon for the frivolities of my life choices.

Thursday 21st June
Matthew 6:7–15

Jesus said, "When you are praying, do not heap up empty phrases as the Gentiles do; for they think that they will be heard because of their many words. Do not be like them, for your Father knows what you need before you ask him.

Pray then in this way:

Our Father in heaven,

hallowed be your name.
Your kingdom come.
Your will be done,
　　on earth as it is in heaven.
Give us this day our daily bread.
And forgive us our debts,
　　as we also have forgiven our debtors.
And do not bring us to the time of trial,
　　but rescue us from the evil one.

For if you forgive others their trespasses, your heavenly Father will also forgive you; but if you do not forgive others, neither will your Father forgive your trespasses."

- The more I pray the Lord's Prayer, the more I realize how this is the expression of all Christian prayer, a real school of prayer. I say it slowly, dwelling gently on each phrase, without hurry, stopping where I find myself feeling inspired or close to the Father.

- I praise God, asking that his will be done and his kingdom come. I ask for my daily bread, trusting that he will never fail me and that I do not need to accumulate reserves. I ask for the ability to forgive and accept forgiveness, and for help and protection in my difficulties.

Friday 22nd June
Matthew 6:19–23

Jesus said, "Do not store up for yourselves treasures on earth, where moth and rust consume and where thieves break in and steal; but store up for yourselves treasures in heaven, where neither moth nor rust consumes and where thieves do not break in and steal. For where your treasure is, there your heart will be also. The eye is the lamp of the body. So, if your eye is healthy, your whole body will be full of light; but if your eye is unhealthy, your whole body will be full of darkness. If then the light in you is darkness, how great is the darkness!"

- When I look at my heart, I may find that it is divided; that is, undecided and torn between different or conflicting loyalties. Its light may be weak, and it may not illuminate my path in life. I look with gratitude

on those persons I admire for their integrity, and I pray for the grace of
an undivided heart.

- If my heart is in darkness, I thank Jesus for his word, which prods me
to walk toward the light.

Saturday 23rd June
Matthew 6:24–34

Jesus said, "No one can serve two masters; for a slave will either hate the
one and love the other, or be devoted to the one and despise the other. You
cannot serve God and wealth. Therefore I tell you, do not worry about your
life, what you will eat or what you will drink, or about your body, what you
will wear. Is not life more than food, and the body more than clothing?
Look at the birds of the air; they neither sow nor reap nor gather into barns,
and yet your heavenly Father feeds them. Are you not of more value than
they? And can any of you by worrying add a single hour to your span of life?
And why do you worry about clothing? Consider the lilies of the field, how
they grow; they neither toil nor spin, yet I tell you, even Solomon in all his
glory was not clothed like one of these. But if God so clothes the grass of the
field, which is alive today and tomorrow is thrown into the oven, will he not
much more clothe you—you of little faith? Therefore do not worry, saying,
'What will we eat?' or 'What will we drink?' or 'What will we wear?' For
it is the Gentiles who strive for all these things; and indeed your heavenly
Father knows that you need all these things. But strive first for the kingdom
of God and his righteousness, and all these things will be given to you as
well. So do not worry about tomorrow, for tomorrow will bring worries of
its own. Today's trouble is enough for today."

- Today I can follow Jesus' advice and look at the birds of the air and at
the lilies of the fields. I reflect on the disaster that our selfishness and
greed bring to the earth, our common home. If left alone, birds and
flowers flourish; when we intervene to grab for ourselves what truly
belongs to all, we endanger earth's beautiful balance. I ask pardon and
pray that humanity learns how to behave responsibly.

- I can also look back at how I have experienced God's providence in my
life. "Do not worry. Today's trouble is enough for today." I ask myself
why I worry so much, and I ask for the grace to trust God and his real
love for me and the whole of humanity. I realize that this trust is not

mere passivity; it also implies a readiness to commit myself to life as a member of the kingdom even as I live in this world.

June 24—June 30

Something to think and pray about each day this week:

Holy Pressure

Imagine for a moment nothing except your kitchen or bathroom sink. Imagine that your sink has a single handle that you can turn on and off rather easily. Behind the wall is a series of interconnected, high-pressure pipes that bring the water into your home from a larger source, a reservoir or a water tower or a local water station. When the water is shut off at your sink, a tiny valve closes that prevents water from flowing. When that valve is closed, the water behind it is under pressure. Extreme pressure. It's sitting there in that pipe and wants badly to be unleashed. Yet you control when the water is turned on, and you also determine how powerful the flow is.

The water is always there. The potential is always just a few centimeters behind a tiny, powerful valve.

You may lift the handle only slightly to get a trickle of water as you wet your toothbrush. You may lift the valve all the way to get a powerful steady stream of water in order to wash your dishes.

Imagine that water is the Holy Spirit, and imagine there is a faucet connected to your heart. Focus on the heart and focus on this faucet, which is connected to a pipe that contains the Holy Spirit. The Spirit is under intense pressure. He's pushing on the valve of your faucet heart. You can feel that pressure when you wake up in the morning, throughout your day at work, when you are stuck in traffic, in the moments before sleep.

It's the holy pressure.

Keep this image in your mind. Turn on the faucet.

—Gary Jansen, *The 15-Minute Prayer Solution*

The Presence of God
Dear Jesus, I come to you today longing for your presence. I desire to love you as you love me. May nothing ever separate me from you.

Freedom
Lord, grant me the grace to have freedom of the Spirit. Cleanse my heart and soul so that I may live joyously in your love.

Consciousness
Where am I with God? With others?
Do I have something to be grateful for? Then I give thanks.
Is there something I am sorry for? Then I ask forgiveness.

The Word
The word of God comes down to us through the Scriptures. May the Holy Spirit enlighten my mind and my heart to respond to the gospel teachings. (Please turn to the Scripture on the following pages. Inspiration points are there should you need them. When you are ready, return here to continue.)

Conversation
How has God's word moved me? Has it left me cold?
Has it consoled me or moved me to act in a new way?
I imagine Jesus standing or sitting beside me;
I turn and share my feelings with him.

Conclusion
I thank God for these moments we have spent together and for any insights I have been given concerning the text.

Sunday 24th June
The Nativity of Saint John the Baptist
Luke 1:57–66, 80

Now the time came for Elizabeth to give birth, and she bore a son. Her neighbors and relatives heard that the Lord had shown his great mercy to her, and they rejoiced with her. On the eighth day they came to circumcise the child, and they were going to name him Zechariah after his father. But his mother said, "No; he is to be called John." They said to her, "None of your relatives has this name." Then they began motioning to his father to find out what name he wanted to give him. He asked for a writing tablet and wrote, "His name is John." And all of them were amazed. Immediately his mouth was opened and his tongue freed, and he began to speak, praising God. Fear came over all their neighbors, and all these things were talked about throughout the entire hill country of Judea. All who heard them pondered them and said, "What then will this child become?" For, indeed, the hand of the Lord was with him. The child grew and became strong in spirit, and he was in the wilderness until the day he appeared publicly to Israel.

- Today we celebrate the birth of John the Baptist. Like many Old Testament figures who played an important role in the history of our salvation, John is born to a sterile woman, in her old age. Our salvation is all God's work. Our world is too self-sufficient to admit we need a savior, but perhaps the present situation—with so much violence and pain—may move more of us to ask God to save us.

- "Indeed the hand of the Lord was with him." I certainly do not have such an important mission as John, but whatever I am being called to do, I know that the hand of the Lord is with me. I thank God for his powerful presence in my life, and I ask him to strengthen my faith.

Monday 25th June
Matthew 7:1–5

Jesus said to the crowds, "Do not judge, so that you may not be judged. For with the judgment you make you will be judged, and the measure you give will be the measure you get. Why do you see the speck in your neighbor's eye, but do not notice the log in your own eye? Or how can you say to your neighbor, 'Let me take the speck out of your eye,' while the log is in your own eye? You hypocrite, first take the log out of your own eye, and then you will see clearly to take the speck out of your neighbor's eye."

- "Who am I to judge?" must rank as one of the best-known phrases of Pope Francis. Perhaps that is because it touches a very sensitive point in our pluralistic culture. How can we ever judge the behavior of others? This can sometimes degenerate into a passive, uncaring attitude. I will not judge you, for you are responsible for your own choices; now do not expect me to help you in any way, for I am not responsible for you at all. Jesus is saying something quite different. He tells you to be careful not to judge others more harshly than you judge yourself and to be free of prejudice because it can cloud your judgement.

- "First take the log out of your own eye." I ask for light to be aware of my prejudices and for strength to remove them. Most of all, I ask for compassion, both for myself and for those whose opinions and behavior I find difficult to accept.

Tuesday 26th June
Matthew 7:6, 12–14

Jesus said to the crowds, "Do not give what is holy to dogs; and do not throw your pearls before swine, or they will trample them under foot and turn and maul you. In everything do to others as you would have them do to you; for this is the law and the prophets. Enter through the narrow gate; for the gate is wide and the road is easy that leads to destruction, and there are many who take it. For the gate is narrow and the road is hard that leads to life, and there are few who find it."

- "In everything do to others as you would have them do to you." The golden rule is challenging because it is so simple; in fact, "this is the law and the prophets." We never seem able to live it fully, even though it is so eminently reasonable. It is not a juridical standard, but rather, it is a standard of true love. A little earlier in Matthew's Gospel, Jesus calls us to love others as we love ourselves.

- Jesus' way is the road that leads to life, yet we need to pass through the narrow door of denying ourselves and carrying our cross every day. I pray for the grace to do this gladly, with inner peace, following in the footsteps of Jesus my brother.

Wednesday 27th June
Matthew 7:15–20

Jesus told the crowds, "Beware of false prophets, who come to you in sheep's clothing but inwardly are ravenous wolves. You will know them by their fruits. Are grapes gathered from thorns, or figs from thistles? In the same way, every good tree bears good fruit, but the bad tree bears bad fruit. A good tree cannot bear bad fruit, nor can a bad tree bear good fruit. Every tree that does not bear good fruit is cut down and thrown into the fire. Thus you will know them by their fruits."

• Jesus warns us to beware of false prophets, and he gives us a concrete and practical guideline for our discernment: look at their fruits. Sometimes our world can confuse us with multiple promises of happiness and well-being while manifesting suffering and loneliness. We need to see that there are not only false prophets who bear bad fruit, but also good prophets whose message is true because it produces good fruit. I pray for the grace of insight and wisdom.

• In this series of passages, I am struck by Jesus' words describing a future judgement; the tree that does not bear good fruit will be cut down and thrown into the fire. I am called, with some urgency, to bear good fruit.

Thursday 28th June
Matthew 7:21–29

"Not everyone who says to me, 'Lord, Lord,' will enter the kingdom of heaven, but only the one who does the will of my Father in heaven. On that day many will say to me, 'Lord, Lord, did we not prophesy in your name, and cast out demons in your name, and do many deeds of power in your name?' Then I will declare to them, 'I never knew you; go away from me, you evildoers.' Everyone then who hears these words of mine and acts on them will be like a wise man who built his house on rock. The rain fell, the floods came, and the winds blew and beat on that house, but it did not fall, because it had been founded on rock. And everyone who hears these words of mine and does not act on them will be like a foolish man who built his house on sand. The rain fell, and the floods came, and the winds blew and beat against that house, and it fell—and great was its fall!" Now when Jesus had finished saying these things, the crowds were astounded at his teaching, for he taught them as one having authority, and not as their scribes.

- This is the grand finale of the Sermon on the Mount, a strong reminder that what counts is our interior life: our heart, and not our words. Jesus once more makes huge claims for himself; if we build our lives on his word, we can withstand the fiercest of problems and storms. How have I made Jesus' word the foundation of my life? I thank him and ask him for his help.

- The people were astounded at his teaching, because he taught them with authority, not like the scribes. The same is true for us; we are moved by people who speak with integrity, not by those whose word is not backed by deeds. I pray for the grace of discernment; I desire to live and speak with integrity.

Friday 29th June
Saints Peter and Paul, Apostles
Matthew 16:13–19

Now when Jesus came into the district of Caesarea Philippi, he asked his disciples, "Who do people say that the Son of Man is?" And they said, "Some say John the Baptist, but others Elijah, and still others Jeremiah or one of the prophets." He said to them, "But who do you say that I am?" Simon Peter answered, "You are the Messiah, the Son of the living God." And Jesus answered him, "Blessed are you, Simon son of Jonah! For flesh and blood has not revealed this to you, but my Father in heaven. And I tell you, you are Peter, and on this rock I will build my church, and the gates of Hades will not prevail against it. I will give you the keys of the kingdom of heaven, and whatever you bind on earth will be bound in heaven, and whatever you loose on earth will be loosed in heaven."

- Saints Peter and Paul are often described as the columns of the faith: Peter was the rock upon which the church was built, and Paul was the apostle to the Gentiles, especially chosen by Christ to carry the good news to those who were not Jews. Today as we celebrate their feast, I reflect on my faith, which is a great gift from God that I received when I was baptized. I reflect also on how my faith grew through the ministry of so many people, beginning with the apostles and extending to my parents, teachers, catechists, parish community, friends, and other witnesses. I thank God for this great gift of faith, and I ask for the ability to know how to transmit it to others, not as a museum piece but as a living reality.

- I also reflect in gratitude that I am called to live my faith with others in the community we call the church. I talk with Jesus about my membership in the church and ask him to help me be a living stone in this, his house. May this house be open to all men and women for all time.

Saturday 30th June
Matthew 8:5–17

When Jesus entered Capernaum, a centurion came to him, appealing to him and saying, "Lord, my servant is lying at home paralyzed, in terrible distress." And he said to him, "I will come and cure him." The centurion answered, "Lord, I am not worthy to have you come under my roof; but only speak the word, and my servant will be healed. For I also am a man under authority, with soldiers under me; and I say to one, 'Go,' and he goes, and to another, 'Come,' and he comes, and to my slave, 'Do this,' and the slave does it." When Jesus heard him, he was amazed and said to those who followed him, "Truly I tell you, in no one in Israel have I found such faith. I tell you, many will come from east and west and will eat with Abraham and Isaac and Jacob in the kingdom of heaven, while the heirs of the kingdom will be thrown into the outer darkness, where there will be weeping and gnashing of teeth." And to the centurion Jesus said, "Go; let it be done for you according to your faith." And the servant was healed in that hour. // When Jesus entered Peter's house, he saw his mother-in-law lying in bed with a fever; he touched her hand, and the fever left her, and she got up and began to serve him. That evening they brought to him many who were possessed with demons; and he cast out the spirits with a word, and cured all who were sick. This was to fulfill what had been spoken through the prophet Isaiah, "He took our infirmities and bore our diseases."

- The Gospels tell us that Jesus spent a lot of his time healing the sick. Yet he was much more than a successful and sought-after healer because his healing was through compassion and solidarity: "he took our infirmities and bore our diseases." This is best seen on Calvary, but he lived this truth throughout his life.

- Jesus makes a surprising comment about the Roman centurion, "In no one in Israel have I found such faith." He praises the unique faith of a pagan. We ask ourselves what faith really is; we may sometimes think that our faith is practically non-existent. What of the faith of those who belong to other religions? What about those people who claim they are unbelievers or atheists? I remember what Jesus said: It is enough if my faith is as big as a mustard seed.

The Thirteenth Week of Ordinary Time
July 1—July 7

Something to think and pray about each day this week:

A Simple Prayer of Review

Begin

Take a few slow breaths. Center yourself and open up to feel God's presence. Ask for God's grace as you enter this time of prayerful reflection.

Give thanks

For music. For composers, instrumentalists, singers, those who help record and distribute the music you love. For the people who introduced you to the songs and melodies you love.

Review

Think of the most beautiful songs and musical pieces you know. It might help to write a list. Choose one. When did you hear it for the first time? What memories or associations does it bring up for you? Think of a time when music made you feel that something good was waiting for you or lifted you beyond the present. Do you feel that way about life as a general rule, or do you tend to think that "the best is behind"? If so, allow God to challenge that notion.

Look ahead

Seek out a piece of music that has always made you feel hopeful. Listen to it again, letting yourself be open to its implicit promise. Tomorrow, go throughout the day trusting that good things await you.

—Ginny Kubitz Moyer, *Taste and See: Experiencing the Goodness of God with Our Five Senses*

The Presence of God

Dear Jesus, today I call on you, but not to ask for anything. I'd like only to dwell in your presence. May my heart respond to your love.

Freedom

God my creator, you gave me life and the gift of freedom. Through your love I exist in this world. May I never take the gift of life for granted. May I always respect others' right to life.

Consciousness

I ask how I am today. Am I particularly tired, stressed, or anxious? If any of these characteristics apply, can I try to let go of the concerns that disturb me?

The Word

The word of God comes down to us through the Scriptures. May the Holy Spirit enlighten my mind and my heart to respond to the gospel teachings. (Please turn to the Scripture on the following pages. Inspiration points are there should you need them. When you are ready, return here to continue.)

Conversation

I begin to talk with Jesus about the Scripture I have just read. What part of it strikes a chord in me? Perhaps the words of a friend—or some story I have heard recently—will rise to the surface in my consciousness. If so, does the story throw light on what the Scripture passage may be saying to me?

Conclusion

Glory be to the Father, and to the Son, and to the Holy Spirit,
As it was in the beginning, is now and ever shall be,
World without end. Amen.

Sunday 1st July
Thirteenth Sunday in Ordinary Time
Mark 5:21–43

When Jesus had crossed again in the boat to the other side, a great crowd gathered round him; and he was by the lake. Then one of the leaders of the synagogue named Jairus came and, when he saw him, fell at his feet and begged him repeatedly, "My little daughter is at the point of death. Come and lay your hands on her, so that she may be made well, and live." // So he went with him. And a large crowd followed him and pressed in on him. Now there was a woman who had been suffering from hemorrhages for twelve years. She had endured much under many physicians, and had spent all that she had; and she was no better, but rather grew worse. She had heard about Jesus, and came up behind him in the crowd and touched his cloak, for she said, "If I but touch his clothes, I will be made well." Immediately her hemorrhage stopped; and she felt in her body that she was healed of her disease. Immediately aware that power had gone forth from him, Jesus turned about in the crowd and said, "Who touched my clothes?" And his disciples said to him, "You see the crowd pressing in on you; how can you say, 'Who touched me?'" He looked all round to see who had done it. But the woman, knowing what had happened to her, came in fear and trembling, fell down before him, and told him the whole truth. He said to her, "Daughter, your faith has made you well; go in peace, and be healed of your disease." // While he was still speaking, some people came from the leader's house to say, "Your daughter is dead. Why trouble the teacher any further?" But overhearing what they said, Jesus said to the leader of the synagogue, "Do not fear, only believe." He allowed no one to follow him except Peter, James, and John, the brother of James. When they came to the house of the leader of the synagogue, he saw a commotion, people weeping and wailing loudly. When he had entered, he said to them, "Why do you make a commotion and weep? The child is not dead but sleeping." And they laughed at him. Then he put them all outside, and took the child's father and mother and those who were with him, and went in where the child was. He took her by the hand and said to her, "Talitha cum," which means, "Little girl, get up!" And immediately the girl got up and began to walk about (she was twelve years of age). At this they were overcome with amazement. He strictly ordered them that no one should know this, and told them to give her something to eat.

- Here we find situations where human solutions fail. "She is at the point of death" . . . "She grew worse" . . . "She is dead." But Jesus confronts human hopelessness. The needs of the sick and the faith of those concerned evoke a compassionate response from him. He is tender to the two women. He calls one, "Daughter!" and the other, "Little girl" (literally "Little lamb").

- In my need, I too can turn to him and find healing. That healing will focus on my heart: my negativity, bad moods, hurtful responses, and hardness. He is always trying to help me grow in love. Then I can in turn become a tender and healing presence to those around me.

Monday 2nd July
Matthew 8:18–22

Now when Jesus saw great crowds around him, he gave orders to go over to the other side. A scribe then approached and said, "Teacher, I will follow you wherever you go." And Jesus said to him, "Foxes have holes, and birds of the air have nests; but the Son of Man has nowhere to lay his head." Another of his disciples said to him, "Lord, first let me go and bury my father." But Jesus said to him, "Follow me, and let the dead bury their own dead."

- Jesus uses the starkest possible words to stress the radical nature of his call. Unlike us, he has no interest in the number of his followers; he cares more about each disciple's commitment and readiness to follow in the footsteps of the master.

- "The Son of Man has nowhere to lay his head." Jesus was born in a manger and died on the cross, outside the city walls. No wonder we discover that following him means some renunciation of material goods and comforts. Am I ready to give up some comfort or certainty of safety?

Tuesday 3rd July
John 20:24–29

But Thomas (who was called the Twin), one of the twelve, was not with them when Jesus came. So the other disciples told him, "We have seen the Lord." But he said to them, "Unless I see the mark of the nails in his hands, and put my finger in the mark of the nails and my hand in his side, I will not believe." // A week later his disciples were again in the house, and Thomas was with them. Although the doors were shut, Jesus came and stood among them and said, "Peace be with you." Then he said to Thomas, "Put your finger here and see my hands. Reach out your hand and put it in my side. Do not doubt but believe." Thomas answered him, "My Lord and my God!" Jesus said to him, "Have you believed because you have seen me? Blessed are those who have not seen and yet have come to believe."

- Thomas refused to believe in the Resurrection until he saw the risen Lord for himself. When he did encounter Jesus and put his hands in Jesus' wounds, Thomas's doubts disappeared and he made the profound act of faith: "My Lord and my God!"

- As the case of Thomas illustrates, even the disciples sometimes had doubts. Jesus meets us wherever we are. He knows that in our walk of faith we face many challenges. I pray, Lord, that when I encounter trials, I still have the courage to proclaim my faith in you.

Wednesday 4th July
Matthew 8:28–34

When Jesus came to the other side, to the country of the Gadarenes, two demoniacs coming out of the tombs met him. They were so fierce that no one could pass that way. Suddenly they shouted, "What have you to do with us, Son of God? Have you come here to torment us before the time?" Now a large herd of swine was feeding at some distance from them. The demons begged him, "If you cast us out, send us into the herd of swine." And he said to them, "'Go!" So they came out and entered the swine; and suddenly, the whole herd rushed down the steep bank into the lake and perished in the water. The swineherds ran off, and on going into the town, they told the whole story about what had happened to the demoniacs. Then the whole town came out to meet Jesus; and when they saw him, they begged him to leave their neighborhood.

• The mission of Jesus transcends all boundaries. He is not afraid to go to the other side—the land of the Gentiles—where the Jews would not normally go. There he encounters the forces of evil in the form of the demoniacs and quells them. However, the people fail to see the power of God at work in Jesus and earnestly ask him to leave.

• Lord, with you close by my side, I have nothing to fear from the forces of darkness in the world. You deliver me from all evil and do everything to ensure that goodness triumphs. Help me trust in your divine power in my life and be attentive to the ways you communicate your message of light.

Thursday 5th July
Matthew 9:1–8

And after getting into a boat he crossed the sea and came to his own town. And just then some people were carrying a paralyzed man lying on a bed. When Jesus saw their faith, he said to the paralytic, "Take heart, son; your sins are forgiven." Then some of the scribes said to themselves, "This man is blaspheming." But Jesus, perceiving their thoughts, said, "Why do you think evil in your hearts? For which is easier, to say, 'Your sins are forgiven,' or to say, 'Stand up and walk'? But so that you may know that the Son of Man has authority on earth to forgive sins"—he then said to the paralytic—"Stand up, take your bed and go to your home." And he stood up and went to his home. When the crowds saw it, they were filled with awe, and they glorified God, who had given such authority to human beings.

• This episode is a reminder of the quality of the mercy Jesus came to proclaim. His first act is to speak to the paralyzed man. His are words of encouragement, the phrase we find so often throughout the Bible: "Take heart . . . your sins are forgiven." Sometimes I might think that I have no sins, or that my sins are too big or shameful to be forgiven by Jesus. But Jesus is upset that the scribes doubt his power to forgive sins, and he is quick to prove he has this power.

• Jesus cured the paralytic when he saw the faith of those who carried him! Who are those I carry in faith, in prayer, in companionship, and in compassion? Who are those whose faith, at one time or another in my life, carried my weak self to Jesus?

Friday 6th July
Matthew 9:9–13

As Jesus was walking along, he saw a man called Matthew sitting at the tax booth; and he said to him, "Follow me." And he got up and followed him. And as he sat at dinner in the house, many tax collectors and sinners came and were sitting with him and his disciples. When the Pharisees saw this, they said to his disciples, "Why does your teacher eat with tax collectors and sinners?" But when he heard this, he said, "Those who are well have no need of a physician, but those who are sick. Go and learn what this means, 'I desire mercy, not sacrifice.' For I have come to call not the righteous but sinners."

- "Why does your teacher eat with tax collectors and sinners?" I ask myself, *Do I hold resentment toward people living on the margins of society or toward anybody who seems to be doing better in life than I am?* I am mindful of how resentments can block the sunlight from my soul. My destructive feelings of anger and hurt affect not only my happiness but also the peace and contentment of those around me.

- Jesus calls me to a better place. He calls me to be merciful to those living on the margins of society, to show them compassion and love. Anger is a luxury I cannot afford. Lord, help me let go of my resentments and instead choose the light of God's wonderful mercy and grace.

Saturday 7th July
Matthew 9:14–17

The disciples of John came to Jesus, saying, "Why do we and the Pharisees fast often, but your disciples do not fast?" And Jesus said to them, "The wedding guests cannot mourn as long as the bridegroom is with them, can they? The days will come when the bridegroom is taken away from them, and then they will fast. No one sews a piece of unshrunk cloth on an old cloak, for the patch pulls away from the cloak, and a worse tear is made. Neither is new wine put into old wineskins; otherwise, the skins burst, and the wine is spilled, and the skins are destroyed; but new wine is put into fresh wineskins, and so both are preserved."

- Being a follower of Jesus is never one-dimensional. To walk with Jesus, I must always remember that there is a time for fasting and a time for celebrating. Am I eager to grow in the understanding of God's word and plan for my life?

- Jesus wants our minds and hearts to be like new wineskins: open and ready to receive the new wine of the Holy Spirit. He doesn't want us to hold rigidly to the past and to resist the ever-new work of his Holy Spirit in our lives. Am I holding tightly to anything that fights God's new work?

Fourteenth Week of Ordinary Time
July 8—July 14

Something to think and pray about each day this week:

Taking Heroic Action

What is a hero? A hero is a person who takes action to help people. That is what the Holy Spirit calls us to do. When the Spirit descended on Mary after the angel Gabriel told her she was to be the mother of Jesus, what did she do? She took action. She packed her things and journeyed to her cousin Elizabeth. To do what? To serve her. When the Holy Spirit descended on Jesus after his baptism by John, what did he do? He took action and did what? He began his ministry and began serving. When the Spirit descended on the apostles at Pentecost, what did they do? They relinquished fear and began serving the people. Not just one group of people but all people, of all nations.

We too are called to serve, to not be afraid. With the Holy Spirit already dwelling in us, there is no time to waste. We need to take action now and assist those around us, whether it's a family member, a friend, a coworker, a stranger on the street, our environment, our nation, or our world.

—Gary Jansen, *The 15-Minute Prayer Solution*

The Presence of God
Dear Lord, as I come to you today, fill my heart, my whole being, with the wonder of your presence. Help me remain receptive to you as I put aside the cares of this world. Fill my mind with your peace.

Freedom
Lord, grant me the grace to be free from the excesses of this life. Let me not get caught up with the desire for wealth. Keep my heart and mind free to love and serve you.

Consciousness
I exist in a web of relationships: links to nature, people, God.
I trace out these links, giving thanks for the life that flows through them.
Some links are twisted or broken; I may feel regret, anger, disappointment.
I pray for the gift of acceptance and forgiveness.

The Word
God speaks to each of us individually. I listen attentively, to hear what he is saying to me. Read the text a few times, then listen. (Please turn to the Scripture on the following pages. Inspiration points are there should you need them. When you are ready, return here to continue.)

Conversation
Jesus, you speak to me through the words of the Gospels. May I respond to your call today. Teach me to recognize your hand at work in my daily living.

Conclusion
I thank God for these moments we have spent together and for any insights I have been given concerning the text.

Sunday 8th July
Fourteenth Sunday in Ordinary Time
Mark 6:1–6a

Jesus left that place and came to his hometown, and his disciples followed him. On the sabbath he began to teach in the synagogue, and many who heard him were astounded. They said, "Where did this man get all this? What is this wisdom that has been given to him? What deeds of power are being done by his hands! Is not this the carpenter, the son of Mary and brother of James and Joses and Judas and Simon, and are not his sisters here with us?" And they took offense at him. Then Jesus said to them, "Prophets are not without honor, except in their hometown, and among their own kin, and in their own house." And he could do no deed of power there, except that he laid his hands on a few sick people and cured them. And he was amazed at their unbelief. Then he went about among the villages teaching.

- People who know us see us in specific contexts: as the youngsters they knew at school, as daughters or sons in a neighborhood family. They have catalogued information about us and put us automatically in categories. Jesus was not immune to this sort of day-by-day assessment and categorization. And, in the same way such thinking limited what Jesus could do in his hometown, others' perceptions of us can threaten to mute the gifts God has placed within us.

- Lord, I am willing to go outward with my life and gifts, to go where they can be nurtured and received. Give me the strength to leave what is familiar for the sake of your kingdom coming alive in me.

Monday 9th July
Matthew 9:18–26

While he was saying these things to them, suddenly a leader of the synagogue came in and knelt before him, saying, "My daughter has just died; but come and lay your hand on her, and she will live." And Jesus got up and followed him, with his disciples. Then suddenly a woman who had been suffering from hemorrhages for twelve years came up behind him and touched the fringe of his cloak, for she said to herself, "If I only touch his cloak, I will be made well." Jesus turned, and seeing her he said, "Take heart, daughter; your faith has made you well." And instantly the woman was made well. When Jesus came to the leader's house and saw the flute-players and the crowd making a commotion, he said, "Go away; for the girl is not dead but sleeping." And they laughed at him. But when the crowd had been put outside, he went in and took her by the hand, and the girl got up. And the report of this spread throughout that district.

- Jesus heals the woman with the hemorrhages because, in his eyes, her action in reaching out and touching the hem of his garment was the supreme act of faith.

- There is no limit to the healing and renewal Jesus can accomplish in my life. When approaching him, do I have the same faith as the woman with the hemorrhages. Do I believe that he can heal me?

Tuesday 10th July
Matthew 9:32–38

After they had gone away, a demoniac who was mute was brought to him. And when the demon had been cast out, the one who had been mute spoke; and the crowds were amazed and said, "Never has anything like this been seen in Israel." But the Pharisees said, "By the ruler of the demons he casts out the demons." // Then Jesus went about all the cities and villages, teaching in their synagogues, and proclaiming the good news of the kingdom, and curing every disease and every sickness. When he saw the crowds, he had compassion for them, because they were harassed and helpless, like sheep without a shepherd. Then he said to his disciples, "The harvest is plentiful, but the laborers are few; therefore ask the Lord of the harvest to send out laborers into his harvest."

- Jesus has deep compassion for the needs of all people. He sees when they are harassed and dejected, wandering and aimless like sheep without a shepherd to guide them. At the same time, he has to contend with the Pharisees, who are not open to listening, seeing, or speaking of his goodness.

- Jesus needs many helpers today. The harvest is as big as ever; people are as lost and rudderless as they have ever been. Where are the laborers? They are not just the bishops, priests, or religious. Every baptized person is called, in some way, to share the good news of Jesus Christ. Each of us has a vocation, a call to serve and to build the kingdom of God. Let us pray today to know our unique vocations.

Wednesday 11th July
Matthew 10:1–7

Then Jesus summoned his twelve disciples and gave them authority over unclean spirits, to cast them out, and to cure every disease and every sickness. These are the names of the twelve apostles: first, Simon, also known as Peter, and his brother Andrew; James son of Zebedee, and his brother John; Philip and Bartholomew; Thomas and Matthew the tax collector; James son of Alphaeus, and Thaddaeus; Simon the Cananaean, and Judas Iscariot, the one who betrayed him. These twelve Jesus sent out with the following instructions: "Go nowhere among the Gentiles, and enter no town of the Samaritans, but go rather to the lost sheep of the house of Israel. As you go, proclaim the good news, 'The kingdom of heaven has come near.'"

- Jesus did not merely call the twelve; he also gave them power to do what he had called them to do as he sent them out. So today, when God calls us, he supplies us with the means to undertake the task at hand. We are never alone; he is always with us.

- No matter where I am in my life, acting as God's messenger, I will always try and live the prayer of Saint Francis: "Lord, make me an instrument of your peace. Where there is hatred, let me sow love; where there is injury, pardon; where there is doubt, faith; where there is despair, hope; where there is darkness, light; where there is sadness, joy. O, Divine Master, grant that I may not so much seek to be consoled as to console; to be understood as to understand; to be loved as to love. For it is in giving that we receive; it is in pardoning that we are pardoned; it is in dying that we are born again to eternal life."

Thursday 12th July
Matthew 10:7–15

"As you go, proclaim the good news, 'The kingdom of heaven has come near.' Cure the sick, raise the dead, cleanse the lepers, cast out demons. You received without payment; give without payment. Take no gold, or silver, or copper in your belts, no bag for your journey, or two tunics, or sandals, or a staff; for laborers deserve their food. Whatever town or village you enter, find out who in it is worthy, and stay there until you leave. As you enter the house, greet it. If the house is worthy, let your peace come upon it; but if it is not worthy, let your peace return to you. If any-one will not welcome you or listen to your words, shake off the dust from your feet as you leave that house or town. Truly I tell you, it will be more tolerable for the land of Sodom and Gomorrah on the day of judgement than for that town."

- Jesus imparts a radical message to his disciples as he sends them out on mission. They are to cast out demons and cleanse lepers, just as he did, and take nothing for the journey—not even a spare tunic or sandals for their feet. It is a rallying call by Jesus to his closest followers to trust completely in the providence and love of God.

- I pray, Lord, that I may cling less to material things and more to your providential presence in my life, which is alive and active in every mo-ment of my day and every decision I make. Help me place all my hope and trust in you—for your love and generosity are never outdone.

Friday 13th July
Matthew 10:16–23

"See, I am sending you out like sheep into the midst of wolves; so be wise as serpents and innocent as doves. Beware of them, for they will hand you over to councils and flog you in their synagogues; and you will be dragged before governors and kings because of me, as a testimony to them and the Gentiles. When they hand you over, do not worry about how you are to speak or what you are to say; for what you are to say will be given to you at that time; for it is not you who speak, but the Spirit of your Father speaking through you. Brother will betray brother to death, and a father his child, and children will rise against parents and have them put to death; and you will be hated by all because of my name. But the one who endures to the end will be saved. When they persecute you in one town, flee to the next; for truly I tell you, you will not have gone through all the towns of Israel before the Son of Man comes."

- I read and hear of Christians being regularly tortured and murdered around the world because of their faith. I must therefore expect oppo-sition from those who oppose the gospel of the Lord.

- Jesus expects us to live outside our comfort zones. He challenges us to defend our faith. Lord, please strengthen my faith and give me courage that I may not shrink back from doing your will.

Saturday 14th July
Matthew 10:24–33

"A disciple is not above the teacher, nor a slave above the master; it is enough for the disciple to be like the teacher, and the slave like the master. If they have called the master of the house Beelzebul, how much more will they malign those of his household! So have no fear of them; for nothing is covered up that will not be uncovered, and nothing secret that will not become known. What I say to you in the dark, tell in the light; and what you hear whispered, proclaim from the housetops. Do not fear those who kill the body but cannot kill the soul; rather fear him who can destroy both soul and body in hell. Are not two sparrows sold for a penny? Yet not one of them will fall to the ground apart from your Father. And even the hairs of your head are all counted. So do not be afraid; you are of more value than many sparrows. Everyone therefore who acknowledges me before others, I also will acknowledge before my Father in heaven; but whoever denies me before others, I also will deny before my Father in heaven."

- Jesus encourages us to focus on what is truly real. The soul will last, but the body will die. Persecutors of the gospel can do no more than this finite world affords them. They may beat you and insult you and even kill you for following Jesus, but they cannot kill your soul or take away your eternal reward.

- Faith in Jesus Christ is a total human experience, not something to practice only on Sundays. Faith without action is dead. I pray therefore that mine may be a living faith and that I may accept God's direction for my life's journey.

Fifteenth Week of Ordinary Time
July 15—July 21

Something to think and pray about each day this week:

The Everyday Splendor

St. Ignatius of Loyola, the founder of the Jesuit order, certainly understood the connection between the physical and the spiritual. He believed that we can find God in all things—a conviction that lies at the core of Ignatian spirituality. Does God really speak to us through a blue sky, through the sound of laughter, through the taste of dinner? Absolutely, St. Ignatius would say. You don't turn your back on the created world to find meaning and purpose; rather, God reveals himself to us through the very concrete stuff of our lives, through our bodies, through the things we experience with our senses. Walter Burghardt, a twentieth-century Jesuit priest, echoes this idea in these beautiful words:

> To be alive is to look. But not merely with my mind—I am not naked intellect. If I am really to respond to the real, my whole being must be alive, vibrating to every throb of the real. Not only mind but eyes; not only eyes but smell and taste, hearing and touching. For reality is not reducible to some far-off, abstract, intangible God-in-the-sky. Reality is pulsing people; reality is fire and water; reality is a rainbow after a summer storm, a gentle doe streaking through a forest; reality is a foaming mug of Michelob, Beethoven's Mass in D, a child lapping a chocolate ice cream cone; reality is a striding woman with wind-blown hair; reality is Christ Jesus. (*Tell the Next Generation: Homilies and Near Homilies*)

Faith is about living life, in all its messy splendor, and doing so with the awareness that God is present throughout it all. It's about recognizing that God speaks to us through our senses and that we can live a richer, more joyful faith if we train ourselves to listen.

—Ginny Kubitz Moyer, *Taste and See: Experiencing the Goodness of God with Our Five Senses*

The Presence of God

God is with me, but even more astounding, God is within me.
Let me dwell for a moment on God's life-giving presence
in my body, in my mind, in my heart,
as I sit here, right now.

Freedom

Lord, may I never take the gift of freedom for granted. You gave me the great blessing of freedom of spirit. Fill my spirit with your peace and joy.

Consciousness

I remind myself that I am in the presence of God, who is my strength in times of weakness and my comforter in times of sorrow.

The Word

I take my time to read the word of God slowly, a few times, allowing myself to dwell on anything that strikes me. (Please turn to the Scripture on the following pages. Inspiration points are there should you need them. When you are ready, return here to continue.)

Conversation

Jesus, you always welcomed little children when you walked on this earth. Teach me to have a childlike trust in you. Teach me to live in the knowledge that you will never abandon me.

Conclusion

Glory be to the Father, and to the Son, and to the Holy Spirit,
As it was in the beginning, is now and ever shall be,
World without end. Amen.

Sunday 15th July
Fifteenth Sunday in Ordinary Time
Mark 6:7–13

Jesus called the twelve and began to send them out two by two, and gave them authority over the unclean spirits. He ordered them to take nothing for their journey except a staff; no bread, no bag, no money in their belts; but to wear sandals and not to put on two tunics. He said to them, "Wherever you enter a house, stay there until you leave the place. If any place will not welcome you and they refuse to hear you, as you leave, shake off the dust that is on your feet as a testimony against them." So they went out and proclaimed that all should repent. They cast out many demons, and anointed with oil many who were sick and cured them.

- Jesus knew that some people were ready for the good news, and that the twelve apostles would find those people as they went. Always there are people on our path who are ready for what we have to say. The Holy Spirit leads us to them, and them to us. We can trust that God draws into our spiritual family those who are waiting to be included.

- Jesus also knew that some people would resist his message and that it would do no good for the apostles to press or argue; they should simply move on. Lord, show me when it is time to move on and leave others alone, knowing that you continue to call each of us. May I respond to people appropriately as I reach out in your love.

Monday 16th July
Matthew 10:34—11:1

Jesus said, "Do not think that I have come to bring peace to the earth; I have not come to bring peace, but a sword.

> For I have come to set a man against his father,
> and a daughter against her mother,
> and a daughter-in-law against her mother-in-law;
> and one's foes will be members of one's own household.

Whoever loves father or mother more than me is not worthy of me; and whoever loves son or daughter more than me is not worthy of me; and whoever does not take up the cross and follow me is not worthy of me. Those who find their life will lose it, and those who lose their life for my sake will find it. // Whoever welcomes you welcomes me, and whoever welcomes me welcomes the one who sent me. Whoever welcomes a prophet in the name of a prophet will receive a prophet's reward; and whoever welcomes a righteous person in the name of a righteous person will receive the reward of the righteous; and whoever gives even a cup of cold water to one of these little ones in the name of a disciple—truly I tell you, none of these will lose their reward." // Now when Jesus had finished instructing his twelve disciples, he went on from there to teach and proclaim his message in their cities.

- Jesus is speaking about the cost of discipleship and puts before the twelve the challenge of taking up the cross as a condition of following him. The litany of references to *welcoming* suggests that it is often through the small things we do—such as giving a cup of water to somebody in need of it—that we can build the kingdom of God.

- Lord, I pray for the grace to go forward in faith with you by recognizing your face in the poor, the suffering, and the needy, and reaching out to them with the same unconditional love that you offer me.

Tuesday 17th July
Matthew 11:20–24

Then Jesus began to reproach the cities in which most of his deeds of power had been done, because they did not repent. "Woe to you, Chorazin! Woe to you, Bethsaida! For if the deeds of power done in you had been done in Tyre and Sidon, they would have repented long ago in sackcloth and ashes. But I tell you, on the day of judgment it will be more tolerable for Tyre and Sidon than for you. And you, Capernaum,

> will you be exalted to heaven?
> No, you will be brought down to Hades.

For if the deeds of power done in you had been done in Sodom, it would have remained until this day. But I tell you that on the day of judgment it will be more tolerable for the land of Sodom than for you."

- Jesus pulls no punches when he scolds the peoples of Chorazin and Bethsaida for not repenting. He also chastises the townspeople of Capernaum for failing to respond adequately to the word of God. Their inertia leaves them accountable in God's eyes.

- Day by day, I also hear the word. Lord, take away my inertia so that I may respond rightly to what you are saying to me.

Wednesday 18th July
Matthew 11:25–27

At that time Jesus said, "I thank you, Father, Lord of heaven and earth, because you have hidden these things from the wise and the intelligent and have revealed them to infants; yes, Father, for such was your gracious will. All things have been handed over to me by my Father; and no one knows the Son except the Father, and no one knows the Father except the Son and anyone to whom the Son chooses to reveal him."

- Do I see myself as wise and intelligent or as an "infant"? Pride keeps us from the love and knowledge of God. It closes the mind to God's truth and wisdom.
- True humility and an open mind can lead us to the love and knowledge of God. Childlike simplicity and humility become the soil in which the grace of God can take root. I am willing, Lord, to become less wise in my own eyes and more willing to learn from you.

Thursday 19th July
Matthew 11:28–30

Jesus said, "Come to me, all you that are weary and are carrying heavy burdens, and I will give you rest. Take my yoke upon you, and learn from me; for I am gentle and humble in heart, and you will find rest for your souls. For my yoke is easy, and my burden is light."

- From the moment Jesus uttered this glorious invitation, it has been a constant support to many people. Today, as I reflect on it, may I be encouraged and comforted.
- I imagine Jesus saying these words to me now. Jesus offers rest for my soul. This invitation opens a refreshing space in my soul by inspiring hope that God is always with me.

Friday 20th July
Matthew 12:1–8

At that time Jesus went through the grainfields on the Sabbath; his disciples were hungry, and they began to pluck heads of grain and to eat. When the Pharisees saw it, they said to him, "Look, your disciples are doing what is not lawful to do on the Sabbath." He said to them, "Have you not read what David did when he and his companions were hungry? He entered the house of God and ate the bread of the Presence, which it was not lawful for him or his companions to eat, but only for the priests. Or have you not read in the law that on the Sabbath the priests in the temple break the Sabbath and yet are guiltless? I tell you, something greater than the temple is here. But if you had known what this means, 'I desire mercy and not sacrifice,' you would not have condemned the guiltless. For the Son of Man is lord of the sabbath."

- I try to imagine Jesus as he moves through the fields. He understands his mission, but he also has a real sense of freedom. His way of proceeding shows that he is not a slave to tradition. Wherever Jesus advances, the darkness retreats. Clarity of purpose and hope remain in his wake.

- The lack of compassion shown by the Pharisees reminds me of the words of Pope Francis: "If our heart is closed, if our heart is made of stone, then the stones will end up in our hands and, then, we will be ready to throw them at someone."

Saturday 21st July
Matthew 12:14–21

The Pharisees went out and conspired against Jesus, how to destroy him. When Jesus became aware of this, he departed. Many crowds followed him, and he cured all of them, and he ordered them not to make him known. This was to fulfill what had been spoken through the prophet Isaiah:

"Here is my servant, whom I have chosen,
    my beloved, with whom my soul is well pleased.
I will put my Spirit upon him,
    and he will proclaim justice to the Gentiles.

He will not wrangle or cry aloud,
    nor will anyone hear his voice in the streets.
He will not break a bruised reed
    or quench a smoldering wick
until he brings justice to victory.
    And in his name the Gentiles will hope."

- How can I walk in Jesus' footsteps and imitate him? Perhaps I can do this by helping refugees, by working for justice, or by taking action to protect the earth. Walking in his footsteps will demand costly love, but it will help me witness to him by being a person for others.

- "He will not break a bruised reed or quench a smoldering wick until he brings justice to victory." To me, this speaks of such radical gentleness toward wounded souls. Alert me, Holy Spirit, when I am moving away from gentleness in my dealings with others.

Sixteenth Week of Ordinary Time
July 22—July 28

Something to think and pray about each day this week:

Sitting in Jesus' Gaze

A few years ago, I read Anthony DeMello's book *Sadhana: A Way to God*. In it, he describes a prayer exercise recommended by St. Teresa of Ávila, one that is deceptively simple: imagine Jesus looking at you, lovingly and humbly. In other words, just sit and let Jesus gaze at you.

The first time I tried it, I imagined Jesus looking straight at me, at close range, with love and humility in his eyes. It felt awkward; my immediate impulse was to look over my shoulder to see who was standing behind me. Then I turned back, and Jesus was still looking at me with infinite love and a smile that seared my heart, and I found myself crying.

I was not prepared for the power of that gaze. Throughout my life I've seen many images of Jesus looking directly at the viewer from a painting or an icon, but they always seem stern and solemn, as if Jesus were reading the hidden sins of humanity as a whole. With this exercise, I was fixed in Jesus' gaze, and it was directed at no one but flawed little me, and Jesus was smiling. I could not escape the love in those eyes, or the fact that it was intended for me. *I'm not worthy*, I kept thinking, but the more I sat there, the more I began to believe that perhaps I am. I started to believe that maybe Jesus is a little easier on me than I am on myself, that he sees my flaws but he also sees beyond them, to the very best of me, the heart of who I really am.

—Ginny Kubitz Moyer, *Taste and See: Experiencing the Goodness of God with Our Five Senses*

The Presence of God
God is with me, but more,
God is within me, giving me existence.
Let me dwell for a moment on God's life-giving presence
in my body, my mind, my heart,
and in the whole of my life.

Freedom
Lord, you created me to live in freedom. May your Holy Spirit guide me
to follow you freely. Instill in my heart a desire to know and love you more
each day.

Consciousness
In God's loving presence I unwind the past day,
starting from now and looking back, moment by moment.
I gather in all the goodness and light, in gratitude.
I attend to the shadows and what they say to me,
seeking healing, courage, forgiveness.

The Word
God speaks to each of us individually. I listen attentively, to hear what he
is saying to me. Read the text a few times, then listen. (Please turn to the
Scripture on the following pages. Inspiration points are there should you
need them. When you are ready, return here to continue.)

Conversation
Jesus, you always welcomed little children when you walked on this earth.
Teach me to have a childlike trust in you. Teach me to live in the knowledge that you will never abandon me.

Conclusion
I thank God for these moments we have spent together and for any insights I have been given concerning the text.

Sunday 22nd July
Sixteenth Sunday in Ordinary Time
Mark 6:30–34

The apostles gathered around Jesus, and told him all that they had done and taught. He said to them, "Come away to a deserted place all by yourselves and rest a while." For many were coming and going, and they had no leisure even to eat. And they went away in the boat to a deserted place by themselves. Now many saw them going and recognized them, and they hurried there on foot from all the towns and arrived ahead of them. As he went ashore, he saw a great crowd; and he had compassion for them, because they were like sheep without a shepherd; and he began to teach them many things.

- Jesus gave his time and energy to people for hours, days on end—and the apostles did as well. But he understood the need for rest and solitude, even in the midst of ministry. If Jesus needed it, can I imagine that I don't?

- Help me, Lord, to sense when it is time for rest—and when it is time to push through the next hour or day because people are in need and you have gifted me with ways to help them.

Monday 23rd July
Matthew 12:38–42

Then some of the scribes and Pharisees said to Jesus, "Teacher, we wish to see a sign from you." But he answered them, "An evil and adulterous generation asks for a sign, but no sign will be given to it except the sign of the prophet Jonah. For just as Jonah was three days and three nights in the belly of the sea monster, so for three days and three nights the Son of Man will be in the heart of the earth. The people of Nineveh will rise up at the judgment with this generation and condemn it, because they repented at the proclamation of Jonah, and see, something greater than Jonah is here! The queen of the South will rise up at the judgment with this generation and condemn it, because she came from the ends of the earth to listen to the wisdom of Solomon, and see, something greater than Solomon is here!"

- I need a spiritual transformation in my life so that I become alive to God. That will be a resurrection for me. Then I can become a helpful sign to this generation.

- True Christians are signs that the world can see and through whom the world can come to know Jesus. People see Jesus through you and me. As Christians, as the church, we are always to witness to God's saving mercy.

Tuesday 24th July
Matthew 12:46–50

While Jesus was still speaking to the crowds, his mother and his brothers were standing outside, wanting to speak to him. Someone told him, "Look, your mother and your brothers are standing outside, wanting to speak to you." But to the one who had told him this, Jesus replied, "Who is my mother, and who are my brothers?" And pointing to his disciples, he said, "Here are my mother and my brothers! For whoever does the will of my Father in heaven is my brother and sister and mother."

- Jesus invites me to become a disciple. This does not mean plodding along after him but becoming a cherished member of his family. Mary is the model disciple; she is fully open to God's will and supports Jesus in his ministry. She is our gentle mother and helps all God's children become brothers and sisters in the Lord. Blessed Mary, thank you for being with us as we follow your son.

- Pope Francis says: "The family is the fundamental locus of the covenant between the Church and God's creation." God's design for our families—biologically and otherwise—is that they create worlds within the larger world in which individuals can thrive, learn to hear God's call on their lives, and move forward in faith. Show me, Lord, how to build up the families around me, whether in homes or in your church.

Wednesday 25th July
Saint James, Apostle
Matthew 20:20–28

Then the mother of the sons of Zebedee came to him with her sons, and kneeling before him, she asked a favor of him. And he said to her, "What do you want?" She said to him, "Declare that these two sons of mine will sit, one at your right hand and one at your left, in your kingdom." But Jesus answered, "You do not know what you are asking. Are you able to drink the cup that I am about to drink?" They said to him, "We are able."

He said to them, "You will indeed drink my cup, but to sit at my right hand and at my left, this is not mine to grant, but it is for those for whom it has been prepared by my Father." // When the ten heard it, they were angry with the two brothers. But Jesus called them to him and said, "You know that the rulers of the Gentiles lord it over them, and their great ones are tyrants over them. It will not be so among you; but whoever wishes to be great among you must be your servant, and whoever wishes to be first among you must be your slave; just as the Son of Man came not to be served but to serve, and to give his life a ransom for many."

- Jesus says that he did not come to be served but to serve. He wants me to use my talents to serve others. How available am I?
- The Ignatian motto is "to love and serve in all things." We are here to serve others, not to bask in comfort and power. The more good things come our way, the more we should serve the needy sisters and brothers of Jesus. Lord, give me a generous heart.

Thursday 26th July
Matthew 13:10–17

Then the disciples came and asked him, "Why do you speak to them in parables?" He answered, "To you it has been given to know the secrets of the kingdom of heaven, but to them it has not been given. For to those who have, more will be given, and they will have an abundance; but from those who have nothing, even what they have will be taken away. The reason I speak to them in parables is that 'seeing they do not perceive, and hearing they do not listen, nor do they understand.' With them indeed is fulfilled the prophecy of Isaiah that says:

'You will indeed listen, but never understand,
    and you will indeed look, but never perceive.
For this people's heart has grown dull,
    and their ears are hard of hearing,
        and they have shut their eyes;
            so that they might not look with their eyes,
    and listen with their ears,
and understand with their heart and turn—
    and I would heal them.'

But blessed are your eyes, for they see, and your ears, for they hear. Truly I tell you, many prophets and righteous people longed to see what you see, but did not see it, and to hear what you hear, but did not hear it."

- What are the secrets of the kingdom of God? To know the Lord Jesus personally, to understand his work of salvation on the cross, and to realize that we are infinitely loved. What a privilege it is to know these things!

- How blessed I am to have the holy Scriptures. But while Jesus speaks to me right now, am I listening to him? Am I open to his word, or do I sit with fingers in my ears?

Friday 27th July
Matthew 13:18–23

"Hear then the parable of the sower. When anyone hears the word of the kingdom and does not understand it, the evil one comes and snatches away what is sown in the heart; this is what was sown on the path. As for what was sown on rocky ground, this is the one who hears the word and immediately receives it with joy; yet such a person has no root, but endures only for a while, and when trouble or persecution arises on account of the word, that person immediately falls away. As for what was sown among thorns, this is the one who hears the word, but the cares of the world and the lure of wealth choke the word, and it yields nothing. But as for what was sown on good soil, this is the one who hears the word and understands it, who indeed bears fruit and yields, in one case a hundredfold, in another sixty, and in another thirty."

- The parable of the sower explains how the word of God is received. Jesus knows that there are different levels of receiving the word. In some, it is allowed to flourish and bear fruit; in others, the word is not given sufficient attention so it endures only a little while.

- The word of God is given to me as a gift. I pray that I will allow its goodness to take root in my life and yield a fertile harvest, leading me in the ways of truth and love.

Saturday 28th July
Matthew 13:24–30

He put before them another parable: "The kingdom of heaven may be compared to someone who sowed good seed in his field; but while everybody was asleep, an enemy came and sowed weeds among the wheat, and then went away. So when the plants came up and bore grain, then the weeds appeared as well. And the slaves of the householder came and said to him, 'Master, did you not sow good seed in your field? Where, then, did these weeds come from?' He answered, 'An enemy has done this.' The slaves said to him, 'Then do you want us to go and gather them?' But he replied, 'No; for in gathering the weeds you would uproot the wheat along with them. Let both of them grow together until the harvest; and at harvest time I will tell the reapers, Collect the weeds first and bind them in bundles to be burned, but gather the wheat into my barn.'"

• While we are still in the season of growth, may I be vigilant as the farmer was. There are weeds among the wheat in my own heart. But let me also be patient, not only with my own weeds but with those of others. In accepting my inadequate self, I can come to accept others.

• Even the church can be a mixed organization, with wheat and weeds growing side by side and looking very much alike. You may have some people who look like faithful disciples, but they're not. The fruit shows what is in the heart; they might look like wheat, but they produce weeds. Lord, may I not be among them.

Seventeenth Week of Ordinary Time
July 29—August 4

Something to think and pray about each day this week:

God's Soft Lap
I'm not going to deny that there is something awesome and amazing and bigger-than-I-can-fathom about God. As someone once observed, if we could understand God, then what we are understanding would not be God. Yet, when I think about terms such as *awesome* and *amazing* in relation to the divine, I tend to assume that they apply to the aspects of God that are majestic and powerful. I need to remind myself that maybe the characteristics of God that are bigger than I can comprehend are also the softer, more comforting ones. I need to understand that God is fathomless depths, all right, but those depths are soothing ones too.

Maybe on those tough days when nothing seems to be going right, I can challenge myself to add a little something to my yoga pants, slippers, and pillow routine. I can take a moment to feel the divine presence enveloping me with warmth. I can ditch any residual echo of God as the metal folding chair and sink into the reality of God as the soft lap, comforting me in both body and soul.

—Ginny Kubitz Moyer, *Taste and See: Experiencing the Goodness of God with Our Five Senses*

The Presence of God

I pause for a moment and think of the love and the grace that God showers on me. I am created in the image and likeness of God; I am God's dwelling place.

Freedom

I am free. When I look at these words in writing, they seem to create in me a feeling of awe. Yes, a wonderful feeling of freedom. Thank you, God.

Consciousness

In the presence of my loving Creator, I look honestly at my feelings over the past day: the highs, the lows, and the level ground. Can I see where the Lord has been present?

The Word

I read the word of God slowly, a few times over, and I listen to what God is saying to me. (Please turn to the Scripture on the following pages. Inspiration points are there should you need them. When you are ready, return here to continue.)

Conversation

Remembering that I am still in God's presence,
I imagine Jesus standing or sitting beside me,
and I say whatever is on my mind, whatever is in my heart,
speaking as one friend to another.

Conclusion

Glory be to the Father, and to the Son, and to the Holy Spirit,
As it was in the beginning, is now and ever shall be,
World without end. Amen.

Sunday 29th July
Seventeenth Sunday in Ordinary Time
John 6:1–15

After this Jesus went to the other side of the Sea of Galilee, also called the Sea of Tiberias. A large crowd kept following him, because they saw the signs that he was doing for the sick. Jesus went up the mountain and sat down there with his disciples. Now the Passover, the festival of the Jews, was near. When he looked up and saw a large crowd coming towards him, Jesus said to Philip, "Where are we to buy bread for these people to eat?" He said this to test him, for he himself knew what he was going to do. Philip answered him, "Six months' wages would not buy enough bread for each of them to get a little." One of his disciples, Andrew, Simon Peter's brother, said to him, "There is a boy here who has five barley loaves and two fish. But what are they among so many people?" Jesus said, "Make the people sit down." Now there was a great deal of grass in the place; so they sat down, about five thousand in all. Then Jesus took the loaves, and when he had given thanks, he distributed them to those who were seated; so also the fish, as much as they wanted. When they were satisfied, he told his disciples, "Gather up the fragments left over, so that nothing may be lost." So they gathered them up, and from the fragments of the five barley loaves, left by those who had eaten, they filled twelve baskets. When the people saw the sign that he had done, they began to say, "This is indeed the prophet who is to come into the world." When Jesus realized that they were about to come and take him by force to make him king, he withdrew again to the mountain by himself.

- Jesus began with what was already present: a few loaves and fishes. When I feel that it's impossible to acquire what is needed, I will try to look first at what I already have.

- The apostles collected all the leftover food, "so that nothing may be lost." Am I careless with the abundance of God? Do I take good care of resources and treasure God's gifts?

Monday 30th July
Matthew 13:31–35

He put before them another parable: "The kingdom of heaven is like a mustard seed that someone took and sowed in his field; it is the smallest of all the seeds, but when it has grown it is the greatest of shrubs and becomes a tree, so that the birds of the air come and make nests in its branches." He told them another parable: "The kingdom of heaven is like yeast that a woman took and mixed in with three measures of flour until all of it was leavened." Jesus told the crowds all these things in parables; without a parable he told them nothing. This was to fulfill what had been spoken through the prophet:

> "I will open my mouth to speak in parables;
> I will proclaim what has been hidden from the foundation of
> the world."

- Jesus often uses images of smallness when describing the heavenly kingdom. Through the wonders of creation God provides living water and radiant sunlight so that the tiny mustard grows over time to become "the greatest of shrubs," firmly rooted in the ground, providing shelter for the many birds who rest in its branches.

- Lord, I pray that I may set my heart on your kingdom first. You invite me to experience the fullness of life you wish to give me. You love me unconditionally and keep me rooted in faith so that I can grow to know you more and experience your great love for me.

Tuesday 31st July
Matthew 13:36–43

Then he left the crowds and went into the house. And his disciples approached him, saying, "Explain to us the parable of the weeds of the field." He answered, "The one who sows the good seed is the Son of Man; the field is the world, and the good seed are the children of the kingdom; the weeds are the children of the evil one, and the enemy who sowed them is the devil; the harvest is the end of the age, and the reapers are angels. Just as the weeds are collected and burned up with fire, so will it be at the end of the age. The Son of Man will send his angels, and they will collect out of his kingdom all causes of sin and all evildoers, and they will throw them into the furnace of fire, where there will be weeping and gnashing of teeth. Then the righteous will shine like the sun in the kingdom of their Father. Let anyone with ears listen!"

- "The Son of Man will send his angels." Jesus is saying that God will sort things out in the end. In the meantime, we are not to assume the role of judges because we cannot tell the weeds from the wheat. I reflect that the ones whom Jesus calls blessed are not those who appear blessed in the eyes of our culture—the winners, we might say—but rather those the culture considers to be losers. The final judgement may be a huge surprise both to winners and losers.

- Dear God, open my heart so that I will be surprised by your grace and mercy. Help me see in every face one who is your beloved child.

Wednesday 1st August
Matthew 13:44–46

"The kingdom of heaven is like treasure hidden in a field, which someone found and hid; then in his joy he goes and sells all that he has and buys that field. Again, the kingdom of heaven is like a merchant in search of fine pearls; on finding one pearl of great value, he went and sold all that he had and bought it.

- What is my pearl, the thing I value most? What is that buried treasure for which I would be willing to sacrifice everything?

- What would the world be like if the pearl we all sought was serving the poor and marginalized and working for peace and justice? Jesus says the world would then become like the kingdom of heaven! Instill in me, Lord, a sense of other people being priceless treasure.

Thursday 2nd August
Matthew 13:47–53

"Again, the kingdom of heaven is like a net that was thrown into the sea and caught fish of every kind; when it was full, they drew it ashore, sat down, and put the good into baskets but threw out the bad. So it will be at the end of the age. The angels will come out and separate the evil from the righteous and throw them into the furnace of fire, where there will be weeping and gnashing of teeth. Have you understood all this?" They answered, "Yes." And he said to them, "Therefore every scribe who has been trained for the kingdom of heaven is like the master of a household who brings out of his treasure what is new and what is old." When Jesus had finished these parables, he left that place.

- Jesus urges us to gather in everyone we possibly can. It's for us to share the good news; it will be for God to sort us all out according to our hearts, our needs, our sins, and our gifts.

- Lord God, may your word take deep root in my heart and transform how I think, discern, and act. May I be a diligent student and faithful disciple of both the Old and the New Testaments.

Friday 3rd August
Matthew 13:54–58

Jesus came to his hometown and began to teach the people in their synagogue, so that they were astounded and said, "Where did this man get this wisdom and these deeds of power? Is not this the carpenter's son? Is not his mother called Mary? And are not his brothers James and Joseph and Simon and Judas? And are not all his sisters with us? Where then did this man get all this?" And they took offense at him. But Jesus said to them, "Prophets are not without honor except in their own country and in their own house." And he did not do many deeds of power there, because of their unbelief.

- The people were astounded at Jesus' teaching. When we experience this—being astounded—it is often a signal that what we are hearing or witnessing is important, even crucial. Have I been astounded lately? Do I resist being moved in such a way that my life might change?

- People take offense for many reasons: personal, political, even financial. When am I most likely to be offended? What aspect of my life would I prefer Jesus not come near or speak to me about?

Saturday 4th August
Matthew 14:1–12

At that time Herod the ruler heard reports about Jesus; and he said to his servants, "This is John the Baptist; he has been raised from the dead, and for this reason these powers are at work in him." For Herod had arrested John, bound him, and put him in prison on account of Herodias, his brother Philip's wife, because John had been telling him, "It is not lawful for you to have her." Though Herod wanted to put him to death, he feared the crowd, because they regarded him as a prophet. But when Herod's birthday came, the daughter of Herodias danced before the company, and she pleased Herod so much that he promised on oath to grant her whatever she might ask. Prompted by her mother, she said, "Give me the head of John the Baptist here on a platter." The king was grieved, yet out of regard for his oaths and for the guests, he commanded it to be given; he sent and had John beheaded in the prison. The head was brought on a platter and given to the girl, who brought it to her mother. His disciples came and took the body and buried it; then they went and told Jesus.

- Herod did not want to execute John that night. He was persuaded by his wife to do so, because he was a weak man. He feared the people who revered John; now he fears the reaction of the guests if he retracts his oath. Lord, give me the courage to do what is right, whether it is popular or not.

- Because Herod was king, he could cut off John's head to avoid having to listen to him. In what ways do I resist hearing unpleasant truth? I may not deal with it violently, but doesn't such resistance do violence to my soul?

Eighteenth Week of Ordinary Time
August 5—August 11

Something to think and pray about each day this week:

Following Our Desires

Ever since I was a child, I've loved honeybees. My grandfather raised them on his retirement farm, and I used to love to help him out at the hives. We'd go to harvest honey or simply to check in on the bees' health. Bees fascinated me for the way that their hard, cooperative work could produce something so sweet and gratuitous.

This summer, in the midst of my summer retreat, I spent some time contemplatively watching bees, their heads nestled into the center of pretty yellow and purple flowers. At that point, I was discerning how to direct my time in the upcoming year. I have many interests and obligations, a lot of energy, and yet also a deep need for contemplation. I want my life to be generative and "for the greater glory of God." Yet, how to choose?

Several bees were heavy with pollen on their legs as they moved from flower to flower. I felt God direct my attention to the fact that bees pollinate as they go about feasting on the nectar that they gather for honey. They do not intend to pollinate; rather, pollination is a side effect as they move from one attractive flower to the next. God's invitation to me was to go to particular activities where I am drawn and to let go of my concerns about where I am being productive. Bees' generative capacities accompany them as they follow their desires, and God was assuring me that following my own deepest desires at work and at home would be generative—whether or not I ever see the effects of my work.

—Marina McCoy on *dotMagis*, the blog of *IgnatianSpirituality.com*
http://www.ignatianspirituality.com/22700/
following-our-deepest-desires-like-the-bees

The Presence of God

I pause for a moment and think of the love and the grace that God showers on me. I am created in the image and likeness of God; I am God's dwelling place.

Freedom

Lord, you granted me the great gift of freedom. In these times, O Lord, grant that I may be free from any form of racism or intolerance. Remind me that we are all equal in your loving eyes.

Consciousness

Knowing that God loves me unconditionally, I can afford to be honest about how I am.

How has the day been, and how do I feel now? I share my feelings openly with the Lord.

The Word

I take my time to read the word of God slowly, a few times, allowing myself to dwell on anything that strikes me. (Please turn to the Scripture on the following pages. Inspiration points are there should you need them. When you are ready, return here to continue.)

Conversation

Sometimes I wonder what I might say if I were to meet you in person, Lord.

I think I might say "Thank you" because you are always there for me.

Conclusion

I thank God for these moments we have spent together and for any insights I have been given concerning the text.

Sunday 5th August
Eighteenth Sunday in Ordinary Time
John 6:24–35

So when the crowd saw that neither Jesus nor his disciples were there, they themselves got into the boats and went to Capernaum looking for Jesus. When they found him on the other side of the lake, they said to him, "Rabbi, when did you come here?" Jesus answered them, "Very truly, I tell you, you are looking for me, not because you saw signs, but because you ate your fill of the loaves. Do not work for the food that perishes, but for the food that endures for eternal life, which the Son of Man will give you. For it is on him that God the Father has set his seal." Then they said to him, "What must we do to perform the works of God?" Jesus answered them, "This is the work of God, that you believe in him whom he has sent." So they said to him, "What sign are you going to give us then, so that we may see it and believe you? What work are you performing? Our ancestors ate the manna in the wilderness; as it is written, 'He gave them bread from heaven to eat.'" Then Jesus said to them, "Very truly, I tell you, it was not Moses who gave you the bread from heaven, but it is my Father who gives you the true bread from heaven. For the bread of God is that which comes down from heaven and gives life to the world." They said to him, "Sir, give us this bread always." Jesus said to them, "I am the bread of life. Whoever comes to me will never be hungry, and whoever believes in me will never be thirsty."

- When God sent down manna from heaven to the Israelites as they starved in the desert, they were delighted at first. However, it did not take them long to grow tired of this food.

- When am I tempted to turn to material things to feed my soul rather than seeking nourishment from the "true bread from heaven"?

Monday 6th August
The Transfiguration of the Lord
Mark 9:2–10

Six days later, Jesus took with him Peter and James and John, and led them up a high mountain apart, by themselves. And he was transfigured before them, and his clothes became dazzling white, such as no one on earth could bleach them. And there appeared to them Elijah with Moses, who were talking with Jesus. Then Peter said to Jesus, "Rabbi, it is good for us to be here; let us make three dwellings, one for you, one for Moses, and one for Elijah." He did not know what to say, for they were terrified. Then a cloud overshadowed them, and from the cloud there came a voice, "This is my Son, the Beloved; listen to him!" Suddenly when they looked around, they saw no one with them any more, but only Jesus. // As they were coming down the mountain, he ordered them to tell no one about what they had seen, until after the Son of Man had risen from the dead. So they kept the matter to themselves, questioning what this rising from the dead could mean.

- Peter cries out in delight and wonder, "Master, it is good for us to be here!" This is how we are surely meant to experience the presence of God: in wonder and delight, the created glorying in the Creator's presence. Too often, we glide along the surface of the spinning earth, never listening to its heartbeat. We look into the depths of the universe and never hear the singing of the stars.

- When did I last sing and make melody to the Lord with all my heart or clap my hands or shout for joy?

Tuesday 7th August
Matthew 14:22–36

Immediately he made the disciples get into the boat and go on ahead to the other side, while he dismissed the crowds. And after he had dismissed the crowds, he went up the mountain by himself to pray. When evening came, he was there alone, but by this time the boat, battered by the waves, was far from the land, for the wind was against them. And early in the morning he came walking towards them on the sea. But when the disciples saw him walking on the sea, they were terrified, saying, "It is a ghost!" And they cried out in fear. But immediately Jesus spoke to them and said, "Take heart, it is I; do not be afraid." // Peter answered him, "Lord, if it is you, command me to come to you on the water." He said, "Come." So Peter got out of the boat, started walking on the water, and came towards Jesus. But when he noticed the strong wind, he became frightened, and beginning to sink, he cried out, "Lord, save me!" Jesus immediately reached out his hand and caught him, saying to him, "You of little faith, why did you doubt?" When they got into the boat, the wind ceased. And those in the boat worshipped him, saying, "Truly you are the Son of God." // When they had crossed over, they came to land at Gennesaret. After the people of that place recognized him, they sent word throughout the region and brought all who were sick to him, and begged him that they might touch even the fringe of his cloak; and all who touched it were healed.

- After all they have been through with Jesus, the disciples still don't understand what he can and will do to care for them. He appears among them and brings his calmness and composure to the chaos. Peter responds with a desire to do miracles, but that desire is soon followed by abject failure, terror, and then worship of Jesus. Is that how we respond to God's invitation sometimes? Can you see yourself in Peter?

- We are this odd bunch of disciples, aren't we? Do we have anything near the faith to which Jesus invited his disciples?

Wednesday 8th August
Matthew 15:21–28

Jesus left that place and went away to the district of Tyre and Sidon. Just then a Canaanite woman from that region came out and started shouting, "Have mercy on me, Lord, Son of David; my daughter is tormented by a demon." But he did not answer her at all. And his disciples came and urged him, saying, "Send her away, for she keeps shouting after us." He answered, "I was sent only to the lost sheep of the house of Israel." But she came and knelt before him, saying, "Lord, help me." He answered, "It is not fair to take the children's food and throw it to the dogs." She said, "Yes, Lord, yet even the dogs eat the crumbs that fall from their masters' table." Then Jesus answered her, "Woman, great is your faith! Let it be done for you as you wish." And her daughter was healed instantly.

- Perhaps this the only example we have in the Gospels of someone who changes Jesus' mind. He appears to exclude the woman from his mission because she is a Canaanite, not a "lost sheep of the house of Israel." But she is persistent and creative in her response, using every ounce of her wit. And underneath her plea is great faith and, after all, that is what Jesus always rewards when asked to heal.

- Can you think of other Gospel examples where Jesus is caught out by a straight-talking woman? Being up front with our desires might not always be the way we choose to be in prayer, but Jesus does not appear to mind too much.

Thursday 9th August
Matthew 16:13–23

Now when Jesus came into the district of Caesarea Philippi, he asked his disciples, "Who do people say that the Son of Man is?" And they said, "Some say John the Baptist, but others Elijah, and still others Jeremiah or one of the prophets." He said to them, "But who do you say that I am?" Simon Peter answered, "You are the Messiah, the Son of the living God." And Jesus answered him, "Blessed are you, Simon son of Jonah! For flesh and blood has not revealed this to you, but my Father in heaven. And I tell you, you are Peter, and on this rock I will build my church, and the gates of Hades will not prevail against it. I will give you the keys of the kingdom of heaven, and whatever you bind on earth will be bound in heaven, and whatever you loose on earth will be loosed in heaven." Then he sternly ordered the disciples not to tell anyone that he was the Messiah. // From that time on, Jesus began to show his disciples that he must go to Jerusalem and undergo great suffering at the hands of the elders and chief priests and scribes, and be killed, and on the third day be raised. And Peter took him aside and began to rebuke him, saying, "God forbid it, Lord! This must never happen to you." But he turned and said to Peter, "Get behind me, Satan! You are a stumbling-block to me; for you are setting your mind not on divine things but on human things."

- Peter makes an extraordinary confession of faith in the master. But when Jesus tells his disciples that he must suffer and be killed, it is too much for Peter. And despite the sharp rebuke, Peter consistently makes the same mistake; right up to the Last Supper when he refuses to allow Jesus to wash his feet. He simply cannot accept that the mission of the one whom he has followed will end in "failure."

- But Jesus' earthly mission is one marked with humility, conflict, and failure. I put myself in Peter's shoes. What will help me embrace humility, conflict, even potential failure?

Friday 10th August
John 12:24–26

Jesus said, "Very truly, I tell you, unless a grain of wheat falls into the earth and dies, it remains just a single grain; but if it dies, it bears much fruit. Those who love their life lose it, and those who hate their life in this world will keep it for eternal life. Whoever serves me must follow me, and where I am, there will my servant be also. Whoever serves me, the Father will honor."

- Jesus is so comfortable with imagery from the garden and the field. He has seen so much of this in his life in a modest rural town. It's comforting to be reminded that Jesus was from such a modest place; his experience was not sophisticated, as we would see it.

- In your experience, what would be the earth in which to set the seed of the word? Where in your life is there soil in which God's word could grow?

Saturday 11th August
Matthew 17:14–20

When they came to the crowd, a man came to him, knelt before him, and said, "Lord, have mercy on my son, for he is an epileptic and he suffers terribly; he often falls into the fire and often into the water. And I brought him to your disciples, but they could not cure him." Jesus answered, "You faithless and perverse generation, how much longer must I be with you? How much longer must I put up with you? Bring him here to me." And Jesus rebuked the demon, and it came out of him, and the boy was cured instantly. Then the disciples came to Jesus privately and said, "Why could we not cast it out?" He said to them, "Because of your little faith. For truly I tell you, if you have faith the size of a mustard seed, you will say to this mountain, 'Move from here to there,' and it will move; and nothing will be impossible for you."

- We ask Jesus, "Why can we not accomplish your work in our lives?" In this reading, Jesus himself supplies the answer: "because of your little faith."

- Lord, grant us the faith that will move mountains—mountains of inertia and apathy, of fear and anxiety, of selfishness and despair.

Nineteenth Week of Ordinary Time
August 12—August 18

Something to think and pray about each day this week:

She's Our Mother Too

At that crucial moment, before fully accomplishing the work his Father had entrusted to him, Jesus said to Mary, "Woman, here is your son." Then he said to his beloved friend, "Here is your mother" (John 19:26–27). These words of the dying Jesus are not chiefly the expression of his devotion and concern for his mother; rather, they are a revelatory formula that manifests the mystery of a special saving mission. Jesus left us his mother to be *our* mother. Only after doing so did Jesus know that "all was now finished" (John 19:28). At the foot of the cross, at the supreme hour of the new creation, Christ led us to Mary. He brought us to her because he did not want us to journey without a mother, and our people read in this maternal image all the mysteries of the Gospel.

The Lord did not want to leave the Church without this icon of womanhood. Mary, who brought him into the world with great faith, also accompanies "the rest of her offspring, those who keep the commandments of God and bear testimony to Jesus" (Rev. 12:17). The close connection between Mary, the Church, and each member of the faithful, based on the fact that each in his or her own way brings forth Christ, has been beautifully expressed by Blessed Isaac of Stella: "In the inspired Scriptures, what is said in a universal sense of the virgin mother, the Church, is understood in an individual sense of the Virgin Mary . . . In a way, every Christian is also believed to be a bride of God's word, a mother of Christ, his daughter and sister, at once virginal and fruitful . . . Christ dwelt for nine months in the tabernacle of Mary's womb. He dwells until the end of the ages in the tabernacle of the Church's faith. He will dwell forever in the knowledge and love of each faithful soul."

—Pope Francis, *The Church of Mercy*

The Presence of God

I pause for a moment
and reflect on God's life-giving presence
in every part of my body,
in everything around me,
in the whole of my life.

Freedom

Many countries are at this moment suffering the agonies of war. I bow my head in thanksgiving for my freedom. I pray for all prisoners and captives.

Consciousness

Knowing that God loves me unconditionally, I look honestly over the past day, its events, and my feelings. Do I have something to be grateful for? Then I give thanks. Is there something I am sorry for? Then I ask forgiveness.

The Word

Now I turn to the Scripture set out for me this day. I read slowly over the words and see if any sentence or sentiment appeals to me. (Please turn to the Scripture on the following pages. Inspiration points are there should you need them. When you are ready, return here to continue.)

Conversation

I know with certainty that there were times when you carried me, Lord. There were times when it was through your strength that I got through the dark times in my life.

Conclusion

Glory be to the Father, and to the Son, and to the Holy Spirit,
As it was in the beginning, is now and ever shall be,
World without end. Amen.

Sunday 12th August
Nineteenth Sunday in Ordinary Time
John 6:41–51

Then the Jews began to complain about him because he said, "I am the bread that came down from heaven." They were saying, "Is not this Jesus, the son of Joseph, whose father and mother we know? How can he now say, 'I have come down from heaven'?" Jesus answered them, "Do not complain among yourselves. No one can come to me unless drawn by the Father who sent me; and I will raise that person up on the last day. It is written in the prophets, 'And they shall all be taught by God.' Everyone who has heard and learned from the Father comes to me. Not that anyone has seen the Father except the one who is from God; he has seen the Father. Very truly, I tell you, whoever believes has eternal life. I am the bread of life. Your ancestors ate the manna in the wilderness, and they died. This is the bread that comes down from heaven, so that one may eat of it and not die. I am the living bread that came down from heaven. Whoever eats of this bread will live forever; and the bread that I will give for the life of the world is my flesh."

- Their personal knowledge of Jesus has made the people skeptical about his claims. Is our sense of awe and wonder blunted by familiarity?

- I am invited daily to the eucharistic table, to eat the bread of eternal life. Do I approach that table with apathy or with a quickening heart? When were my eyes last opened, and when did I last recognize Christ in the breaking of the bread?

Monday 13th August
Matthew 17:22–27

As they were gathering in Galilee, Jesus said to them, "The Son of Man is going to be betrayed into human hands, and they will kill him, and on the third day he will be raised." And they were greatly distressed. When they reached Capernaum, the collectors of the temple tax came to Peter and said, "Does your teacher not pay the temple tax?" He said, "Yes, he does." And when he came home, Jesus spoke of it first, asking, "What do you think, Simon? From whom do kings of the earth take toll or tribute? From their children or from others?" When Peter said, "From others," Jesus said to him, "Then the children are free. However, so that we do not give offense to them, go to the lake and cast a hook; take the first fish that comes up; and when you open its mouth, you will find a coin; take that and give it to them for you and me."

- Imagine touring the country with a group of followers who are "greatly distressed." It seems that the disciples are beginning to understand that this wandering mission is to end in failure and disgrace. If they have been distressed by his words, then they are beginning to see that he is serious.

- Jesus' casual dealings with the revenue authorities can hardly have comforted Peter. Jesus appears to hold the system in contempt. What do you make of this scene? Try to sit with it for a while.

Tuesday 14th August
Matthew 18:1–5, 10, 12–14

At that time the disciples came to Jesus and asked, "Who is the greatest in the kingdom of heaven?" He called a child, whom he put among them, and said, "Truly I tell you, unless you change and become like children, you will never enter the kingdom of heaven. Whoever becomes humble like this child is the greatest in the kingdom of heaven. Whoever welcomes one such child in my name welcomes me. . . . Take care that you do not despise one of these little ones; for, I tell you, in heaven their angels continually see the face of my Father in heaven. . . . What do you think? If a shepherd has a hundred sheep, and one of them has gone astray, does he not leave the ninety-nine on the mountains and go in search of the one that went astray? And if he finds it, truly I tell you, he rejoices over it more than over the ninety-nine that never went astray. So it is not the will of your Father in heaven that one of these little ones should be lost."

- Jesus is telling us very clearly that every life is precious in his eyes. Every person I meet is invaluable and irreplaceable. Jesus turns conventional attitudes upside down: the "little ones," the people the world does not rate as important, are the most precious of all. Will my attitudes today reflect this?

- If I were the only person in the world needing salvation, Jesus would still die for me. Does that thrill me or terrify me? Why?

Wednesday 15th August
The Assumption of the Blessed Virgin Mary
Luke 1:39–56

In those days Mary set out and went with haste to a Judean town in the hill country, where she entered the house of Zechariah and greeted Elizabeth. When Elizabeth heard Mary's greeting, the child leapt in her womb. And Elizabeth was filled with the Holy Spirit and exclaimed with a loud cry, "Blessed are you among women, and blessed is the fruit of your womb. And why has this happened to me, that the mother of my Lord comes to me? For as soon as I heard the sound of your greeting, the child in my womb leapt for joy. And blessed is she who believed that there would be a fulfillment of what was spoken to her by the Lord."
And Mary said,

> "My soul magnifies the Lord,
>> and my spirit rejoices in God my Savior,
> for he has looked with favor on the lowliness of his servant.
>> Surely, from now on all generations will call me blessed;
> for the Mighty One has done great things for me,
>> and holy is his name.
> His mercy is for those who fear him
>> from generation to generation.
> He has shown strength with his arm;
>> he has scattered the proud in the thoughts of their hearts.
> He has brought down the powerful from their thrones,
>> and lifted up the lowly;
> he has filled the hungry with good things,
>> and sent the rich away empty.
> He has helped his servant Israel,
>> in remembrance of his mercy,
> according to the promise he made to our ancestors,
>> to Abraham and to his descendants forever."

And Mary remained with her for about three months and then returned to her home.

- There are moments for all of us when, just like expectant mothers, we know that we have been blessed. Sometimes it may be only a gradual realization in difficult circumstances.

- Pope Francis opens his letter *Evangelii Gaudium*: "The joy of the Gospel fills the hearts and lives of all who encounter Jesus. Those who accept this offer of salvation are set free from sin, sorrow, inner emptiness and loneliness. . . . I understand the grief of people who have to endure great suffering, yet slowly but surely we all have to let the joy of faith slowly revive as a quiet yet firm trust, even amid the greatest distress." Is there a particular line of this extract that resonates with you or jars you?

Thursday 16th August
Matthew 18:21—19:1

Then Peter came and said to him, "Lord, if another member of the church sins against me, how often should I forgive? As many as seven times?" Jesus said to him, "Not seven times, but, I tell you, seventy-seven times. // "For this reason the kingdom of heaven may be compared to a king who wished to settle accounts with his slaves. When he began the reckoning, one who owed him ten thousand talents was brought to him; and, as he could not pay, his lord ordered him to be sold, together with his wife and children and all his possessions, and payment to be made. So the slave fell on his knees before him, saying, 'Have patience with me, and I will pay you everything.' And out of pity for him, the lord of that slave released him and forgave him the debt. But that same slave, as he went out, came upon one of his fellow-slaves who owed him a hundred denarii; and seizing him by the throat, he said, 'Pay what you owe.' Then his fellow slave fell down and pleaded with him, 'Have patience with me, and I will pay you.' But he refused; then he went and threw him into prison until he should pay the debt. When his fellow slaves saw what had happened, they were greatly distressed, and they went and reported to their lord all that had taken place. Then his lord summoned him and said to him, 'You wicked slave! I forgave you all that debt because you pleaded with me. Should you not have had mercy on your fellow slave, as I had mercy on you?' And in anger his lord handed him over to be tortured until he should pay his entire debt. So my heavenly Father will also do to every

one of you, if you do not forgive your brother or sister from your heart."
// When Jesus had finished saying these things, he left Galilee and went
to the region of Judea beyond the Jordan.

- Pope Francis describes mercy this way: "We need constantly to contemplate the mystery of mercy. It is a wellspring of joy, serenity, and
peace. Our salvation depends on it." Today, I will carry the word *mercy*
everywhere I go and allow it to work in my mind and heart.

- Jesus affirms that mercy is not only an action of the Father, it becomes
a criterion for ascertaining who his true children are. In short, we are
called to show mercy because mercy has first been shown to us.

Friday 17th August
Matthew 19:3–12

Some Pharisees came to him, and to test him they asked, "Is it lawful for
a man to divorce his wife for any cause?" He answered, "Have you not
read that the one who made them at the beginning 'made them male and
female', and said, 'For this reason a man shall leave his father and mother
and be joined to his wife, and the two shall become one flesh'? So they are
no longer two, but one flesh. Therefore what God has joined together, let
no one separate." They said to him, "Why then did Moses command us
to give a certificate of dismissal and to divorce her?" He said to them, "It
was because you were so hard-hearted that Moses allowed you to divorce
your wives, but at the beginning it was not so. And I say to you, whoever
divorces his wife, except for unchastity, and marries another commits
adultery." // His disciples said to him, "If such is the case of a man with
his wife, it is better not to marry." But he said to them, "Not everyone
can accept this teaching, but only those to whom it is given. For there are
eunuchs who have been so from birth, and there are eunuchs who have
been made eunuchs by others, and there are eunuchs who have made
themselves eunuchs for the sake of the kingdom of heaven. Let anyone
accept this who can."

- Rabbi Jesus knows his Scripture! He restates God's standards in the
face of human hard-heartedness. As a result, the disciples' doubts
about marriage seem entirely understandable. But some situations re-
quire careful pastoral discernment. Pope Francis states: "The Church's
way, from the time of the Council of Jerusalem, has always been the

way of Jesus, the way of mercy and reinstatement . . .The way of the Church is not to condemn anyone forever; it is to pour out the balm of God's mercy on all those who ask for it with a sincere heart."

- Are you in touch with somebody struggling in marriage or a commitment to celibate service?

Saturday 18th August
Matthew 19:13–15

Then little children were being brought to him in order that he might lay his hands on them and pray. The disciples spoke sternly to those who brought them; but Jesus said, "Let the little children come to me, and do not stop them; for it is to such as these that the kingdom of heaven belongs." And he laid his hands on them and went on his way.

- What a warm-hearted person Jesus is! He wants to hug little children, and he's inspired by the spontaneous gesture of parents bringing their children to him for his blessing.

- But once again his disciples (can we be included here?) get it profoundly wrong. It seems they consider the parents' gesture a problem, not on the program, and not to be encouraged. When am I most tempted to shoo away children or to think that spending time with them is unimportant in the larger scheme of things?

The Twentieth Week of Ordinary Time
August 19—August 25

Something to think and pray about each day this week:

One Ordinary Marvelous Day

Twenty years from now—should you live so long—you will have opportunity to reflect on the summer you're living in right now. Imagine that you are already years into your future, and it's a mild summer day, and you take a few moments to remember *this* day.

What moments of this day will stand out as highlights?
What worries will seem, in retrospect, not worth worrying about?
What errands do you wish you had skipped?
Which conversations helped your soul?
Which people had a good impact on your day?
What scents were in the air?
How many dogs, cats, birds, and other creatures did you notice and
    enjoy?
What was your favorite meal of the day, and why?
What did the air feel like, when you walked through the afternoon?
Which sounds added to your contentment or joy?
What did the sky look like when evening came?
How did you make a loving impact on someone else's day?
Where did you encounter God, on this ordinary, marvelous day?

—Watch a video version of this reflection by Vinita Hampton Wright
https://www.youtube.com/watch?v=e_zO0CctvsE

The Presence of God

I remind myself that I am in the presence of God, who is my strength in times of weakness and my comforter in times of sorrow.

Freedom

Saint Ignatius thought that a thick and shapeless tree trunk would never believe that it could become a statue, admired as a miracle of sculpture, and would never submit itself to the chisel of the sculptor, who sees by her genius what she can make of it. I ask for the grace to let myself be shaped by my loving Creator.

Consciousness

Dear Lord, help me to remember that you gave me life. Teach me to slow down, to be still and enjoy the pleasures created for me. To be aware of the beauty that surrounds me: the marvel of mountains, the calmness of lakes, the fragility of a flower petal. I need to remember that all these things come from you.

The Word

In this expectant state of mind, please turn to the text for the day with confidence. Believe that the Holy Spirit is present and may reveal whatever the passage has to say to you. Read reflectively, listening with a third ear to what may be going on in your heart. (Please turn to the Scripture on the following pages. Inspiration points are there should you need them. When you are ready, return here to continue.)

Conversation

What feelings are rising in me as I pray and reflect on God's word? I imagine Jesus himself sitting or standing near me, and I open my heart to him.

Conclusion

I thank God for these moments we have spent together and for any insights I have been given concerning the text.

Sunday 19th August
Twentieth Sunday in Ordinary Time
John 6:51–58

"I am the living bread that came down from heaven. Whoever eats of this bread will live forever; and the bread that I will give for the life of the world is my flesh." The Jews then disputed among themselves, saying, "How can this man give us his flesh to eat?" So Jesus said to them, "Very truly, I tell you, unless you eat the flesh of the Son of Man and drink his blood, you have no life in you. Those who eat my flesh and drink my blood have eternal life, and I will raise them up on the last day; for my flesh is true food and my blood is true drink. Those who eat my flesh and drink my blood abide in me, and I in them. Just as the living Father sent me, and I live because of the Father, so whoever eats me will live because of me. This is the bread that came down from heaven, not like that which your ancestors ate, and they died. But the one who eats this bread will live forever."

- There can hardly be a more graphic or a more surprising description of the indissoluble participation of one life in another. In Hebrew, the expression "flesh and blood" means the whole being. The reality of Christ's presence at the Eucharist is beyond our comprehension. We are asked not to understand it, but to experience it.

- "Abide in me" is a phrase Jesus uses over and over again. He invites us to take him into ourselves and become one with him. How might I take today's reading, along with "abide in me," to the table when I next partake of the Eucharist?

Monday 20th August
Matthew 19:16–22

Then someone came to Jesus and said, "Teacher, what good deed must I do to have eternal life?" And he said to him, "Why do you ask me about what is good? There is only one who is good. If you wish to enter into life, keep the commandments." He said to him, "Which ones?" And Jesus said, "You shall not murder; you shall not commit adultery; you shall not steal; you shall not bear false witness; Honor your father and mother; also, you shall love your neighbor as yourself." The young man said to him, "I have kept all these; what do I still lack?" Jesus said to him, "If you wish to be perfect, go, sell your possessions, and give the money to the poor, and you will have treasure in heaven; then come, follow me." When the young man heard this word, he went away grieving, for he had many possessions.

• Interestingly, the commandments Jesus recites to the rich young man do not include the first three, which all relate to our relationship with God. Instead, he lists those that address our relationships with one another. The message is clear: we do not live in isolation. Love for our neighbor is the door to eternal life.

• What attachments in my life are holding me back from a deeper relationship with my neighbor and with God?

Tuesday 21st August
Matthew 19:23–30

Then Jesus said to his disciples, "Truly I tell you, it will be hard for a rich person to enter the kingdom of heaven. Again I tell you, it is easier for a camel to go through the eye of a needle than for someone who is rich to enter the kingdom of God." When the disciples heard this, they were greatly astounded and said, "Then who can be saved?" But Jesus looked at them and said, "For mortals it is impossible, but for God all things are possible." // Then Peter said in reply, "Look, we have left everything and followed you. What then will we have?" Jesus said to them, "Truly I tell you, at the renewal of all things, when the Son of Man is seated on the throne of his glory, you who have followed me will also sit on twelve thrones, judging the twelve tribes of Israel. And everyone who has left houses or brothers or sisters or father or mother or children or fields, for my name's sake, will receive a hundredfold, and will inherit eternal life. But many who are first will be last, and the last will be first."

• The "Eye of the Needle" was the name for a very small gate into Jerusalem. How often Jesus notices everyday things and uses them as images to convey his message. Yet again Jesus raises the standard for those who want to enter the kingdom of God, and again the disciples are exasperated.

• Jesus often goes to the extreme to convey a truth. We may be tempted to drift away in disillusionment. Or we can wait for the word of mercy he invariably adds. Can I trust what he says about eternal life?

Wednesday 22nd August
The Queenship of the Blessed Virgin Mary
Matthew 20:1–16

Jesus said to his disciples, "For the kingdom of heaven is like a landowner who went out early in the morning to hire laborers for his vineyard. After agreeing with the laborers for the usual daily wage, he sent them into his vineyard. When he went out about nine o'clock, he saw others standing idle in the marketplace; and he said to them, 'You also go into the vineyard, and I will pay you whatever is right.' So they went. When he went out again about noon and about three o'clock, he did the same. And about five o'clock he went out and found others standing around; and he said to them, 'Why are you standing here idle all day?' They said to him, 'Because no one has hired us.' He said to them, 'You also go into the vineyard.' When evening came, the owner of the vineyard said to his manager, 'Call the laborers and give them their pay, beginning with the last and then going to the first.' When those hired about five o'clock came, each of them received the usual daily wage. Now when the first came, they thought they would receive more; but each of them also received the usual daily wage. And when they received it, they grumbled against the landowner, saying, 'These last worked only one hour, and you have made them equal to us who have borne the burden of the day and the scorching heat.' But he replied to one of them, 'Friend, I am doing you no wrong; did you not agree with me for the usual daily wage? Take what belongs to you and go; I choose to give to this last the same as I give to you. Am I not allowed to do what I choose with what belongs to me? Or are you envious because I am generous?' So the last will be first, and the first will be last'."

- Scripture scholar Nicholas King, SJ, describes God's generosity this way: "God is utterly generous (generosity is the quality that defines God), and we do not lose out because God has been equally generous to those undeserving people next door."

- Tolerance and generosity would seem to be the qualities most recognizable in those closest to Jesus. Does it surprise you that this may not always be the case? Why do you think these qualities do not shine more in the followers of Jesus? What has your own experience been?

Thursday 23rd August
Matthew 22:1–14

Once more Jesus spoke to them in parables, saying: "The kingdom of heaven may be compared to a king who gave a wedding banquet for his son. He sent his slaves to call those who had been invited to the wedding banquet, but they would not come. Again he sent other slaves, saying, 'Tell those who have been invited: Look, I have prepared my dinner, my oxen and my fat calves have been slaughtered, and everything is ready; come to the wedding banquet.' But they made light of it and went away, one to his farm, another to his business, while the rest seized his slaves, maltreated them, and killed them. The king was enraged. He sent his troops, destroyed those murderers, and burned their city. Then he said to his slaves, 'The wedding is ready, but those invited were not worthy. Go therefore into the main streets, and invite everyone you find to the wedding banquet.' Those slaves went out into the streets and gathered all whom they found, both good and bad; so the wedding hall was filled with guests. But when the king came in to see the guests, he noticed a man there who was not wearing a wedding robe, and he said to him, 'Friend, how did you get in here without a wedding robe?' And he was speechless. Then the king said to the attendants, 'Bind him hand and foot, and throw him into the outer darkness, where there will be weeping and gnashing of teeth.' For many are called, but few are chosen."

- This is an altogether strange little parable and the treatment meted out to the guest without the party clothes seems particularly harsh: tied up and dumped at the edge of town. If you turn up at a party under-dressed you certainly stick out like a sore thumb, unless, of course, you couldn't care less.

- The guests are of all types, good and bad, and every one of them is dressed up appropriately. They took the trouble to follow the dress code, and this shows respect for the host. Except for the careless one who appears to have no respect. Could it be that the kingdom is open to the strong and the weak but not to the careless?

Friday 24th August
Saint Bartholomew

John 1:45–51

Philip found Nathanael and said to him, "We have found him about whom Moses in the law and also the prophets wrote, Jesus son of Joseph from Nazareth." Nathanael said to him, "Can anything good come out of Nazareth?" Philip said to him, "Come and see." When Jesus saw Nathanael coming toward him, he said of him, "Here is truly an Israelite in whom there is no deceit!" Nathanael asked him, "Where did you get to know me?" Jesus answered, "I saw you under the fig tree before Philip called you." Nathanael replied, "Rabbi, you are the Son of God! You are the King of Israel!" Jesus answered, "Do you believe because I told you that I saw you under the fig tree? You will see greater things than these." And he said to him, "Very truly, I tell you, you will see heaven opened and the angels of God ascending and descending upon the Son of Man."

• Nathanael seems cynical about Jesus at first. But then Jesus shows Nathanael that he knows him more profoundly than he could have imagined. Jesus saw Nathanael under the fig tree. And the significance of this is known only to Nathanael. Then, as Peter so often does, he throws himself at the feet of Jesus professing the utmost faith in him.

• Has anyone ever seen your personal life deeply and in a way that confirmed the best in you, while understanding the worst? Does such intimate knowledge by another person build you up or threaten you? Could you allow Jesus to look at your life and your behavior in all its forms, both good and bad?

Saturday 25th August

Matthew 23:1–12

Then Jesus said to the crowds and to his disciples, "The scribes and the Pharisees sit on Moses' seat; therefore, do whatever they teach you and follow it; but do not do as they do, for they do not practice what they teach. They tie up heavy burdens, hard to bear, and lay them on the shoulders of others; but they themselves are unwilling to lift a finger to move them. They do all their deeds to be seen by others; for they make their phylacteries broad and their fringes long. They love to have the place of honor at banquets and the best seats in the synagogues, and to be greeted with respect in the marketplaces, and to have people call them rabbi. But you are not to be called rabbi, for you have one teacher, and you are all students. And call no one your father on earth, for you have one Father—the one in heaven. Nor are you to be called instructors, for you have one instructor, the Messiah. The greatest among you will be your servant. All who exalt themselves will be humbled, and all who humble themselves will be exalted."

• Jesus described quite vividly how important it was to certain people to be known, admired, and honored. Not much has changed, has it? When am I tempted to seek the higher position, the more high-profile place at the table or in the room?

• On a more sobering note, Jesus described how those who should be leaders have actually burdened the people they are supposed to help. When have I seen this happen, and where? Church? A workplace? A club or organization? In my own family? Show me, Lord, how to honor others and care for them.

The Twenty-First Week of Ordinary Time
August 26—September 1

Something to think and pray about each day this week:

Less Room for the Weeds

In late summer, when gardening columns advise being vigilant about pulling weeds, I was noticing their relative absence in areas of the garden where I've planted hardy perennials over the years. Where the hostas, butterfly bush, and echinacea grow, there are fewer weeds to pull. Even the most vigilant weeding cannot replace the effectiveness of cultivating plants through tending to water and soil, and then letting sunshine and God do the rest!

God tends to us like a divine gardener who encourages what is good within. Jesus tells us of the wheat and weeds that must grow up together until harvest; we all have some of each within. Yet Jesus also uses images such as yeast in bread, lilies in the field, and the multiplication of loaves to show God's desire for us is to keep growing us in Christ.

We, too, can tend to the complexity and sometimes messiness of ourselves and our relationships by cultivating what is already loving and good rather than just avoiding the bad. Then we may find that as we tend to the growth of love, there is less and less room for the weeds.

—Marina McCoy on *dotMagis*, the blog of *IgnatianSpirituality.com*
http://www.ignatianspirituality.com/19664/
tending-to-the-growth-of-love

The Presence of God

I remind myself that, as I sit here now,
God is gazing on me with love and holding me in being.
I pause for a moment and think of this.

Freedom

"There are very few people who realize what God would make of them
if they abandoned themselves into his hands, and let themselves be formed
by his grace" (Saint Ignatius). I ask for the grace to trust myself totally to
God's love.

Consciousness

Where do I sense hope, encouragement, and growth in my life? By looking back over the past few months, I may be able to see which activities
and occasions have produced rich fruit. If I do notice such areas, I will
determine to give those areas both time and space in the future.

The Word

Lord Jesus, you became human to communicate with me.
You walked and worked on this earth.
You endured the heat and struggled with the cold.
All your time on this earth was spent in caring for humanity.
You healed the sick, you raised the dead.
Most important of all, you saved me from death.
(Please turn to the Scripture on the following pages. Inspiration points
are there should you need them. When you are ready, return here to
continue.)

Conversation

What is stirring in me as I pray? Am I consoled, troubled, left cold? I
imagine Jesus standing or sitting at my side, and I share my feelings with
him.

Conclusion

Glory be to the Father, and to the Son, and to the Holy Spirit,
As it was in the beginning, is now and ever shall be,
World without end. Amen.

Sunday 26th August
Twenty-First Sunday in Ordinary Time
John 6:60–69

When many of his disciples heard it, they said, "This teaching is difficult; who can accept it?" But Jesus, being aware that his disciples were complaining about it, said to them, "Does this offend you? Then what if you were to see the Son of Man ascending to where he was before? It is the spirit that gives life; the flesh is useless. The words that I have spoken to you are spirit and life. But among you there are some who do not believe." For Jesus knew from the first who were the ones that did not believe, and who was the one that would betray him. And he said, "For this reason I have told you that no one can come to me unless it is granted by the Father." // Because of this many of his disciples turned back and no longer went about with him. So Jesus asked the twelve, "Do you also wish to go away?" Simon Peter answered him, "Lord, to whom can we go? You have the words of eternal life. We have come to believe and know that you are the Holy One of God."

- The disciples understood that, no matter how confusing or troubling it might be to follow Jesus, there was no place else to go. When we hear the truth and know it is the truth, that narrows down all other choices, doesn't it?

- Lord, there are days when I waver; I flirt with the idea of going someplace else, of forgetting about being your disciple. Maybe I'm weary, or maybe I'm resisting some part of your message. May your Holy Spirit remind me that you have the words of life, and that is enough.

Monday 27th August
Matthew 23:13–22

Jesus said, "But woe to you, scribes and Pharisees, hypocrites! For you lock people out of the kingdom of heaven. For you do not go in yourselves, and when others are going in, you stop them. Woe to you, scribes and Pharisees, hypocrites! For you cross sea and land to make a single convert, and you make the new convert twice as much a child of hell as yourselves. Woe to you, blind guides, who say, 'Whoever swears by the sanctuary is bound by nothing, but whoever swears by the gold of the sanctuary is bound by the oath.' You blind fools! For which is greater, the gold or the sanctuary that has made the gold sacred? And you say, 'Whoever swears by the altar is bound by nothing, but whoever swears by the gift that is on the altar is bound by the oath.' How blind you are! For which is greater, the gift or the altar that makes the gift sacred? So whoever swears by the altar, swears by it and by everything on it; and whoever swears by the sanctuary, swears by it and by the one who dwells in it; and whoever swears by heaven, swears by the throne of God and by the one who is seated upon it."

- We cannot minimize the force of Jesus' message in this scene. He lays out the sins of the men who should be leading the people of Israel, showing them God's mercy and great care. But they are not, and Jesus does not hold back this scathing rebuke. We hear his anger as well as his mercy—anger toward leaders who do not lead, and mercy toward those who should be receiving leadership.

- I am reminded that it is a grave responsibility to possess any form of leadership. God will hold me responsible, and he will judge me by how merciful I was. Did I tend those in my charge? Did I use the position for my own agenda? Did I forget that God is always present and waiting for me to act with justice?

Tuesday 28th August
Matthew 23:23–26

Jesus said, "Woe to you, scribes and Pharisees, hypocrites! For you tithe mint, dill, and cummin, and have neglected the weightier matters of the law: justice and mercy and faith. It is these you ought to have practiced without neglecting the others. You blind guides! You strain out a gnat but swallow a camel! Woe to you, scribes and Pharisees, hypocrites! For you clean the outside of the cup and of the plate, but inside they are full of greed and self-indulgence. You blind Pharisee! First clean the inside of the cup, so that the outside also may become clean."

- Institutionalized religion always runs the risk of insincerity or, in the worst case, hypocrisy. Interestingly, the only people Jesus denounces in the Gospel are these Pharisees and their like. He accuses them of not understanding God because they don't see the importance of the fundamentals: justice, mercy, and faith.

- Very often it takes one person to see and to state what is going wrong and to reset the priorities. Jesus does this again and again in his dealings with "sinners," who are those whose behavior runs contrary to the Jewish law. He heals, and he forgives sins where Pharisees and others rush to condemn and even destroy. Is my life fueled more by Jesus' kind of energy or by the energy that fueled the Pharisees?

Wednesday 29th August
Mark 6:17–29

For Herod himself had sent men who arrested John, bound him, and put him in prison on account of Herodias, his brother Philip's wife, because Herod had married her. For John had been telling Herod, "It is not lawful for you to have your brother's wife." And Herodias had a grudge against him, and wanted to kill him. But she could not, for Herod feared John, knowing that he was a righteous and holy man, and he protected him. When he heard him, he was greatly perplexed; and yet he liked to listen to him. But an opportunity came when Herod on his birthday gave a banquet for his courtiers and officers and for the leaders of Galilee. When his daughter Herodias came in and danced, she pleased Herod and his guests; and the king said to the girl, "Ask me for whatever you wish, and I will give it." And he solemnly swore to her, "Whatever you ask me, I will give you, even half of my kingdom." She went out and said to her mother, "What should I ask for?" She replied, "The head of John the baptizer." Immediately she rushed back to the king and requested, "I want you to give me at once the head of John the Baptist on a platter." The king was deeply grieved; yet out of regard for his oaths and for the guests, he did not want to refuse her. Immediately the king sent a soldier of the guard with orders to bring John's head. He went and beheaded him in the prison, brought his head on a platter, and gave it to the girl. Then the girl gave it to her mother. When his disciples heard about it, they came and took his body, and laid it in a tomb.

- This horrible scene opens with the totally corrupt Herod at a royal banquet. We can only imagine the sumptuousness of the feast and the entertainments laid on. And then through his selfish cupidity he is cornered into taking the life of John, the outspoken Baptist, and adding that horror to the entertainments of the evening. Nothing is sacred to this king.

- Contrast this with the quiet humility of John's disciples, who mercifully look after his body and honor it with burial. What a sorrowful and humble group; they bring some humanity to this awful scene. Does it remind me of any contemporary situations?

Thursday 30th August
Matthew 24:42–51

Jesus said, "Keep awake therefore, for you do not know on what day your Lord is coming. But understand this: if the owner of the house had known in what part of the night the thief was coming, he would have stayed awake and would not have let his house be broken into. Therefore you also must be ready, for the Son of Man is coming at an unexpected hour. Who then is the faithful and wise slave, whom his master has put in charge of his household, to give the other slaves their allowance of food at the proper time? Blessed is that slave whom his master will find at work when he arrives. Truly I tell you, he will put that one in charge of all his possessions. But if that wicked slave says to himself, 'My master is delayed,' and he begins to beat his fellow slaves, and eats and drinks with drunkards, the master of that slave will come on a day when he does not expect him and at an hour that he does not know. He will cut him in pieces and put him with the hypocrites, where there will be weeping and gnashing of teeth."

- So often Jesus uses extreme—even scary—examples of wicked behavior followed by dreadful punishment to communicate his point. Here he's counselling attentiveness, and it's always good to be reminded of the need to remain attentive.

- Often it is the hardest thing in the world to change just a little bit. But the rewards far outweigh the effort. Is there something small that you could take on now that might just change your whole mentality and, with it, your world?

Friday 31st August
Matthew 25:1–13

Jesus said to his disciples, "Then the kingdom of heaven will be like this. Ten bridesmaids took their lamps and went to meet the bridegroom. Five of them were foolish, and five were wise. When the foolish took their lamps, they took no oil with them; but the wise took flasks of oil with their lamps. As the bridegroom was delayed, all of them became drowsy and slept. But at midnight there was a shout, 'Look! Here is the bridegroom! Come out to meet him.' Then all those bridesmaids got up and trimmed their lamps. The foolish said to the wise, 'Give us some of your oil, for our lamps are going out.' But the wise replied, 'No! there will not be enough for you and for us; you had better go to the dealers and buy some for yourselves.' And while they went to buy it, the bridegroom came, and those who were ready went with him into the wedding banquet; and the door was shut. Later the other bridesmaids came also, saying, 'Lord, lord, open to us.' But he replied, 'Truly I tell you, I do not know you.' Keep awake therefore, for you know neither the day nor the hour."

- You can feel the disappointment of the foolish bridesmaids who were caught up in the present moment without thinking of the greater moment to come. You can also feel the sting of the matter-of-fact way the wise bridesmaids dismiss the foolish ones.

- What does Jesus mean that the kingdom of heaven will be like this? Does he mean that we need to be attentive and prepared? Prepared for what? For the moment when our energies can be applied to the right thing, at the right time? What can I do, here and now, to be prepared for the moment when Jesus will bring an opportunity my way?

Saturday 1st September
Matthew 25:14–30

Jesus said, "For it is as if a man, going on a journey, summoned his slaves and entrusted his property to them; to one he gave five talents, to another two, to another one, to each according to his ability. Then he went away. The one who had received the five talents went off at once and traded with them, and made five more talents. In the same way, the one who had the two talents made two more talents. But the one who had received the one talent went off and dug a hole in the ground and hid his master's money. After a long time the master of those slaves came and settled accounts with them. Then the one who had received the five talents came forward, bringing five more talents, saying, 'Master, you handed over to me five talents; see, I have made five more talents.' His master said to him, 'Well done, good and trustworthy slave; you have been trustworthy in a few things, I will put you in charge of many things; enter into the joy of your master.' And the one with the two talents also came forward, saying, 'Master, you handed over to me two talents; see, I have made two more talents.' His master said to him, 'Well done, good and trustworthy slave; you have been trustworthy in a few things, I will put you in charge of many things; enter into the joy of your master.' Then the one who had received the one talent also came forward, saying, 'Master, I knew that you were a harsh man, reaping where you did not sow, and gathering where you did not scatter seed; so I was afraid, and I went and hid your talent in the ground. Here you have what is yours.' But his master replied, 'You wicked and lazy slave! You knew, did you, that I reap where I did not sow, and gather where I did not scatter? Then you ought to have invested my money with the bankers, and on my return I would have received what was my own with interest. So take the talent from him, and give it to the one with the ten talents. For to all those who have, more will be given, and they will have an abundance; but from those who have nothing, even what they have will be taken away. As for this worthless slave, throw him into the outer darkness, where there will be weeping and gnashing of teeth.'"

- Focus first on all those servants who did a fine job for their master. Their reward? To enter the joy of their master. You can imagine all sorts of celebrations, gifts, a sense of fulfillment, and general happiness all around. A "talent" was a huge amount at the time, so the master was entrusting his servants with a great deal. He must have been delighted with their work. The opposite was true for the one who received only one talent. There's no reason to believe that the servant with one talent was a bad man; he only opted for security and not for risk. Which servant would I have been?

- As Pope Francis describes those who live a "tomb-psychology" in the church: "Let us not allow ourselves to be robbed of the joy of evangelization! Disillusioned with reality, with the Church, and with themselves, they experience a constant temptation to cling to a faint melancholy, lacking in hope, which seizes the heart like 'the most precious of the devil's potions.' Called to radiate light and communicate life, in the end they are caught up in things that generate only darkness and inner weariness, and slowly consume all zeal for the apostolate. For all this, I repeat: Let us not allow ourselves to be robbed of the joy of evangelization!"

The Twenty-Second Week of Ordinary Time
September 2—September 8

Something to think and pray about each day this week:

Love without Strings Attached

When we have no fear of losing that which cannot be taken away from us, *we become capable of actively seeking the good of others.* We usually want the best for our loved ones: spouses, parents, children, siblings, close friends. We see them—especially our family—as an extension of ourselves. But we do not have to confine our charitable attitudes to that inner circle. We need to expand that circle and love an ever-expanding population, until we have mastered the technique of seeing every human being as another self and loving them accordingly.

This doesn't mean that we have to develop feelings of affection for everyone we meet. Actively seeking the good of others is something that we can achieve with a sense of detachment. This kind of love is called "disinterested" love. It doesn't sound very loving to be disinterested, but that's not what the term means. Disinterested love is love that has no regard for oneself. Is it possible to love others without seeking to be loved in return? Yes, but only when one knows at the very core of his or her being, that he or she is already loved by God.

To love without strings attached is how God loves. It's the kind of love that we're referring to when we say that "God is love." This is a love that wants what is best for others based on the recognition that they, like us, are made in the image and likeness of God. This enables us to live according to the Golden Rule, doing unto others as we would have done unto ourselves, namely because others are "another self."

—Joe Paprocki, *7 Keys to Spiritual Wellness*

The Presence of God
Lord, help me to be fully alive to your holy presence. Enfold me in your love. Let my heart become one with yours.
My soul longs for your presence, Lord. When I turn my thoughts to You, I find peace and contentment.

Freedom
Your death on the cross has set me free. I can live joyously and freely without fear of death. Your mercy knows no bounds.

Consciousness
At this moment, Lord, I turn my thoughts to you.
I will leave aside my chores and preoccupations.
I will take rest and refreshment in your presence.

The Word
The word of God comes down to us through the Scriptures.
May the Holy Spirit enlighten my mind and my heart
to respond to the gospel teachings:
to love my neighbor as myself,
to care for my sisters and brothers in Christ.
(Please turn to the Scripture on the following pages. Inspiration points are there should you need them. When you are ready, return here to continue.)

Conversation
Begin to talk to Jesus about the Scripture you have just read. What part of it strikes a chord in you? Perhaps the words of a friend—or some story you have heard recently—will slowly rise to the surface of your consciousness. If so, does the story throw light on what the Scripture passage may be saying to you?

Conclusion
I thank God for these moments we have spent together and for any insights I have been given concerning the text.

Sunday 2nd September
Twenty-Second Sunday in Ordinary Time
Mark 7:1–8, 14–15, 21–23

Now when the Pharisees and some of the scribes who had come from Jerusalem gathered around him, they noticed that some of his disciples were eating with defiled hands, that is, without washing them. (For the Pharisees, and all the Jews, do not eat unless they thoroughly wash their hands, thus observing the tradition of the elders; and they do not eat anything from the market unless they wash it; and there are also many other traditions that they observe, the washing of cups, pots, and bronze kettles.) So the Pharisees and the scribes asked him, "Why do your disciples not live according to the tradition of the elders, but eat with defiled hands?" He said to them, "Isaiah prophesied rightly about you hypocrites, as it is written,

'This people honors me with their lips,
     but their hearts are far from me;
in vain do they worship me,
     teaching human precepts as doctrines.'

You abandon the commandment of God and hold to human tradition." // Then he called the crowd again and said to them, "Listen to me, all of you, and understand: there is nothing outside a person that by going in can defile, but the things that come out are what defile. . . . For it is from within, from the human heart, that evil intentions come: fornication, theft, murder, adultery, avarice, wickedness, deceit, licentiousness, envy, slander, pride, folly. All these evil things come from within, and they defile a person."

- Jesus often impresses upon us the need to act upon his word. It is not enough to honor him with our lips. One can argue with words, but deeds speak for themselves.

- Jesus' word is planted deep in me, and I pray, inspired by the message from the letter of the Apostle James: Let me be a doer of the word, and not a forgetful hearer. If I am a doer that acts, I shall be blessed in my doing.

Monday 3rd September
Luke 4:16–30

When he came to Nazareth, where he had been brought up, he went to the synagogue on the sabbath day, as was his custom. He stood up to read, and the scroll of the prophet Isaiah was given to him. He unrolled the scroll and found the place where it was written:

> "The Spirit of the Lord is upon me,
>> because he has anointed me
>>> to bring good news to the poor.
> He has sent me to proclaim release to the captives
>> and recovery of sight to the blind,
>>> to let the oppressed go free,
> to proclaim the year of the Lord's favor."

And he rolled up the scroll, gave it back to the attendant, and sat down. The eyes of all in the synagogue were fixed on him. Then he began to say to them, "Today this scripture has been fulfilled in your hearing." All spoke well of him and were amazed at the gracious words that came from his mouth. They said, "Is not this Joseph's son?" He said to them, "Doubtless you will quote to me this proverb, 'Doctor, cure yourself!' And you will say, 'Do here also in your hometown the things that we have heard you did at Capernaum.'" And he said, "Truly I tell you, no prophet is accepted in the prophet's hometown. But the truth is, there were many widows in Israel in the time of Elijah, when the heaven was shut up for three years and six months, and there was a severe famine over all the land; yet Elijah was sent to none of them except to a widow at Zarephath in Sidon. There were also many lepers in Israel in the time of the prophet Elisha, and none of them was cleansed except Naaman the Syrian." When they heard this, all in the synagogue were filled with rage. They got up, drove him out of the town, and led him to the brow of the hill on which their town was built, so that they might hurl him off the cliff. But he passed through the midst of them and went on his way.

• As he preached about inclusion, Jesus found himself excluded. His listeners were appalled at his message. Is there anyone in my community whom I fail to accept?

- Familiarity with Jesus left his listeners unimpressed. The Word of God made flesh was reading the word of God to them, and it fell upon deaf ears. Today, let me consciously look for the extraordinary among the ordinary.

Tuesday 4th September
Luke 4:31–37

Jesus went down to Capernaum, a city in Galilee, and was teaching them on the sabbath. They were astounded at his teaching, because he spoke with authority. In the synagogue there was a man who had the spirit of an unclean demon, and he cried out with a loud voice, "Let us alone! What have you to do with us, Jesus of Nazareth? Have you come to destroy us? I know who you are, the Holy One of God." But Jesus rebuked him, saying, "Be silent, and come out of him!" When the demon had thrown him down before them, he came out of him without having done him any harm. They were all amazed and kept saying to one another, "What kind of utterance is this? For with authority and power he commands the unclean spirits, and out they come!" And a report about him began to reach every place in the region.

- The man possessed claims to know who Jesus really is, "the Holy One of God." But Jesus deals with the evil spirit without delay. Is he ensuring that the wrong interpretation of him doesn't spread? His actions certainly leave people wondering.

- What is clear to all, whatever the evil spirits utter about him, is that Jesus has power and authority. They were impressed by how he intervened in these difficult cases. Can you think of a moment when, with speed and prudence, you intervened to put a situation right?

Wednesday 5th September
Luke 4:38–44

After leaving the synagogue he entered Simon's house. Now Simon's mother-in-law was suffering from a high fever, and they asked him about her. Then he stood over her and rebuked the fever, and it left her. Immediately she got up and began to serve them. As the sun was setting, all those who had any who were sick with various kinds of diseases brought them to him; and he laid his hands on each of them and cured them. Demons also came out of many, shouting, "You are the Son of God!" But he rebuked them and would not allow them to speak, because they knew that he was the Messiah. // At daybreak he departed and went into a deserted place. And the crowds were looking for him; and when they reached him, they wanted to prevent him from leaving them. But he said to them, "I must proclaim the good news of the kingdom of God to the other cities also; for I was sent for this purpose." So he continued proclaiming the message in the synagogues of Judea.

- Pope Francis challenges our tendency to see evangelization as a dangerous poison rather than a joyful response to God's love: "At a time when we most need a missionary dynamism which will bring salt and light to the world, many lay people fear that they may be asked to undertake some apostolic work and they seek to avoid any responsibility that may take away from their free time. For example, it has become very difficult today to find trained parish catechists willing to persevere in this work for some years" (Evangelii Gaudium #81).

- When I meditate on the word evangelization, how do I react? What has that word meant to me in the past. What would I like it to mean—and how would I like to experience it?

Thursday 6th September
Luke 5:1–11

Once while Jesus was standing beside the lake of Gennesaret, and the crowd was pressing in on him to hear the word of God, he saw two boats there at the shore of the lake; the fishermen had gone out of them and were washing their nets. He got into one of the boats, the one belonging to Simon, and asked him to put out a little way from the shore. Then he sat down and taught the crowds from the boat. When he had finished speaking, he said to Simon, "Put out into the deep water and let down your nets for a catch." Simon answered, "Master, we have worked all night long but have caught nothing. Yet if you say so, I will let down the nets." When they had done this, they caught so many fish that their nets were beginning to break. So they signaled to their partners in the other boat to come and help them. And they came and filled both boats, so that they began to sink. But when Simon Peter saw it, he fell down at Jesus' knees, saying, "Go away from me, Lord, for I am a sinful man!" For he and all who were with him were amazed at the catch of fish that they had taken; and so also were James and John, sons of Zebedee, who were partners with Simon. Then Jesus said to Simon, "Do not be afraid; from now on you will be catching people." When they had brought their boats to shore, they left everything and followed him.

- Peter knows better than Jesus. Are there occasions when I think that God should have arranged things differently? Can I speak to God about that now?

- "Do not be afraid." What do I fear at the moment? I calm my soul and speak to Jesus about these fears.

Friday 7th September
Luke 5:33–39

Then the Pharisees and the scribes said to Jesus, "John's disciples, like the disciples of the Pharisees, frequently fast and pray, but your disciples eat and drink." Jesus said to them, "You cannot make wedding guests fast while the bridegroom is with them, can you? The days will come when the bridegroom will be taken away from them, and then they will fast in those days." He also told them a parable: "No one tears a piece from a new garment and sews it on an old garment; otherwise the new will be torn, and the piece from the new will not match the old. And no one puts new wine into old wineskins; otherwise the new wine will burst the skins and will be spilled, and the skins will be destroyed. But new wine must be put into fresh wineskins. And no one after drinking old wine desires new wine, but says, 'The old is good.'"

- Many of us lament that the Jews and Christians, religious cousins, have had such a poor relationship with such dreadful consequences. The old wineskins of the Old Testament did not manage to accommodate the new wine of Jesus' message.

- How often do I pray for a reconciliation of the two faiths? Do I take steps to understand and work for greater harmony between them? Do I try to see the situation from the Jewish point of view? I spend some time to speak with Jesus about this.

Saturday 8th September
The Nativity of the Blessed Virgin Mary
Matthew 1:1–16, 18–23

An account of the genealogy of Jesus the Messiah, the son of David, the son of Abraham. // Abraham was the father of Isaac, and Isaac the father of Jacob, and Jacob the father of Judah and his brothers, and Judah the father of Perez and Zerah by Tamar, and Perez the father of Hezron, and Hezron the father of Aram, and Aram the father of Aminadab, and Aminadab the father of Nahshon, and Nahshon the father of Salmon, and Salmon the father of Boaz by Rahab, and Boaz the father of Obed by Ruth, and Obed the father of Jesse, and Jesse the father of King David. And David was the father of Solomon by the wife of Uriah. . . . Now the birth of Jesus the Messiah took place in this way. When his mother Mary had been engaged to Joseph, but before they lived together, she was found to be with child from the Holy Spirit. Her husband Joseph, being a righteous man and unwilling to expose her to public disgrace, planned to dismiss her quietly. But just when he had resolved to do this, an angel of the Lord appeared to him in a dream and said, "Joseph, son of David, do not be afraid to take Mary as your wife, for the child conceived in her is from the Holy Spirit. She will bear a son, and you are to name him Jesus, for he will save his people from their sins." All this took place to fulfill what had been spoken by the Lord through the prophet:

"Look, the virgin shall conceive and bear a son,
       and they shall name him Emmanuel,
   which means, 'God is with us.'"

- Emmanuel means "God is with us." This is the most consoling of statements. Often I am lonely and wish for company; I sometimes feel that there is no one around for me. Especially as I get older, I sense that I am on a lonely journey. But here is good news: God is with me! This is my salvation, that God is never far away.

- This message is repeated over and over in Scripture, so let me take it seriously, as Mary and the others did. Instead of running away from solitude when it comes, I can use it as an opportunity to be with my God. God is with me, so let me be with God!

The Twenty-Third Week of Ordinary Time
September 9—September 15

Something to think and pray about each day this week:

The Spiritual Value of Imagination

Imagination is often accused of being out of touch with reality. In reality, imagination is the capacity to see beyond reality to an alternate reality. Imagination is the key to navigating, deciphering, and transcending the reality that meets the eye so that we can recognize unseen reality. Imagination is not foolishness. Albert Einstein asserted that "imagination is more important than knowledge." When a young mother asked Einstein what she should read to her son so that he could grow up to be a brilliant thinker like him, he replied, "Fairy tales." When she asked what she should read him next, Einstein replied, "More fairy tales!" Einstein said, "When I examine myself and my methods of thought, I come to the conclusion that the gift of fantasy has meant more to me than any talent for abstract, positive thinking."

Imagination is at the heart of the gospel message. If any part of the gospel could be called Jesus' core message, it would be the Sermon on the Mount, a lengthy discourse brimming with imaginative concepts climaxed in the Beatitudes. It takes great imagination to recognize the blessings of being poor, of peacemaking, of being meek, of mourning, of hungering for justice, and of being persecuted for righteousness sake. It takes great imagination to turn the other cheek, to love your enemies, and to pray for those who persecute you. Jesus tells us that this is the reality of the kingdom of God—a reality that is in our midst, albeit unseen. By his very existence—his incarnation—Jesus transformed this unseen reality into a seen reality.

—Joe Paprock, *7 Keys to Spiritual Wellness*

The Presence of God

The more we call on God the more we can feel God's presence. Day by day we are drawn closer to the loving heart of God.

Freedom

I am free. When I look at these words in writing, they seem to create in me a feeling of awe. Yes, a wonderful feeling of freedom. Thank you, God.

Consciousness

Help me, Lord, become more conscious of your presence. Teach me to recognize your presence in others. Fill my heart with gratitude for the times your love has been shown to me through the care of others.

The Word

The word of God comes down to us through the Scriptures. May the Holy Spirit enlighten my mind and my heart to respond to the gospel teachings. (Please turn to the Scripture on the following pages. Inspiration points are there should you need them. When you are ready, return here to continue.)

Conversation

Conversation requires talking and listening.
As I talk to Jesus, may I also learn to pause and listen.
I picture the gentleness in his eyes and the love in his smile.
I can be totally honest with Jesus as I tell him my worries and cares.
I will open my heart to Jesus as I tell him my fears and doubts.
I will ask him to help me place myself fully in his care, knowing that he always desires good for me.

Conclusion

Glory be to the Father, and to the Son, and to the Holy Spirit,
As it was in the beginning, is now and ever shall be,
World without end. Amen.

Sunday 9th September
Twenty-Third Sunday in Ordinary Time
Mark 7:31–37

Then Jesus returned from the region of Tyre, and went by way of Sidon towards the Sea of Galilee, in the region of the Decapolis. They brought to him a deaf man who had an impediment in his speech; and they begged him to lay his hand on him. He took him aside in private, away from the crowd, and put his fingers into his ears, and he spat and touched his tongue. Then looking up to heaven, he sighed and said to him, "Ephphatha," that is, "Be opened." And immediately his ears were opened, his tongue was released, and he spoke plainly. Then Jesus ordered them to tell no one; but the more he ordered them, the more zealously they proclaimed it. They were astounded beyond measure, saying, "He has done everything well; he even makes the deaf to hear and the mute to speak."

- Jesus heals this man in private, whereas in other encounters his work is quite public. Why did he take this man aside? What needs did the man have that others may not have noticed? I pray to grow in my ability to be attentive to others, especially those I'm trying to help.

- "He has done everything well." This recalls the Genesis creation story, in which God does all things well. Now the new creation is dawning in Jesus, and I am one who is being restored. If this does not bring me joy, what will?

Monday 10th September
Luke 6:6–11

On another sabbath Jesus entered the synagogue and taught, and there was a man there whose right hand was withered. The scribes and the Pharisees watched him to see whether he would cure on the sabbath, so that they might find an accusation against him. Even though he knew what they were thinking, he said to the man who had the withered hand, "Come and stand here." He got up and stood there. Then Jesus said to them, "I ask you, is it lawful to do good or to do harm on the sabbath, to save life or to destroy it?" After looking around at all of them, he said to him, "Stretch out your hand." He did so, and his hand was restored.

But they were filled with fury and discussed with one another what they might do to Jesus.

- Jesus rebukes the scribes and the Pharisees for their narrow-mindedness and rigid approach to the rule of the law. Their practice of religion lacked compassion and love, key principles of the gospel message.

- What lesson do I draw from this incident? I ask the Lord to enlighten me about the Pharisees. What were their bad points? What good was in them?

Tuesday 11th September
Luke 6:12–19

Now during those days Jesus went out to the mountain to pray; and he spent the night in prayer to God. And when day came, he called his disciples and chose twelve of them, whom he also named apostles: Simon, whom he named Peter, and his brother Andrew, and James, and John, and Philip, and Bartholomew, and Matthew, and Thomas, and James son of Alphaeus, and Simon, who was called the Zealot, and Judas son of James, and Judas Iscariot, who became a traitor. // He came down with them and stood on a level place, with a great crowd of his disciples and a great multitude of people from all Judea, Jerusalem, and the coast of Tyre and Sidon. They had come to hear him and to be healed of their diseases; and those who were troubled with unclean spirits were cured. And all in the crowd were trying to touch him, for power came out from him and healed all of them.

- Jesus prayed all night to prepare for this momentous decision, choosing the twelve apostles. He then healed the great multitude of people who gathered from afar.

- In what way do I see myself as an apostle? What kind of healing do I need? In what ways can I touch Jesus?

Wednesday 12th September
Luke 6:20–26

Jesus looked up at his disciples and said:

> "Blessed are you who are poor,
>   for yours is the kingdom of God.

"Blessed are you who are hungry now,
　　for you will be filled.
"Blessed are you who weep now,
　　for you will laugh.

"Blessed are you when people hate you, and when they exclude you, revile you, and defame you on account of the Son of Man. Rejoice on that day and leap for joy, for surely your reward is great in heaven; for that is what their ancestors did to the prophets.

"But woe to you who are rich,
　　for you have received your consolation.
"Woe to you who are full now,
　　for you will be hungry.
"Woe to you who are laughing now,
　　for you will mourn and weep.

"Woe to you when all speak well of you, for that is what their ancestors did to the false prophets."

- I speak out to the Lord about my reaction to this passage. Does it mean that this world is no more than a waiting room for another and better one? Is it truly desirable not to have the good things of this time and place because these things make me less likely to seek what is eternal?

- Can I identify treasure that is eternal? Can I mourn the worldly riches I have, in that they tend to make me less sensitive to others' needs?

Thursday 13th September
Luke 6:27–38

"But I say to you that listen, Love your enemies, do good to those who hate you, bless those who curse you, pray for those who abuse you. If any-one strikes you on the cheek, offer the other also; and from anyone who takes away your coat do not withhold even your shirt. Give to everyone who begs from you; and if anyone takes away your goods, do not ask for them again. Do to others as you would have them do to you. // "If you love those who love you, what credit is that to you? For even sinners love those who love them. If you do good to those who do good to you, what credit is that to you? For even sinners do the same. If you lend to those from whom you hope to receive, what credit is that to you? Even sinners lend to sinners, to receive as much again. But love your enemies, do good, and lend, expecting nothing in return. Your reward will be great, and you will be children of the Most High; for he is kind to the ungrateful and the wicked. Be merciful, just as your Father is merciful. // "Do not judge, and you will not be judged; do not condemn, and you will not be condemned. Forgive, and you will be forgiven; give, and it will be given to you. A good measure, pressed down, shaken together, running over, will be put into your lap; for the measure you give will be the measure you get back."

- Jesus, again you turn our thinking upside down! Love of enemies is so contrary to human nature, but that is what you demand of us. But I am what you call a sinner because, when others offend me, I close my heart to them and punish them as best I can.

- You ask me now to bring my enemies into my heart and show mercy to them. Lord, change my heart or I will never become "a child of the Most High." Let me spend time pondering how merciful you are to me, even when I am ungrateful and wicked. That will make me pause before judging and condemning my enemies.

Friday 14th September
The Exaltation of the Holy Cross
John 3:13–17

"No one has ascended into heaven except the one who descended from heaven, the Son of Man. And just as Moses lifted up the serpent in the wilderness, so must the Son of Man be lifted up, that whoever believes in him may have eternal life. For God so loved the world that he gave his only Son, so that everyone who believes in him may not perish but may have eternal life. Indeed, God did not send the Son into the world to condemn the world, but in order that the world might be saved through him."

- In the cross of Christ is our freedom. In some way only God knows, this death brings us life. Have I thought about this lately? For a few moments now, I meditate on the wonder of this.

- The cross is the icon of great faith, hope, and love. As I gaze and contemplate Christ on the cross, I ask the Lord for his redemptive and healing love that embraces the whole world.

Saturday 15th September
Our Lady of Sorrows
John 19:25–27

Meanwhile, standing near the cross of Jesus were his mother, and his mother's sister, Mary the wife of Clopas, and Mary Magdalene. When Jesus saw his mother and the disciple whom he loved standing beside her, he said to his mother, "Woman, here is your son." Then he said to the disciple, "Here is your mother." And from that hour the disciple took her into his own home.

- Saint John is the only evangelist to depict Mary at the foot of the cross. He did this to make the theological point that she has a place of special importance beside the disciple "whom Jesus loved" at the cross and as a founder of the community of disciples that Jesus left.

- Mary is the first Christian who heard the word, accepted it, and followed it. Ask her to intercede for you in receiving that grace from her son.

The Twenty-Fourth Week of Ordinary Time
September 16—September 22

Something to think and pray about each day this week:

The Awareness Prayer

Practice an extended period of private prayer, reflection, meditation, pondering, percolating—whatever you want to call it. But do *something* on a regular basis to engage in a conscious dialogue with your inner self and with God. If every waking moment is crowded with input and stimulation, your soul's voice is being drowned out. You'll eventually begin to experience spiritual numbness . . . a blasé feeling. Without prayer, you run the risk of avoiding issues that may lead you to self-destructive thoughts, feelings, and behaviors. Not making time to pay attention to your soul each day is like driving around with God in the back seat of the car, but with the music turned on so loud that you can't hear a word he's saying.

One of the simplest ways of getting in touch with your soul on a daily basis is to practice the Daily Examen, a method of prayer that was taught by St. Ignatius of Loyola. (See one version of the Examen here.) By praying this way, you become more aware of how God has been present to you in the past and therefore, more attuned to how he is acting in the present. It's like turning down the volume on the car stereo and asking God, "I'm sorry, did you say something?" This practice does not typically result in some kind of ecstasy or ongoing feeling of euphoria. It simply puts us in touch with what our soul is pondering (often without our conscious awareness); thus, it enables us to avoid behaviors that bring only temporary relief from the gnawing itch at our core. The result is that our soul grows and we generally feel more alive.

—Joe Paprocki, *7 Keys to Spiritual Wellness*

The Presence of God
"Be still and know that I am God!" Lord, your words lead us to the calmness and greatness of your presence.

Freedom
"In these days, God taught me as a schoolteacher teaches a pupil" (Saint Ignatius). I remind myself that there are things God has to teach me yet, and I ask for the grace to hear them and let them change me.

Consciousness
How am I really feeling? Lighthearted? Heavyhearted? I may be very much at peace, happy to be here.
Equally, I may be frustrated, worried or angry.
I acknowledge how I really am. It is the real me whom the Lord loves.

The Word
God speaks to each of us individually. I listen attentively, to hear what he is saying to me. Read the text a few times, then listen. (Please turn to the Scripture on the following pages. Inspiration points are there should you need them. When you are ready, return here to continue.)

Conversation
Do I notice myself reacting as I pray with the word of God? Do I feel challenged, comforted, angry? Imagining Jesus sitting or standing by me, I speak out my feelings, as one trusted friend to another.

Conclusion
I thank God for these moments we have spent together and for any insights I have been given concerning the text.

Sunday 16th September
Twenty-Fourth Sunday in Ordinary Time
Mark 8:27–35

Jesus went on with his disciples to the villages of Caesarea Philippi; and on the way he asked his disciples, "Who do people say that I am?" And they answered him, "John the Baptist; and others, Elijah; and still others, one of the prophets." He asked them, "But who do you say that I am?" Peter answered him, "You are the Messiah." And he sternly ordered them not to tell anyone about him. // Then he began to teach them that the Son of Man must undergo great suffering, and be rejected by the elders, the chief priests, and the scribes, and be killed, and after three days rise again. He said all this quite openly. And Peter took him aside and began to rebuke him. But turning and looking at his disciples, he rebuked Peter and said, "Get behind me, Satan! For you are setting your mind not on divine things but on human things." // He called the crowd with his disciples, and said to them, "If any want to become my followers, let them deny themselves and take up their cross and follow me. For those who want to save their life will lose it, and those who lose their life for my sake, and for the sake of the gospel, will save it."

• This is a painful scene: first Peter rebukes Jesus, then Jesus rebukes Peter. We can sympathize with Peter, because which of us can bear the thought of our best friend being tortured and killed? But Jesus tells Peter that God's plans are so much bigger than he imagines.

• Someone has said that God's dreams come to us several sizes too large! It takes us time to grow into them. What about my inner growth; have I stopped growing at some point, so that God cannot do more creative work with me?

Monday 17th September
Luke 7:1–10

After Jesus had finished all his sayings in the hearing of the people, he entered Capernaum. A centurion there had a slave whom he valued highly, and who was ill and close to death. When he heard about Jesus, he sent some Jewish elders to him, asking him to come and heal his slave. When they came to Jesus, they appealed to him earnestly, saying, "He is worthy of having you do this for him, for he loves our people, and it is he who built our synagogue for us." And Jesus went with them, but when he was not far from the house, the centurion sent friends to say to him, "Lord, do not trouble yourself, for I am not worthy to have you come under my roof; therefore I did not presume to come to you. But only speak the word, and let my servant be healed. For I also am a man set under authority, with soldiers under me; and I say to one, 'Go,' and he goes, and to another, 'Come,' and he comes, and to my slave, 'Do this,' and the slave does it." When Jesus heard this he was amazed at him, and turning to the crowd that followed him, he said, "I tell you, not even in Israel have I found such faith." When those who had been sent returned to the house, they found the slave in good health.

• The centurion had the humility to know that Jesus was holy and he was not. But he had the faith to believe that Jesus could and would help him. Lord, please help these two qualities—humility and faith—grow in my life, side by side.

• What kind of faith had the centurion? We would like to have a strong trust in God that he will make all things well. Speak to the Lord about your trust, what strengthens it and what undermines it.

Tuesday 18th September
Luke 7:11–17

Soon afterwards Jesus went to a town called Nain, and his disciples and a large crowd went with him. As he approached the gate of the town, a man who had died was being carried out. He was his mother's only son, and she was a widow; and with her was a large crowd from the town. When the Lord saw her, he had compassion for her and said to her, "Do not weep." Then he came forward and touched the bier, and the bearers stood still. And he said, "Young man, I say to you, rise!" The dead man sat up and began to speak, and Jesus gave him to his mother. Fear seized all of them; and they glorified God, saying, "A great prophet has risen among us!" and "God has looked favorably on his people!" This word about him spread throughout Judea and all the surrounding country.

• How many mothers have hoped and prayed for something like this to happen! What do I pray for when I see a young mother walking behind the coffin of her son?

- I ask the Lord to help me appreciate the need to pray for what people need and not only for what they desire. The bereaved mother usually requires the grace to cope with the sadness and to face life with courage and trust in God.

Wednesday 19th September
Luke 7:31–35

Jesus said, "To what then will I compare the people of this generation, and what are they like? They are like children sitting in the marketplace and calling to one another,

> 'We played the flute for you, and you did not dance;
> we wailed, and you did not weep.'

For John the Baptist has come eating no bread and drinking no wine, and you say, 'He has a demon'; the Son of Man has come eating and drinking, and you say, 'Look, a glutton and a drunkard, a friend of tax-collectors and sinners!' Nevertheless, wisdom is vindicated by all her children."

- Jesus here is trying to shake us up! I can remain unmoved no matter what God does for me. Sometimes the pain of others does not move my heart. I can be hard to please; psychologists speak of people who live lives of "a thousand little disgusts"! Gratitude and praise for God's goodness can be weak and faltering in me.

- Jesus, pull me out of my numb state so that I can respond to your love in whatever form it comes.

Thursday 20th September
Luke 7:36–50

One of the Pharisees asked Jesus to eat with him, and he went into the Pharisee's house and took his place at the table. And a woman in the city, who was a sinner, having learned that he was eating in the Pharisee's house, brought an alabaster jar of ointment. She stood behind him at his feet, weeping, and began to bathe his feet with her tears and to dry them with her hair. Then she continued kissing his feet and anointing them with the ointment. Now when the Pharisee who had invited him saw it, he said to himself, "If this man were a prophet, he would have known who and what kind of woman this is who is touching him—that she is a sinner." Jesus spoke up and said to him, "Simon, I have something to say to you." "Teacher," he replied, "speak." "A certain creditor had two debtors; one owed five hundred denarii, and the other fifty. When they could not pay, he cancelled the debts for both of them. Now which of them will love him more?" Simon answered, "I suppose the one for whom he cancelled the greater debt." And Jesus said to him, "You have judged rightly." Then turning towards the woman, he said to Simon, "Do you see this woman? I entered your house; you gave me no water for my feet, but she has bathed my feet with her tears and dried them with her hair. You gave me no kiss, but from the time I came in she has not stopped kissing my feet. You did not anoint my head with oil, but she has anointed my feet with ointment. Therefore, I tell you, her sins, which were many, have been forgiven; hence she has shown great love. But the one to whom little is forgiven, loves little." Then he said to her, "Your sins are forgiven." But those who were at the table with him began to say among themselves, "Who is this who even forgives sins?" And he said to the woman, "Your faith has saved you; go in peace."

- Here we see how God's mercy really verges on the scandalous; we need to look at it at length to be able to penetrate its depths.

- What would my reaction have been if I had been the Pharisee or one of the other guests? Would I have been scandalized by the woman's behavior and by Jesus' reaction? Or can I imagine myself as the woman herself, unable to control my gratitude?

Friday 21st September
Matthew 9:9–13

As Jesus was walking along, he saw a man called Matthew sitting at the tax booth; and he said to him, "Follow me." And he got up and followed him. And as he sat at dinner in the house, many tax collectors and sinners came and were sitting with him and his disciples. When the Pharisees saw this, they said to his disciples, "Why does your teacher eat with tax collectors and sinners?" But when he heard this, he said, "Those who are well have no need of a physician, but those who are sick. Go and learn what this means, 'I desire mercy, not sacrifice.' For I have come to call not the righteous but sinners."

- "Go and learn what this means, 'I desire mercy, not sacrifice.'" Jesus does not let the Pharisees off the hook. He is quoting an Old Testament Scripture that they should know well. But they have forgotten it—or allowed other values to push it aside.

- I can learn, and I can change. Jesus expected the Pharisees to go back and study what they had neglected. He was not asking the impossible. Lord, may I cultivate a heart that wants to learn your ways.

Saturday 22nd September
Luke 8:4–15

When a great crowd gathered and people from town after town came to him, he said in a parable: "A sower went out to sow his seed; and as he sowed, some fell on the path and was trampled on, and the birds of the air ate it up. Some fell on the rock; and as it grew up, it withered for lack of moisture. Some fell among thorns, and the thorns grew with it and choked it. Some fell into good soil, and when it grew, it produced a hundredfold." As he said this, he called out, "Let anyone with ears to hear listen!" // Then his disciples asked him what this parable meant. He said, "To you it has been given to know the secrets of the kingdom of God; but to others I speak in parables, so that

> 'looking they may not perceive,
>   and listening they may not understand.'

"Now the parable is this: The seed is the word of God. The ones on the path are those who have heard; then the devil comes and takes away the word from their hearts, so that they may not believe and be saved. The ones on the rock are those who, when they hear the word, receive it with joy. But these have no root; they believe only for a while and in a time of testing fall away. As for what fell among the thorns, these are the ones who hear; but as they go on their way, they are choked by the cares and riches and pleasures of life, and their fruit does not mature. But as for that in the good soil, these are the ones who, when they hear the word, hold it fast in an honest and good heart, and bear fruit with patient endurance."

- Here we have a parable and its interpretation. The interpretation is probably from the early church. The seed of faith comes to us in varying circumstances, and its fate depends in part on what our disposition to it is.

- At the moment, what steps am I taking to see that the faith I have is flourishing like a seed in good soil? Are there thorns choking it? If so, what are these thorns?

The Twenty-Fifth Week of Ordinary Time
September 23—September 29

Something to think and pray about each day this week:

Finding God's Fire

Since spiritual wellness is all about being aligned with the Spirit, we should ask, What is God fired up about? I think he is most fired up by selfless love. Mercy. Compassion. Justice. God's great imagination envisions a world in which the hungry are fed, the thirsty are given drink, the sick are tended to, the homeless are sheltered, the imprisoned are visited, the naked are clothed, and the estranged are welcomed. A healthy spirituality compels us to be present to people in need, offering them the possibility of seeing the presence of God, which is obstructed by the pain in their lives. Dorothy Day insisted that everything a baptized person should do every day should be directly or indirectly related to the corporal and spiritual works of mercy. She knew that God's fire could be found there. If you are looking for God—the goal of spirituality—these are the places to look. As the traditional Christian hymn *Ubi Caritas* reminds us: "Where charity and love prevail, there God is ever found."

The God we seek is on fire, has a mission, and invites you and me to be a part of it.

Imagine that.

—Joe Paprocki, *7 Keys to Spiritual Wellness*

The Presence of God

To be present is to arrive as one is and open up to the other.
At this instant, as I arrive here, God is present waiting for me.
God always arrives before me, desiring to connect with me
even more than my most intimate friend.
I take a moment and greet my loving God.

Freedom

Leave me here / freely all alone In cell where never sunlight shone / Should
no one ever speak to me. / This golden silence makes me free!

> —Part of a poem by Bl. Titus Brandsma, written while he was a
> prisoner at Dachau concentration camp

Consciousness

Where am I with God? With others?
Do I have something to be grateful for? Then I give thanks.
Is there something I am sorry for? Then I ask forgiveness.

The Word

I take my time to read the word of God slowly, a few times, allowing myself to dwell on anything that strikes me. (Please turn to the Scripture on the following pages. Inspiration points are there should you need them. When you are ready, return here to continue.)

Conversation

How has God's word moved me? Has it left me cold?
Has it consoled me or moved me to act in a new way?
I imagine Jesus standing or sitting beside me;
I turn and share my feelings with him.

Conclusion

Glory be to the Father, and to the Son, and to the Holy Spirit,
As it was in the beginning, is now and ever shall be,
World without end. Amen.

Sunday 23rd September
Twenty-Fifth Sunday in Ordinary Time
Mark 9:30–37

They went on from there and passed through Galilee. Jesus did not want anyone to know it; for he was teaching his disciples, saying to them, "The Son of Man is to be betrayed into human hands, and they will kill him, and three days after being killed, he will rise again." But they did not understand what he was saying and were afraid to ask him. // Then they came to Capernaum; and when he was in the house he asked them, "What were you arguing about on the way?" But they were silent, for on the way they had argued with one another who was the greatest. He sat down, called the twelve, and said to them, "Whoever wants to be first must be last of all and servant of all." Then he took a little child and put it among them; and taking it in his arms, he said to them, "Whoever welcomes one such child in my name welcomes me, and whoever welcomes me welcomes not me but the one who sent me."

- It's odd that, after Jesus reveals that he will be killed, his disciples break into argument over who is the greatest. What was that about? Were they simply avoiding the topic of Jesus' death? Or were they already wondering who might take his place? Clearly, they were still thinking that God's kingdom had something like a worldly structure.

- Rather than a kingdom of hierarchy and power plays, God's kingdom thrives on kindness, openness, humility, and hearts that do not hunger for power but would rather sit with a child. What qualities show up in my life? When am I most likely to slide into a worldview in which honor and influence mean more to me than attentiveness and kindness?

Monday 24th September
Luke 8:16–18

Jesus said to his disciples, "No one after lighting a lamp hides it under a jar, or puts it under a bed, but puts it on a lampstand, so that those who enter may see the light. For nothing is hidden that will not be disclosed, nor is anything secret that will not become known and come to light. Then pay attention to how you listen; for to those who have, more will be given; and from those who do not have, even what they seem to have will be taken away."

- Commentators have struggled to interpret this short passage. What do you make of it? In what way do you make it part of your prayer?
- Are you conscious of your call to be a light for others, an inviting light to lead them to Christ? What is your reaction to being given that task? Ask the Lord to help you to see and accept that role.

Tuesday 25th September
Luke 8:19–21

Then Jesus' mother and his brothers came to him, but they could not reach him because of the crowd. And he was told, "Your mother and your brothers are standing outside, wanting to see you." But he said to them, "My mother and my brothers are those who hear the word of God and do it."

- It is worth comparing this passage with the parallel passages in Matthew and particularly in Mark. Here, the family of the Lord is praised, but in Mark they are sidelined. The attitude toward Mary and the family of Jesus developed during the New Testament period; the family of the Lord gains its distinction from hearing the word of God and doing it.
- Ask the Lord to help you see the ways you may best hear his word and do it and ways to sharpen your hearing and develop your keenness to follow him.

Wednesday 26th September
Luke 9:1–6

Then Jesus called the twelve together and gave them power and authority over all demons and to cure diseases, and he sent them out to proclaim the kingdom of God and to heal. He said to them, "Take nothing for your journey, no staff, nor bag, nor bread, nor money—not even an extra tunic. Whatever house you enter, stay there, and leave from there. Wherever they do not welcome you, as you are leaving that town shake the dust off your feet as a testimony against them." They departed and went through the villages, bringing the good news and curing diseases everywhere.

- "Take nothing for your journey!" Pope Francis dreams of a poor church for the poor. Like the disciples in the Gospel scene, the church today must depend on God, not on property, power, or prestige. The only riches that matter are the riches of the good news.

- Today's disciples need to be focused solely on God; only then will the power of God's grace be free to work through us unrestrictedly. In this way, we will bring good news to a world that has lost its way, and we will cure its diseases everywhere.

Thursday 27th September
Luke 9:7–9

Now Herod the ruler heard about all that had taken place, and he was perplexed, because it was said by some that John had been raised from the dead, by some that Elijah had appeared, and by others that one of the ancient prophets had arisen. Herod said, "John I beheaded; but who is this about whom I hear such things?" And he tried to see him.

- Herod was a Jew, but he benefited in his role as king. That is, he was the one Rome allowed to sit as ruler of the Jewish population. He beheaded John the Baptist, which is a sign that Herod was more focused on keeping his position than he was interested in a spiritual quest.
- How do you react to Herod's perplexity? Let it stimulate you to ask the fundamental question, "Who is Jesus for me?"

Friday 28th September
Luke 9:18–22

Once when Jesus was praying alone, with only the disciples near him, he asked them, "Who do the crowds say that I am?" They answered, "John the Baptist; but others, Elijah; and still others, that one of the ancient prophets has arisen." He said to them, "But who do you say that I am?" Peter answered, "The Messiah of God." He sternly ordered and commanded them not to tell anyone, saying, "The Son of Man must undergo great suffering, and be rejected by the elders, chief priests, and scribes, and be killed, and on the third day be raised."

- This passage explicitly brings up the fundamental question: who is Jesus for me? And it asks that question not in a merely intellectual sense but in a personal one. Is he a leader, a friend, a judge, a teacher, a father, or a combination of all?

- Pray about this, asking the Lord to clarify your sense of Jesus and to strengthen your commitment to him.

Saturday 29th September
John 1:47–51

When Jesus saw Nathanael coming towards him, he said of him, "Here is truly an Israelite in whom there is no deceit!" Nathanael asked him, "Where did you come to know me?" Jesus answered, "I saw you under the fig tree before Philip called you." Nathanael replied, "Rabbi, you are the Son of God! You are the King of Israel!" Jesus answered, "Do you believe because I told you that I saw you under the fig tree? You will see greater things than these." And he said to him, "Very truly, I tell you, you will see heaven opened and the angels of God ascending and descending upon the Son of Man."

- Jesus witnessed some aspect of Nathanael that seemed to surprise him; there are also hidden and secret aspects of my life that are known and valued by God.

- Jesus lifts Nathanael's eyes from the everyday and prompts him to think of heaven. I might consider my hoped-for destination and see how my daily concerns are enlightened and brought into another perspective.

The Twenty-Sixth Week of Ordinary Time
September 30—October 6

Something to think and pray about each day this week:

Prayers or Demands?

What if God's answer to one of our prayers is "no"? We **are** given this answer at times. Sometimes when we are told "no" we easily accept the answer we are given, because what we are asking for is something that really did not matter that much. Occasionally, though, we find ourselves being told "no" when every part of our being wants the answer to be "yes." What happens to our relationship with God then? Does our relationship with God completely fall apart? Does our entire relationship with God depend on God answering our prayers?

We are invited into a relationship with God that trusts that our prayers are heard yet does not demand our prayers be answered. We are invited into a relationship of confidence that God can answer our prayers, yet at the same time, we are invited into a relationship that asks us for complete surrender to God's way. The relationship we are invited into with God is not an insurance policy that guarantees we get what we want. However, we are promised that God hears us and will be with us every step of the way.

—Becky Eldredge on *dotMagis*, the blog of *IgnatianSpirituality.com*
http://www.ignatianspirituality.com/14524/what-if-the-answer-is-no

The Presence of God
What is present to me is what has a hold on my becoming.
I reflect on the presence of God always there in love,
amidst the many things that have a hold on me.
I pause and pray that I may let God
affect my becoming in this precise moment.

Freedom
By God's grace I was born to live in freedom. Free to enjoy the pleasures
he created for me. Dear Lord, grant that I may live as you intended, with
complete confidence in your loving care.

Consciousness
To be conscious about something is to be aware of it.
Dear Lord, help me to remember that you gave me life.
Thank you for the gift of life.
Teach me to slow down, to be still and enjoy the pleasures created for me.
To be aware of the beauty that surrounds me: the marvel of mountains,
the calmness of lakes, the fragility of a flower petal. I need to remember
that all these things come from you.

The Word
God speaks to each of us individually. I listen attentively, to hear what he
is saying to me. Read the text a few times, then listen. (Please turn to the
Scripture on the following pages. Inspiration points are there should you
need them. When you are ready, return here to continue.)

Conversation
I begin to talk with Jesus about the Scripture I have just read. What part
of it strikes a chord in me? Perhaps the words of a friend—or some story
I have heard recently—will rise to the surface in my consciousness. If so,
does the story throw light on what the Scripture passage may be saying
to me?

Conclusion
Glory be to the Father, and to the Son, and to the Holy Spirit,
As it was in the beginning, is now and ever shall be,
World without end. Amen.

Sunday 30th September
Twenty-Sixth Sunday in Ordinary Time
Mark 9:38–43, 45, 47–48

John said to him, "Teacher, we saw someone casting out demons in your name, and we tried to stop him, because he was not following us." But Jesus said, "Do not stop him; for no one who does a deed of power in my name will be able soon afterwards to speak evil of me. Whoever is not against us is for us. For truly I tell you, whoever gives you a cup of water to drink because you bear the name of Christ will by no means lose the reward. // If any of you put a stumbling block before one of these little ones who believe in me, it would be better for you if a great millstone were hung around your neck and you were thrown into the sea. If your hand causes you to stumble, cut it off; it is better for you to enter life maimed than to have two hands and to go to hell, to the unquenchable fire. And if your foot causes you to stumble, cut it off; it is better for you to enter life lame than to have two feet and to be thrown into hell. And if your eye causes you to stumble, tear it out; it is better for you to enter the kingdom of God with one eye than to have two eyes and to be thrown into hell, where their worm never dies, and the fire is never quenched."

- The followers of Jesus are not meant to be an exclusive group that despises the good work others do. We are encouraged to work with other Christians, and indeed with anyone of good will. The old slogan, "Outside the Church there is no salvation" was a stumbling block to many good people, and now it must be left aside.

- Boasting has no place in the kingdom of God. The Holy Spirit blows like the wind wherever it pleases and is at work incognito in every heart. God has a large imagination and labors to orchestrate all things for the world's good. What stirrings of the Holy Spirit do I sense today?

Monday 1st October
Luke 9:46–50

An argument arose among them as to which one of them was the greatest. But Jesus, aware of their inner thoughts, took a little child and put it by his side, and said to them, "Whoever welcomes this child in my name welcomes me, and whoever welcomes me welcomes the one who sent me; for the least among all of you is the greatest." John answered, "Master, we saw someone casting out demons in your name, and we tried to stop him, because he does not follow with us." But Jesus said to him, "Do not stop him; for whoever is not against you is for you."

- This is a strange argument to have just after the Lord had told his followers that he was going to be betrayed. It shows that his disciples had not grasped his words, the truth of which would become perfectly clear at the time of his passion.

- Try to remember when you have entertained thoughts that were completely contrary to the message of Jesus. How did you cope? Ask the Lord to help you see when this tends to happen and to give you the power to reject such thoughts.

Tuesday 2nd October
Matthew 18:1–5, 10

At that time the disciples came to Jesus and asked, "Who is the greatest in the kingdom of heaven?" He called a child, whom he put among them, and said, "Truly I tell you, unless you change and become like children, you will never enter the kingdom of heaven. Whoever becomes humble like this child is the greatest in the kingdom of heaven. Whoever welcomes one such child in my name welcomes me. Take care that you do not despise one of these little ones; for, I tell you, in heaven their angels continually see the face of my Father in heaven."

- Jesus cares for us individually through our guardian angel. Do I believe that I am personally cared for by God? To believe this is a great gift of faith. We are asked to trust God like little children, whose nature is to trust.

- I can thank God for his care, observing the signs of it in my life, and ask him to help me develop a deeper relationship with him.

Wednesday 3rd October
Luke 9:57–62

As they were going along the road, someone said to Jesus, "I will follow you wherever you go." And Jesus said to him, "Foxes have holes, and birds of the air have nests; but the Son of Man has nowhere to lay his head." To another he said, "Follow me." But he said, "Lord, first let me go and bury my father." But Jesus said to him, "Let the dead bury their own dead; but as for you, go and proclaim the kingdom of God." Another said, "I will follow you, Lord; but let me first say farewell to those at my home." Jesus said to him, "No one who puts a hand to the plow and looks back is fit for the kingdom of God."

- This is an example of the Hebrew way of teaching by exaggeration. Jesus was making a strong point about commitment, not telling people to neglect their families.

- Is there a sense in which you could say to yourself that "having put your hand to the plow, you looked back"? What were the consequences? If you have never done this, what are the issues that might tempt you to do so? Speak to the Lord about these.

Thursday 4th October
Luke 10:1–12

After this the Lord appointed seventy others and sent them on ahead of him in pairs to every town and place where he himself intended to go. He said to them, "The harvest is plentiful, but the laborers are few; therefore ask the Lord of the harvest to send out laborers into his harvest. Go on your way. See, I am sending you out like lambs into the midst of wolves. Carry no purse, no bag, no sandals; and greet no one on the road. Whatever house you enter, first say, 'Peace to this house!' And if anyone is there who shares in peace, your peace will rest on that person; but if not, it will return to you. Remain in the same house, eating and drinking whatever they provide, for the laborer deserves to be paid. Do not move about from house to house. Whenever you enter a town and its people welcome you, eat what is set before you; cure the sick who are there, and say to them, 'The kingdom of God has come near to you.' But whenever you enter a town and they do not welcome you, go out into its streets and say, 'Even the dust of your town that clings to our feet, we wipe off in protest against you. Yet know this: the kingdom of God has come near.' I tell you, on that day it will be more tolerable for Sodom than for that town."

- What an awesome responsibility and privilege the Lord has bestowed on me, together with others, to carry the message of God's love and mercy to the world. I ask him therefore to give me the wisdom, courage, and strength to carry on his ministry.

- Today is the feast day of Saint Francis of Assisi. We find him appealing because he was capable of embodying the gospel spirit. On his feast day I ask him to help me be more Christ-like. I also pray for Pope Francis, who so often asks for our prayers.

Friday 5th October
Luke 10:13–16

Jesus said to his disciples, "Woe to you, Chorazin! Woe to you, Bethsaida! For if the deeds of power done in you had been done in Tyre and Sidon, they would have repented long ago, sitting in sackcloth and ashes. But at the judgment it will be more tolerable for Tyre and Sidon than for you. And you, Capernaum,

> will you be exalted to heaven?
> No, you will be brought down to Hades.

"Whoever listens to you listens to me, and whoever rejects you rejects me, and whoever rejects me rejects the one who sent me."

- These are some of the "hard sayings" of Jesus in which he warns of retribution to those who do not listen to those sent by Jesus. He especially singles out those who were privileged to observe his deeds. We have been privileged and have benefitted from the examples of martyrs and saints and the solid social structure of the church which supports our faith.
- Ask the Lord to deepen your appreciation of the faith and the supports that the church community affords us.

Saturday 6th October
Luke 10:17–24

The seventy returned with joy, saying, "Lord, in your name even the demons submit to us!" He said to them, "I watched Satan fall from heaven like a flash of lightning. See, I have given you authority to tread on snakes and scorpions, and over all the power of the enemy; and nothing will hurt you. Nevertheless, do not rejoice at this, that the spirits submit to you, but rejoice that your names are written in heaven." // At that same hour Jesus rejoiced in the Holy Spirit and said, "I thank you, Father, Lord of heaven and earth, because you have hidden these things from the wise and the intelligent and have revealed them to infants; yes, Father, for such was your gracious will. All things have been handed over to me by my Father; and no one knows who the Son is except the Father, or who the Father is except the Son and anyone to whom the Son chooses to reveal him." // Then turning to the disciples, Jesus said to them privately, "Blessed are the eyes that see what you see! For I tell you that many prophets and kings desired to see what you see, but did not see it, and to hear what you hear, but did not hear it."

- Religion can give rise to all sorts of false manifestations or mistaken priorities. Jesus warns his close friends to be careful of what to look for in religious belonging—not the external feel-good factors but the quality of our relationship with God.

- Jesus seems unable to contain his happiness at the Father's showing himself to the little ones. I ask to be counted among these, not among those who consider themselves wise and intelligent. I pray to be able to do this with the same freedom of spirit that Jesus had, free from all hint of cynicism or moral superiority.

The Twenty-Seventh Week of Ordinary Time
October 7—October 13

Something to think and pray about each day this week:

Prepared for Prayer

The life founded on prayer must also involve preparation and knowledge of the short- and long-term demands. Many people similarly approach the idea of prayer with romantic notions and good intentions but find the realities of their lives squelching their enthusiasm. I doubt that any endeavor exempts us from having to make choices; prayer, like anything else, means prioritizing. There are hundreds of ways we can spend our time, and so if we are to devote time to prayer, then we must be prepared for what it involves. More than that, though, we must have a sense that what we are doing is worthwhile. It is difficult to remain committed to anything that seems like a waste of time. In the short run, this means trusting those who are already used to doing the activity. Novice athletes trust their coaches and their peers who have been in training for some time, using them as models for where they eventually want to be. Christians trust Jesus and the saints, who are similarly models to follow in their single-minded pursuit of holiness. We need saints—not just those historical figures revered by the church but also those ordinary people in our lives who quietly testify to the work of God in our midst.

—Tim Muldoon, *The Ignatian Workout*

The Presence of God
"Be still and know that I am God!" Lord, your words lead us to the calmness and greatness of your presence.

Freedom
Everything has the potential to draw forth from me a fuller love and life. Yet my desires are often fixed, caught, on illusions of fulfillment. I ask that God, through my Freedom, may orchestrate my desires in a vibrant loving melody rich in harmony.

Consciousness
I exist in a web of relationships: links to nature, people, God.
I trace out these links, giving thanks for the life that flows through them.
Some links are twisted or broken; I may feel regret, anger, disappointment.
I pray for the gift of acceptance and forgiveness.

The Word
I read the word of God slowly, a few times over, and I listen to what God is saying to me. (Please turn to the Scripture on the following pages. Inspiration points are there should you need them. When you are ready, return here to continue.)

Conversation
Jesus, you speak to me through the words of the Gospels. May I respond to your call today. Teach me to recognize your hand at work in my daily living.

Conclusion
I thank God for these moments we have spent together and for any insights I have been given concerning the text.

Sunday 7th October
Twenty-Seventh Sunday in Ordinary Time
Mark 10:2–16

Some Pharisees came, and to test him they asked, "Is it lawful for a man to divorce his wife?" He answered them, "What did Moses command you?" They said, "Moses allowed a man to write a certificate of dismissal and to divorce her." But Jesus said to them, "Because of your hardness of heart he wrote this commandment for you. But from the beginning of creation, 'God made them male and female.' 'For this reason a man shall leave his father and mother and be joined to his wife, and the two shall become one flesh.' So they are no longer two, but one flesh. Therefore what God has joined together, let no one separate." // Then in the house the disciples asked him again about this matter. He said to them, "Whoever divorces his wife and marries another commits adultery against her; and if she divorces her husband and marries another, she commits adultery." // People were bringing little children to him in order that he might touch them; and the disciples spoke sternly to them. But when Jesus saw this, he was indignant and said to them, "Let the little children come to me; do not stop them; for it is to such as these that the kingdom of God belongs. Truly I tell you, whoever does not receive the kingdom of God as a little child will never enter it." And he took them up in his arms, laid his hands on them, and blessed them.

- The unity and love of a happy marriage is a gift from God. Unfortunately, many married people, for various reasons, have been unable to live this gift fully. As in other areas, our inability to live the ideal gives us much reason to turn to the grace and healing of Jesus.

- I can pray today for all married couples. May the compassion of Christ touch all those who are experiencing or have experienced difficulty in marriage.

Monday 8th October
Luke 10:25–37

Just then a lawyer stood up to test Jesus. "Teacher," he said, "what must I do to inherit eternal life?" He said to him, "What is written in the law? What do you read there?" He answered, "You shall love the Lord your God with all your heart, and with all your soul, and with all your strength, and with all your mind; and your neighbor as yourself." And he said to him, "You have given the right answer; do this, and you will live." // But wanting to justify himself, he asked Jesus, "And who is my neighbor?" // Jesus replied, "A man was going down from Jerusalem to Jericho, and fell into the hands of robbers, who stripped him, beat him, and went away, leaving him half dead. Now by chance a priest was going down that road; and when he saw him, he passed by on the other side. So likewise a Levite, when he came to the place and saw him, passed by on the other side. But a Samaritan while travelling came near him; and when he saw him, he was moved with pity. He went to him and bandaged his wounds, having poured oil and wine on them. Then he put him on his own animal, brought him to an inn, and took care of him. The next day he took out two denarii, gave them to the innkeeper, and said, 'Take care of him; and when I come back, I will repay you whatever more you spend.' Which of these three, do you think, was a neighbor to the man who fell into the hands of the robbers?" He said, "The one who showed him mercy." Jesus said to him, "Go and do likewise."

- Who is my neighbor? This is a fundamental question that each of us must answer. I dwell on this question, and as I struggle to answer it, I ask Jesus to help me answer it as a true disciple of his.

- I also listen to his advice, to go and do likewise, using mercy with my neighbor in real life. As I look at the faces of those who inhabit my days, I ask for the grace of an open and merciful heart similar to the Father's.

Tuesday 9th October
Luke 10:38–42

Now as they went on their way, Jesus entered a certain village, where a woman named Martha welcomed him into her home. She had a sister named Mary, who sat at the Lord's feet and listened to what he was saying. But Martha was distracted by her many tasks; so she came to him and asked, "Lord, do you not care that my sister has left me to do all the work by myself? Tell her then to help me." But the Lord answered her, "Martha, Martha, you are worried and distracted by many things; there is need of only one thing. Mary has chosen the better part, which will not be taken away from her."

- Jesus may seem to be preferring contemplation to action, praising Mary and criticizing Martha. Yet, he cannot be telling us to be content with sitting down to listen to his word, for he always insists that true listening to his word means putting it into practice. His objection to Martha is that she is too worried and distracted by many things to be able to listen to him. Do I merit the same reproach? I ask for a pure heart, focused on what will not be taken away.

- If Jesus were to say my name twice—lovingly, yet firmly—what do I imagine him saying to me?

Wednesday 10th October
Luke 11:1–4

Jesus was praying in a certain place, and after he had finished, one of his disciples said to him, "Lord, teach us to pray, as John taught his disciples." He said to them, "When you pray, say:

Father, hallowed be your name.
　　Your kingdom come.
　　Give us each day our daily bread.
　　And forgive us our sins,
　　　　for we ourselves forgive everyone indebted to us.
　　And do not bring us to the time of trial."

- "Teach us how to pray." This is certainly a prayer that is never refused. So I make it my own today, while thanking God for all that he has taught me already.

- It is Jesus himself who is teaching me to pray through these words. I pray the Our Father slowly, word by word, letting each word echo in my heart as it evokes what is deepest in me to rise in prayer to the Father.

Thursday 11th October
Luke 11:5–13

And he said to them, "Suppose one of you has a friend, and you go to him at midnight and say to him, 'Friend, lend me three loaves of bread; for a friend of mine has arrived, and I have nothing to set before him.' And he answers from within, 'Do not bother me; the door has already been locked, and my children are with me in bed; I cannot get up and give you anything.' I tell you, even though he will not get up and give him anything because he is his friend, at least because of his persistence he will get up and give him whatever he needs. "So I say to you, Ask, and it will be given you; search, and you will find; knock, and the door will be opened for you. For everyone who asks receives, and everyone who searches finds, and for everyone who knocks, the door will be opened. Is there anyone among you who, if your child asks for a fish, will give a snake instead of a fish? Or if the child asks for an egg, will give a scorpion? If you then, who are evil, know how to give good gifts to your children, how much more will the heavenly Father give the Holy Spirit to those who ask him!"

- Do I believe that prayer "works"? I recall those instances in which my persistence in prayer paid off. I ask myself if this persistence was just hard-headedness or if it helped me become more open to God's love and care for me and my loved ones. I ask Jesus now to teach me to pray better.

- I pray for childlike trust in God and his love for me. I pray for the ability to trust him when my prayers are not answered, and I ask for the comfort and wisdom of his Holy Spirit.

Friday 12th October
Luke 11:15–26

But some of them said, "He casts out demons by Beelzebul, the ruler of the demons." Others, to test him, kept demanding from him a sign from heaven. But he knew what they were thinking and said to them, "Every kingdom divided against itself becomes a desert, and house falls on house. If Satan also is divided against himself, how will his kingdom stand?—for you say that I cast out the demons by Beelzebul. Now if I cast out the demons by Beelzebul, by whom do your exorcists cast them out? Therefore they will be your judges. But if it is by the finger of God that I cast out the demons, then the kingdom of God has come to you. When a strong man, fully armed, guards his castle, his property is safe. But when one stronger than he attacks him and overpowers him, he takes away his armor in which he trusted and divides his plunder. Whoever is not with me is against me, and whoever does not gather with me scatters.

// "When the unclean spirit has gone out of a person, it wanders through waterless regions looking for a resting place, but not finding any, it says, 'I will return to my house from which I came.' When it comes, it finds it swept and put in order. Then it goes and brings seven other spirits more evil than itself, and they enter and live there; and the last state of that person is worse than the first."

- "The kingdom of God has come to you." I note the sense of urgency in these words, the pressing invitation to take sides and commit myself fully to God's kingdom.

- Like the opponents of Jesus, instead of accepting that his actions and presence often are mysterious, we sometimes say incredibly stupid things about God. I bow in adoration before his saving presence in our complex and violent world.

Saturday 13th October
Luke 11:27–28

While Jesus was speaking, a woman in the crowd raised her voice and said to him, "Blessed is the womb that bore you and the breasts that nursed you!" But he said, "Blessed rather are those who hear the word of God and obey it!"

- I join this woman in her praise of the mother of Jesus, the woman who brought him up, taught him how to relate to others, educated his heart to become so compassionate, and was the first one to talk to him about God and prayer. I remember that she is also my mother.

- I wonder at the power of Jesus' reply. Mary's greatness comes from her openness and obedience to God's word. I ask her to help me be like her in this.

The Twenty-Eighth Week of Ordinary Time
October 14—October 20

Something to think and pray about each day this week:

Prayer That Pervades

People unaccustomed to regular prayer need to be encouraged that the practice is worthwhile, even though, on many occasions, it isn't particularly fun. The examples of Jesus and the saints remind us that seeking God's will always is the source of their joy, even in the midst of terrible suffering. These people show us single-minded devotion to prayer and how the things they do with their lives arise from prayer. For them, prayer is the very lifeblood of their souls; it is what nourishes them to face difficulty and maintain trust in God's ultimate care for them. Prayer pervades every aspect of their lives; their lives become prayer.

Over time, the practices that command our greatest care eventually become the essence of our lives, and prayer is no different. Jesus' life was a constant testament to God; but even Jesus withdrew in important cases to be alone with God. Seeing God in all things can enable us, like Jesus, to make any part of our lives a prayer. But also like Jesus, we must make time for when we must be alone with God.

—Tim Muldoon, *The Ignatian Workout*

The Presence of God
"Come to me, all you who are weary and are carrying heavy burdens, and I will give you rest." Here I am, Lord. I come to seek your presence. I long for your healing power.

Freedom
God is not foreign to my freedom. The Spirit breathes life into my most intimate desires, gently nudging me toward all that is good. I ask for the grace to let myself be enfolded by the Spirit.

Consciousness
I remind myself that I am in the presence of the Lord. I will take refuge in his loving heart. He is my strength in times of weakness. He is my comforter in times of sorrow.

The Word
I take my time to read the word of God slowly, a few times, allowing myself to dwell on anything that strikes me. (Please turn to the Scripture on the following pages. Inspiration points are there should you need them. When you are ready, return here to continue.)

Conversation
Jesus, you always welcomed little children when you walked on this earth. Teach me to have a childlike trust in you. Teach me to live in the knowledge that you will never abandon me.

Conclusion
Glory be to the Father, and to the Son, and to the Holy Spirit,
As it was in the beginning, is now and ever shall be,
World without end. Amen.

Sunday 14th October
Twenty-Eighth Sunday in Ordinary Time
Mark 10:17–30

As he was setting out on a journey, a man ran up and knelt before him, and asked him, "Good Teacher, what must I do to inherit eternal life?" Jesus said to him, "Why do you call me good? No one is good but God alone. You know the commandments: 'You shall not murder; You shall not commit adultery; You shall not steal; You shall not bear false witness; You shall not defraud; Honor your father and mother.'" He said to him, "Teacher, I have kept all these since my youth." Jesus, looking at him, loved him and said, "You lack one thing; go, sell what you own, and give the money to the poor, and you will have treasure in heaven; then come, follow me." When he heard this, he was shocked and went away grieving, for he had many possessions. // Then Jesus looked around and said to his disciples, "How hard it will be for those who have wealth to enter the kingdom of God!" And the disciples were perplexed at these words. But Jesus said to them again, "Children, how hard it is to enter the kingdom of God! It is easier for a camel to go through the eye of a needle than for someone who is rich to enter the kingdom of God." They were greatly astounded and said to one another, "Then who can be saved?" Jesus looked at them and said, "For mortals it is impossible, but not for God; for God all things are possible." // Peter began to say to him, "Look, we have left everything and followed you." Jesus said, "Truly I tell you, there is no one who has left house or brothers or sisters or mother or father or children or fields, for my sake and for the sake of the good news, who will not receive a hundredfold now in this age—houses, brothers and sisters, mothers and children, and fields, with persecutions—and in the age to come eternal life."

- Today we are reminded of the difficulty that comes from being too attached to things and forgetting that true fulfillment comes from the love of God and the love of others. It is a great blessing to be free enough to use things for the purpose of loving. Without God, this kind of loving is impossible. I ask him for his help.

- What are my honest struggles in following Jesus? What do I fear he will ask me to give up? What do I cling to, unsure that grace will be enough? I pray now for the grace to trust with open hands.

Monday 15th October
Luke 11:29–32

When the crowds were increasing, Jesus began to say, "This generation is an evil generation; it asks for a sign, but no sign will be given to it except the sign of Jonah. For just as Jonah became a sign to the people of Nineveh, so the Son of Man will be to this generation. The queen of the South will rise at the judgment with the people of this generation and condemn them, because she came from the ends of the earth to listen to the wisdom of Solomon, and see, something greater than Solomon is here! The people of Nineveh will rise up at the judgment with this generation and condemn it, because they repented at the proclamation of Jonah, and see, something greater than Jonah is here!"

- We all ask for signs from time to time, for we think they will give us greater certainty in what we believe. Apparitions, miracles, and other sensational events seem to be important not only for the contemporaries of Jesus but also for us. Yet Jesus insists that the real sign is his own person; in him God has become a human being, and whoever sees him sees the Father. Looking for other signs will not get us anywhere.

- Today is the feast day of Saint Teresa of Ávila, who reminds me why I must carry on Jesus' ministry to the world: "Christ has no body on earth but yours; no hands but yours; no feet but yours. Yours are the eyes through which the compassion of Christ looks out to the world. Yours are the feet with which he is to go about doing good. Yours are the hands with which he is to bless others now." How do I respond to this saint's words today?

Tuesday 16th October
Luke 11:37–41

While Jesus was speaking, a Pharisee invited him to dine with him; so he went in and took his place at the table. The Pharisee was amazed to see that he did not first wash before dinner. Then the Lord said to him, "Now you Pharisees clean the outside of the cup and of the dish, but inside you are full of greed and wickedness. You fools! Did not the one who made the outside make the inside also? So give for alms those things that are within; and see, everything will be clean for you."

- There is a Pharisee in all of us, big or small, who prefers cleaning the outside of the cup to tackling the greed and wickedness inside. The only way to deal with this conflict is to make the prayer of the publican in the temple my own: "Have pity on me, a sinner."

- Jesus sees a link between almsgiving and purification of the heart. Elsewhere he insists that true almsgiving must be sincere and not done to elicit the admiration of others; it is not what we give but why and how we give it. How do I react to those who ask for my material help? What does my reaction to the current migrant crisis tell me about the state of my heart? I pray for real freedom to love those in need.

Wednesday 17th October
Luke 11:42–46

"But woe to you Pharisees! For you tithe mint and rue and herbs of all kinds, and neglect justice and the love of God; it is these you ought to have practiced, without neglecting the others. Woe to you Pharisees! For you love to have the seat of honor in the synagogues and to be greeted with respect in the marketplaces. Woe to you! For you are like unmarked graves, and people walk over them without realizing it." // One of the lawyers answered him, "Teacher, when you say these things, you insult us too." And he said, "Woe also to you lawyers! For you load people with burdens hard to bear, and you yourselves do not lift a finger to ease them."

- Once again, I let myself be impressed by the harshness of Jesus' words to the Pharisees. He must have found it very difficult to stomach religious hypocrisy, especially when it came from the leaders—those entrusted with the care of God's people.

- He accuses lawyers of imposing heavy burdens on people and then not helping them carry them. I pray for the church, for my religious leaders, and for my religious community not to be guilty of such behavior. May we be a sign of compassion and solidarity in a world where so many people carry heavy burdens.

Thursday 18th October
Luke 10:1–9

After this the Lord appointed seventy others and sent them on ahead of him in pairs to every town and place where he himself intended to go. He said to them, "The harvest is plentiful, but the laborers are few; therefore ask the Lord of the harvest to send out laborers into his harvest. Go on your way. See, I am sending you out like lambs into the midst of wolves. Carry no purse, no bag, no sandals; and greet no one on the road. Whatever house you enter, first say, 'Peace to this house!' And if anyone is there who shares in peace, your peace will rest on that person; but if not, it will return to you. Remain in the same house, eating and drinking whatever they provide, for the laborer deserves to be paid. Do not move about from house to house. Whenever you enter a town and its people welcome you, eat what is set before you; cure the sick who are there, and say to them, 'The kingdom of God has come near to you.'"

• On today, the feast day of Saint Luke, I pray in deep gratitude for him and the other evangelists. It is through them that I, and millions of others, can get to know Jesus and choose to follow him.

• I ask for the grace to be ready and willing to spread the joy of the gospel wherever I am, relying above all on the power Jesus gives me to carry out the mission. I ask to be one of the laborers sent out to the abundant harvest.

Friday 19th October
Luke 12:1–7

Meanwhile, when the crowd gathered by the thousands, so that they trampled on one another, Jesus began to speak first to his disciples, "Beware of the yeast of the Pharisees, that is, their hypocrisy. Nothing is covered up that will not be uncovered, and nothing secret that will not become known. Therefore whatever you have said in the dark will be heard in the light, and what you have whispered behind closed doors will be proclaimed from the housetops. I tell you, my friends, do not fear those who kill the body, and after that can do nothing more. But I will warn you whom to fear: fear him who, after he has killed, has authority to cast into hell. Yes, I tell you, fear him! Are not five sparrows sold for two pennies? Yet not one of them is forgotten in God's sight. But even the hairs of your head are all counted. Do not be afraid; you are of more value than many sparrows."

- "Do not be afraid; you are of more value than many sparrows." I let the gentle force of these words enter my heart and inspire me with God's provident care for me personally. I remain in wonder and gratitude.

- Jesus once again warns us of hypocrisy, this time comparing it to the yeast which, though small in quantity, can wreak great damage to my life and that of others. Very often I am not aware of my own hypocrisy, so I ask for the grace of light in my heart.

Saturday 20th October
Luke 12:8–12

Jesus said to the disciples, "And I tell you, everyone who acknowledges me before others, the Son of Man also will acknowledge before the angels of God; but whoever denies me before others will be denied before the angels of God. And everyone who speaks a word against the Son of Man will be forgiven; but whoever blasphemes against the Holy Spirit will not be forgiven. When they bring you before the synagogues, the rulers, and the authorities, do not worry about how you are to defend yourselves or what you are to say; for the Holy Spirit will teach you at that very hour what you ought to say."

- Sometimes I find myself unwilling to acknowledge Jesus before others. I am afraid or embarrassed, or I simply don't know what to say. I ask Jesus for the grace to be his witness before others and to believe in his promise that the Holy Spirit will teach me what to say every time.

- What does it mean to blaspheme against the Holy Spirit? These words of Jesus are confusing and disturbing to me, so I take them to him in prayer.

The Twenty-Ninth Week of Ordinary Time
October 21—October 27

Something to think and pray about each day this week:

Unprayed-for Answers

A friend of mine is one of those people who is always cheerful and positive even though it seems as though she encounters more than her fair share of rotten luck in her life. As a result of all of her lousy luck, she has some pretty interesting stories to share. My favorite is the story of the night she woke up to two police officers standing at the foot of her bed in her home as she slept. By some odd set of circumstances, the front door of her house had been left wide open late at night. Her neighbor worried about her and her family and called the police, who immediately went to the house and searched every room prior to waking my friend to tell her everything was OK (and to please, lock her door next time). I think I would have had a heart attack to wake up to two police officers standing over my bed in the middle of the night! Indeed, God was watching out for my friend that night and sent help in the form of a concerned neighbor and the policemen.

Sometimes Jesus sends help when we don't even realize we need it. I'm reminded that sometimes our prayers are answered before we ever pray them. Recently I heard someone speaking of "unanswered prayers," and it occurred to me that while we seem to notice those a lot (or at least what we may perceive to be unanswered prayers), we sometimes miss the "un-prayed-for answers."

—Cara Callbeck on *dotMagis*, the blog of *IgnatianSpirituality.com*
http://www.ignatianspirituality.com/18773/un-prayed-for-answers

The Presence of God

"I am standing at the door, knocking" says the Lord. What a wonderful privilege that the Lord of all creation desires to come to me. I welcome his presence.

Freedom

I will ask God's help
to be free from my own preoccupations,
to be open to God in this time of prayer,
to come to know, love, and serve God more.

Consciousness

In God's loving presence I unwind the past day,
starting from now and looking back, moment by moment.
I gather in all the goodness and light, in gratitude.
I attend to the shadows and what they say to me,
seeking healing, courage, forgiveness.

The Word

Now I turn to the Scripture set out for me this day. I read slowly over the words and see if any sentence or sentiment appeals to me. (Please turn to the Scripture on the following pages. Inspiration points are there should you need them. When you are ready, return here to continue.)

Conversation

Sometimes I wonder what I might say if I were to meet you in person, Lord.
I think I might say "Thank you" because you are always there for me.

Conclusion

I thank God for these moments we have spent together and for any insights I have been given concerning the text.

Sunday 21st October
Twenty-Ninth Sunday in Ordinary Time
Mark 10:35–45

James and John, the sons of Zebedee, came forward to him and said to him, "Teacher, we want you to do for us whatever we ask of you." And he said to them, "What is it you want me to do for you?" And they said to him, "Grant us to sit, one at your right hand and one at your left, in your glory." But Jesus said to them, "You do not know what you are asking. Are you able to drink the cup that I drink, or be baptized with the baptism that I am baptized with?" They replied, "We are able." Then Jesus said to them, "The cup that I drink you will drink; and with the baptism with which I am baptized, you will be baptized; but to sit at my right hand or at my left is not mine to grant, but it is for those for whom it has been prepared." // When the ten heard this, they began to be angry with James and John. So Jesus called them and said to them, "You know that among the Gentiles those whom they recognize as their rulers lord it over them, and their great ones are tyrants over them. But it is not so among you; but whoever wishes to become great among you must be your servant, and whoever wishes to be first among you must be slave of all. For the Son of Man came not to be served but to serve, and to give his life a ransom for many."

- The request of the apostles brings to light our natural desires to be approved of and rewarded in worldly terms. Jesus tells us his definition of real greatness: service to and care of others.

- How do I experience Jesus serving me? Do I allow myself to think of Jesus as my servant and what that means? Today I spend time with this thought. I invite the Holy Spirit to remind me of when Jesus' servant-hood has touched my life.

Monday 22nd October
Luke 12:13–21

Someone in the crowd said to Jesus, "Teacher, tell my brother to divide the family inheritance with me." But he said to him, "Friend, who set me to be a judge or arbitrator over you?" And he said to them, "Take care! Be on your guard against all kinds of greed; for one's life does not consist in the abundance of possessions." Then he told them a parable: "The land of a rich man produced abundantly. And he thought to himself, 'What should I do, for I have no place to store my crops?' Then he said, 'I will do this: I will pull down my barns and build larger ones, and there I will store all my grain and my goods. And I will say to my soul, Soul, you have ample goods laid up for many years; relax, eat, drink, be merry.' But God said to him, 'You fool! This very night your life is being demanded of you. And the things you have prepared, whose will they be?' So it is with those who store up treasures for themselves but are not rich toward God."

- "Be on your guard against all kinds of greed." So much in our world seems to be motivated by greed, so that if I am not on my guard, I too will let greed influence my decisions. I look at my life's motivations in the light of God's word.

- "You fool." I ask for true wisdom to see what is important and lasting in my life and for the courage to choose it over what is transient and temporary.

Tuesday 23rd October
Luke 12:35–38

Jesus said to his disciples, "Be dressed for action and have your lamps lit; be like those who are waiting for their master to return from the wedding banquet, so that they may open the door for him as soon as he comes and knocks. Blessed are those slaves whom the master finds alert when he comes; truly I tell you, he will fasten his belt and have them sit down to eat, and he will come and serve them. If he comes during the middle of the night, or near dawn, and finds them so, blessed are those slaves."

- When we are fully involved in anything, our attention is complete. At other times, we tend to put things off. It's a great gift to be alert to the fact that we have come from God and are going back to God. This helps put our whole life into a proper perspective. Closeness to Jesus is what keeps this awareness alive.

- What can I do, Lord, to be more prepared for your presence in my life? I want to participate with you in the work you do in the world. Some days, I am not prepared, but I want to work on that.

Wednesday 24th October
Luke 12:39–48

Jesus said, "But know this: if the owner of the house had known at what hour the thief was coming, he would not have let his house be broken into. You also must be ready, for the Son of Man is coming at an unexpected hour." // Peter said, "Lord, are you telling this parable for us or for everyone?" And the Lord said, "Who then is the faithful and prudent manager whom his master will put in charge of his slaves, to give them their allowance of food at the proper time? Blessed is that slave whom his master will find at work when he arrives. Truly I tell you, he will put that one in charge of all his possessions. But if that slave says to himself, 'My master is delayed in coming,' and if he begins to beat the other slaves, men and women, and to eat and drink and get drunk, the master of that slave will come on a day when he does not expect him and at an hour that he does not know, and will cut him in pieces, and put him with the unfaithful. That slave who knew what his master wanted, but did not prepare himself or do what was wanted, will receive a severe beating. But one who did not know and did what deserved a beating will receive a light beating. From everyone to whom much has been given, much will be required; and from one to whom much has been entrusted, even more will be demanded."

- Jesus never tells us to be afraid of his coming, for he comes to save us. But he does insist that we be watchful so that we won't be caught unawares or unprepared. I do that by living the present moment as fully as I can, trying to be as aware as I can of the presence of God in every moment of my life.

- I pray for the grace to be aware of all my gifts and of the responsibility they bring with them. I ask that this become a source of joy and gratitude for me, and never a burden.

Thursday 25th October
Luke 12:49–53

Jesus said to the crowds, "I came to bring fire to the earth, and how I wish it were already kindled! I have a baptism with which to be baptized, and what stress I am under until it is completed! Do you think that I have come to bring peace to the earth? No, I tell you, but rather division! From now on five in one household will be divided, three against two and two against three; they will be divided:

> father against son
>> and son against father,
> mother against daughter
>> and daughter against mother,
> mother-in-law against her daughter-in-law
>> and daughter-in-law against mother-in-law."

- So often Christians look like a discouraged group with little passion in their lives for what they believe in. Yet we have chosen to follow someone who came to bring fire on earth and who is passionate about kindling it.

- Living my faith passionately will certainly involve me in conflict, even at the deepest levels of my life and relationships. I ask for freedom and wisdom to be able to deal well with such conflicts.

Friday 26th October
Luke 12:54–59

Jesus also said to the crowds, "When you see a cloud rising in the west, you immediately say, 'It is going to rain'; and so it happens. And when you see the south wind blowing, you say, 'There will be scorching heat'; and it happens. You hypocrites! You know how to interpret the appearance of earth and sky, but why do you not know how to interpret the present time? // "And why do you not judge for yourselves what is right? Thus, when you go with your accuser before a magistrate, on the way make an effort to settle the case, or you may be dragged before the judge, and the judge hand you over to the officer, and the officer throw you in prison. I tell you, you will never get out until you have paid the very last penny."

- We seem to be living in a world that is very flat, a world that finds it next to impossible to think beyond the pragmatic and the immediate. Jesus challenges us to "interpret the present time" and behave wisely.

- To read the spiritual signs of the times requires spiritual depth and awareness. This comes from conversation with God. It develops in meditative silence and in moments when we meditate on Scripture or contemplate God's presence in daily life. I pray to be faithful to the spiritual practices that can prepare me for true wisdom.

Saturday 27th October
Luke 13:1–9

At that very time there were some present who told him about the Galileans whose blood Pilate had mingled with their sacrifices. He asked them, "Do you think that because these Galileans suffered in this way they were worse sinners than all other Galileans? No, I tell you; but unless you repent, you will all perish as they did. Or those eighteen who were killed when the tower of Siloam fell on them—do you think that they were worse offenders than all the others living in Jerusalem? No, I tell you; but unless you repent, you will all perish just as they did." // Then he told this parable: "A man had a fig tree planted in his vineyard; and he came looking for fruit on it and found none. So he said to the gardener, 'See here! For three years I have come looking for fruit on this fig tree, and still I find none. Cut it down! Why should it be wasting the soil?' He replied, 'Sir, let it alone for one more year, until I dig round it and put manure on it. If it bears fruit next year, well and good; but if not, you can cut it down.'"

- The gardener is confident that if he makes another effort the fig tree can bear fruit, despite appearances. I too can be involved in what looks like an impossible situation with someone close to me, in my own family, or in the work place. I pray to be as merciful as the gardener in this parable was.

- Saint John Paul II was a massive presence in the church and in the world for more than a quarter of a century. I thank God for what I know I have received through this great pope. I pray to God for Pope Francis and ask him to send us holy and wise leaders.

The Thirtieth Week of Ordinary Time
October 28—November 3

Something to think and pray about each day this week:

The Saints We Were Meant to Be

Believing that all of us are called to be saints has profound implications for daily life. An acceptance of what the Second Vatican Council termed the "universal call to holiness" imbues even the most hidden moments of one's life with a special grace.

The universal call to holiness is an invitation to be ourselves. It's also an invitation to remember the sacramentality of everyday life and to realize the great goal that God has set for us: sanctity. It is what the saints came to realize, sometimes in an instant, sometimes over the course of many years, whether they were born in first-century Palestine, thirteenth-century France, or twentieth-century America. Whether they lived in a quiet cloistered monastery in Lisieux, in a lonely desert tent in Morocco, or in the grand papal palace in the Vatican. Whether they worked alongside the poorest of the poor in Calcutta, with the plague victims in Rome, or with the gentiles of Asia Minor. Whether they succumbed to illness early in life, were martyred in middle age, or died after a long life of perfect health.

The call to sanctity is an invitation to friendship with God. It is a call that transformed the lives of the saints into gifts to the One who loved them into being. The invitation to holiness is a lifelong call to draw closer to God, who wants nothing more than to encounter us as the people we are and the saints we are meant to be.

—James Martin, SJ, *My Life with the Saints 10th Anniversary Edition*

The Presence of God

"Be still and know that I am God!" Lord, your words lead us to the calmness and greatness of your presence.

Freedom

If God were trying to tell me something, would I know?
If God were reassuring me or challenging me, would I notice?
I ask for the grace to be free of my own preoccupations
and open to what God may be saying to me.

Consciousness

In the presence of my loving Creator, I look honestly at my feelings over the past day: the highs, the lows, and the level ground. Can I see where the Lord has been present?

The Word

In this expectant state of mind, please turn to the text for the day with confidence. Believe that the Holy Spirit is present and may reveal whatever the passage has to say to you. Read reflectively, listening with a third ear to what may be going on in your heart. (Please turn to the Scripture on the following pages. Inspiration points are there should you need them. When you are ready, return here to continue.)

Conversation

Remembering that I am still in God's presence,
I imagine Jesus standing or sitting beside me,
and I say whatever is on my mind, whatever is in my heart,
speaking as one friend to another.

Conclusion

Glory be to the Father, and to the Son, and to the Holy Spirit,
As it was in the beginning, is now and ever shall be,
World without end. Amen.

Sunday 28th October
Thirtieth Sunday in Ordinary Time
Mark 10:46–52

They came to Jericho. As he and his disciples and a large crowd were leaving Jericho, Bartimaeus son of Timaeus, a blind beggar, was sitting by the roadside. When he heard that it was Jesus of Nazareth, he began to shout out and say, "Jesus, Son of David, have mercy on me!" Many sternly ordered him to be quiet, but he cried out even more loudly, "Son of David, have mercy on me!" Jesus stood still and said, "Call him here." And they called the blind man, saying to him, "Take heart; get up, he is calling you." So throwing off his cloak, he sprang up and came to Jesus. Then Jesus said to him, "What do you want me to do for you?" The blind man said to him, "My teacher, let me see again." Jesus said to him, "Go; your faith has made you well." Immediately he regained his sight and followed him on the way.

- Theologian Michel de Verteuil has a wonderful prayer in connection with this story: "Lord, there are many people sitting at the side of the road, shouting to us to have pity on them, but they often shout in strange ways: by behaving badly in the classroom; by taking drugs and alcohol; by sulking, remaining silent or locked up in their rooms; sometimes by insisting that they are happy to be at the side of the road while others pass by. Lord, like Jesus, we need to stop all that we are doing so that we can hear them express their deep longing to have their sight restored to them."

- I imagine Jesus saying about me, "Call her here! Call him here!" and then saying, "What do you want me to do for you?" How would I answer?

Monday 29th October
Luke 13:10–17

Now Jesus was teaching in one of the synagogues on the sabbath. And just then there appeared a woman with a spirit that had crippled her for eighteen years. She was bent over and was quite unable to stand up straight. When Jesus saw her, he called her over and said, "Woman, you are set free from your ailment." When he laid his hands on her, immediately she stood up straight and began praising God. But the leader of the synagogue, indignant because Jesus had cured on the sabbath, kept saying to the crowd, "There are six days on which work ought to be done; come on those days and be cured, and not on the sabbath day." But the Lord answered him and said, "You hypocrites! Does not each of you on the sabbath untie his ox or his donkey from the manger, and lead it away to give it water? And ought not this woman, a daughter of Abraham whom Satan bound for eighteen long years, be set free from this bondage on the sabbath day?" When he said this, all his opponents were put to shame; and the entire crowd was rejoicing at all the wonderful things that he was doing.

• For Jesus, mercy and compassion are paramount, trumping all other considerations. This is certainly a challenging position. I imagine myself present in the synagogue, and I observe my spontaneous reaction during the argument between Jesus and the head of the synagogue. I ask for a heart that is like the heart of Jesus, always compassionate and ready to defend the poor and suffering.

• I wonder at how easily religion can become a source of hard-heartedness rather than Christ-like mercy. I ask for light to be aware of my prejudices and of the rationalizations that justify them.

Tuesday 30th October
Luke 13:18–21

Jesus said therefore, "What is the kingdom of God like? And to what should I compare it? It is like a mustard seed that someone took and sowed in the garden; it grew and became a tree, and the birds of the air made nests in its branches." // And again he said, "To what should I compare the kingdom of God? It is like yeast that a woman took and mixed in with three measures of flour until all of it was leavened."

• Jesus was so optimistic when he spoke of the kingdom! For him, even a small beginning was sufficient, for he was convinced that the kingdom of God generates power and dynamism. As I look around my world, I ask myself if I share this conviction or if I find myself acting like a prophet of doom and gloom.

• The yeast can change the dough only if it is integrated with it. Engagement and presence seem to be what matter to Jesus. I pray for a church and a Christian community that is totally engaged with and in the world, like yeast in dough.

Wednesday 31st October
Luke 13:22–30

Jesus went through one town and village after another, teaching as he made his way to Jerusalem. Someone asked him, "Lord, will only a few be saved?" He said to them, "Strive to enter through the narrow door; for many, I tell you, will try to enter and will not be able. When once the owner of the house has got up and shut the door, and you begin to stand outside and to knock at the door, saying, 'Lord, open to us,' then in reply he will say to you, 'I do not know where you come from.' Then you will begin to say, 'We ate and drank with you, and you taught in our streets.' But he will say, 'I do not know where you come from; go away from me, all you evildoers!' There will be weeping and gnashing of teeth when you see Abraham and Isaac and Jacob and all the prophets in the kingdom of God, and you yourselves thrown out. Then people will come from east and west, from north and south, and will eat in the kingdom of God. Indeed, some are last who will be first, and some are first who will be last."

- Unlike Jesus, we are sometimes too concerned about numbers, as if they were the most important sign of the presence of God's kingdom and of its power to save the world. Jesus asks us to concentrate on entering through the narrow door. This phrase has given rise to all sorts of negative spiritualities, but what Jesus is saying is to take up the cross and follow him every day of our lives. It is the cross that will bring us joy and everlasting life.

- He also foretells that we will be surprised by those who enter and those who don't. However hard we try, we find ourselves excluding persons or groups from salvation. Jesus invites us to be wary of judging others and to believe that all can be open to God's loving offer of salvation.

Thursday 1st November
All Saints
Matthew 5:1–12a

When Jesus saw the crowds, he went up the mountain; and after he sat down, his disciples came to him. Then he began to speak, and taught them, saying:

"Blessed are the poor in spirit, for theirs is the kingdom of heaven.
"Blessed are those who mourn, for they will be comforted.
"Blessed are the meek, for they will inherit the earth.
"Blessed are those who hunger and thirst for righteousness, for they will be filled.
"Blessed are the merciful, for they will receive mercy.
"Blessed are the pure in heart, for they will see God.
"Blessed are the peacemakers, for they will be called children of God.
"Blessed are those who are persecuted for righteousness' sake, for theirs is the kingdom of heaven.
"Blessed are you when people revile you and persecute you and utter all kinds of evil against you falsely on my account. Rejoice and be glad, for your reward is great in heaven, for in the same way they persecuted the prophets who were before you."

- These verses from Scripture are called the Beatitudes. To live or be with these attitudes is a gift from God, and they are a summary of the full Christian life. The life of Jesus is the fulfillment of all of them.

- Pick out scenes in Jesus' life in which he demonstrates the Beatitudes in his approach to interacting with others. When have you felt a special resonance with one of the Beatitudes?

Friday 2nd November
The Commemoration of All the Faithful Departed (All Souls' Day)
John 6:37–40

"Everything that the Father gives me will come to me, and anyone who comes to me I will never drive away; for I have come down from heaven, not to do my own will, but the will of him who sent me. And this is the will of him who sent me, that I should lose nothing of all that he has given me, but raise it up on the last day. This is indeed the will of my Father, that all who see the Son and believe in him may have eternal life; and I will raise them up on the last day."

- For Christians, the dead are not gone from our lives forever; they continue to exist and to be part of our community. Some are enjoying the fullness of life with Christ in heaven; others are awaiting that enjoyment in a state that Catholics call purgatory. We pray today that their wait may be short-lived.

- This Gospel reading can underpin our prayer. It offers us Christ's assurance that he will raise us all up on the last day because that is the will of his Father. What phrase from this reading speaks to you most powerfully?

Saturday 3rd November
Luke 14:1, 7–11

On one occasion when Jesus was going to the house of a leader of the Pharisees to eat a meal on the sabbath, they were watching him closely. When he noticed how the guests chose the places of honor, he told them a parable. "When you are invited by someone to a wedding banquet, do not sit down at the place of honor, in case someone more distinguished than you has been invited by your host; and the host who invited both of you may come and say to you, 'Give this person your place,' and then in disgrace you would start to take the lowest place. But when you are invited, go and sit down at the lowest place, so that when your host comes, he may say to you, 'Friend, move up higher'; then you will be honored in the presence of all who sit at the table with you. For all who exalt themselves will be humbled, and those who humble themselves will be exalted."

- We are often surprised and even shocked at the lengths people go to for the sake of receiving honor. In our efforts to be acknowledged, we can end up humiliating ourselves. The desire for honor is a powerful, deep-seated force, and we need God's help to be free of it.

- Saint Ignatius suggests that we ask insistently for the grace to be able to make the same choices Jesus made: to ask to be like him in refusing honors and to choose to be humble and even humiliated, as he was. I ask for the freedom to accept humiliations calmly and gracefully when they come.

The Thirty-First Week of Ordinary Time
November 4—November 10

Something to think and pray about each day this week:

A Sense of God's Promise

The meadow exploded with life. It felt as if I were biking through a science experiment. Fat grasshoppers jumped among the daisies and black-eyed Susans, bees hummed above the Queen Anne's lace, little brown crickets sang underneath pale blue thistles, and cardinals and robins darted from branch to branch. The air was fresh, and the field sang the words of creation.

One warm spring morning, I stopped to catch my breath in the middle of the field. I must have been ten or eleven years old. My schoolbooks, heavy in the bike's metal basket, swung violently to the side, and I almost lost my math homework to the grasshopper and crickets. Standing astride my bike, I could see much going on around me—so much color, so much activity, so much *life*. Looking toward my school on the horizon, I felt so happy to be alive. And I wanted both to possess and to be a part of all I saw around me. I can still see myself in this meadow, in the warm air, surrounded by creation, more clearly than any other memory from childhood.

Looking back, I believe that I was feeling a sense of God's *promise*: an invitation to limitless joy.

—James Martin, SJ, *My Life with the Saints 10th Anniversary Edition*

The Presence of God

As I sit here, the beating of my heart,
the ebb and flow of my breathing, the movements of my mind
are all signs of God's ongoing creation of me.
I pause for a moment and become aware
of this presence of God within me.

Freedom

It is so easy to get caught up
with the trappings of wealth in this life.
Grant, O Lord, that I may be free
from greed and selfishness.
Remind me that the best things in life are free:
Love, laughter, caring, and sharing.

Consciousness

Knowing that God loves me unconditionally, I can afford to be honest
about how I am.
How has the day been, and how do I feel now? I share my feelings openly
with the Lord.

The Word

Lord Jesus, you became human to communicate with me.
You walked and worked on this earth.
You endured the heat and struggled with the cold.
All your time on this earth was spent in caring for humanity.
You healed the sick, you raised the dead.
Most important of all, you saved me from death.
(Please turn to the Scripture on the following pages. Inspiration points
are there should you need them. When you are ready, return here to
continue.)

Conversation

Sometimes I wonder what I might say if I were to meet you in person,
Lord.
I think I might say "Thank you" because you are always there for me.

Conclusion

I thank God for these moments we have spent together and for any insights I have been given concerning the text.

Sunday 4th November
Thirty-First Sunday in Ordinary Time
Mark 12:28b–34

One of the scribes came near and heard them disputing with one another, and seeing that Jesus answered them well, he asked him, "Which commandment is the first of all?" Jesus answered, "The first is, 'Hear, O Israel: the Lord our God, the Lord is one; you shall love the Lord your God with all your heart, and with all your soul, and with all your mind, and with all your strength.' The second is this, 'You shall love your neighbor as yourself.' There is no other commandment greater than these." Then the scribe said to him, "You are right, Teacher; you have truly said that 'he is one, and besides him there is no other'; and 'to love him with all the heart, and with all the understanding, and with all the strength,' and 'to love one's neighbor as oneself,'—this is much more important than all whole burnt offerings and sacrifices." When Jesus saw that he answered wisely, he said to him, "You are not far from the kingdom of God." After that no one dared to ask him any question.

- What would it feel like—be like—to love God with all my strength? Have I seen that kind of love in anyone else?
- Jesus told the scribe that he was not far from the kingdom of God. What did he mean by that? Was the man's understanding coming closer to the reality of the kingdom? When have I felt close to the kingdom of God? What was on my mind? What was I doing?

Monday 5th November
Luke 14:12–14

Jesus said also to the one who had invited him, "When you give a luncheon or a dinner, do not invite your friends or your brothers or your relatives or rich neighbors, in case they may invite you in return, and you would be repaid. But when you give a banquet, invite the poor, the crippled, the lame, and the blind. And you will be blessed, because they cannot repay you, for you will be repaid at the resurrection of the righteous."

- So much of our behavior and decision making is determined, or at least influenced, by the expectations and behavior of others. Jesus uses a simple, yet telling, example to challenge us to give freely without expecting anything back. We can do this only if we are aware that we have received freely.

- First-century Christian writers used to say that it will be the poor who will welcome us at the doors of heaven. Will they know me well enough to let me in? Do those in need have an important place in my heart?

Tuesday 6th November
Luke 14:15–24

One of the dinner guests, on hearing this, said to Jesus, "Blessed is anyone who will eat bread in the kingdom of God!" Then Jesus said to him, "Someone gave a great dinner and invited many. At the time for the dinner he sent his slave to say to those who had been invited, 'Come; for everything is ready now.' But they all alike began to make excuses. The first said to him, 'I have bought a piece of land, and I must go out and see it; please accept my apologies.' Another said, 'I have bought five yoke of oxen, and I am going to try them out; please accept my apologies.' Another said, 'I have just been married, and therefore I cannot come.' So the slave returned and reported this to his master. Then the owner of the house became angry and said to his slave, 'Go out at once into the streets and lanes of the town and bring in the poor, the crippled, the blind, and the lame.' And the slave said, 'Sir, what you ordered has been done, and there is still room.' Then the master said to the slave, 'Go out into the roads and lanes, and compel people to come in, so that my house may be filled. For I tell you, none of those who were invited will taste my dinner.'"

- Portraying the kingdom of God as a festive meal is common in the Bible. We receive the invitation, "Come, for everything is ready now." What is our response? The meal may be ready, but are we? Where are our priorities? Do we want to enter the kingdom where God reigns, or do we prefer to follow our own agenda?

- Notice how the invitation becomes more and more inclusive as the story develops. We may be surprised at who we find beside us when we are seated at the heavenly feast. Is our own hospitality so inclusive?

Wednesday 7th November
Luke 14:25–33

Now large crowds were travelling with him; and he turned and said to them, "Whoever comes to me and does not hate father and mother, wife and children, brothers and sisters, yes, and even life itself, cannot be my disciple. Whoever does not carry the cross and follow me cannot be my disciple. For which of you, intending to build a tower, does not first sit down and estimate the cost, to see whether he has enough to complete it? Otherwise, when he has laid a foundation and is not able to finish, all who see it will begin to ridicule him, saying, 'This fellow began to build and was not able to finish.' Or what king, going out to wage war against another king, will not sit down first and consider whether he is able with ten thousand to oppose the one who comes against him with twenty thousand? If he cannot, then, while the other is still far away, he sends a delegation and asks for the terms of peace. So therefore, none of you can become my disciple if you do not give up all your possessions.

- Jesus here teaches about the cost of discipleship. That there is a cost is illustrated by the stories of the builder and the king. A true disciple does not simply drift unreflectively through life but is aware of the seriousness of the commitment. When was the last time I counted the cost of following the way of Jesus?

- Some people balk at Jesus' use of the word hate (v. 26). He is using a rhetorical device (deliberate exaggeration) to emphasize a point. In Matthew 10:37 he explains his meaning: "Whoever loves father or mother more than me is not worthy of me." It is a matter of priorities.

Thursday 8th November
Luke 15:1–10

Now all the tax-collectors and sinners were coming near to listen to him. And the Pharisees and the scribes were grumbling and saying, "This fellow welcomes sinners and eats with them." So he told them this parable: "Which one of you, having a hundred sheep and losing one of them, does not leave the ninety-nine in the wilderness and go after the one that is lost until he finds it? When he has found it, he lays it on his shoulders and rejoices. And when he comes home, he calls together his friends and neighbors, saying to them, 'Rejoice with me, for I have found my sheep that was lost.' Just so, I tell you, there will be more joy in heaven over one sinner who repents than over ninety-nine righteous people who need no repentance. // "Or what woman having ten silver coins, if she loses one of them, does not light a lamp, sweep the house, and search carefully until she finds it? When she has found it, she calls together her friends and neighbors, saying, 'Rejoice with me, for I have found the coin that I had lost.' Just so, I tell you, there is joy in the presence of the angels of God over one sinner who repents."

- Even apart from sin, there are many other ways in which we can become "lost" as we journey through life. Have you had such an experience? Do you feel lost now?

- While these parables can stand on their own, note the context in which Jesus tells them. He has drawn criticism from the Pharisees and scribes because he shares table fellowship with "tax collectors and sinners." Are we ready to take abuse for our efforts to be inclusive?

Friday 9th November
John 2:13–22

The Passover of the Jews was near, and Jesus went up to Jerusalem. In the temple he found people selling cattle, sheep, and doves, and the money changers seated at their tables. Making a whip of cords, he drove all of them out of the temple, both the sheep and the cattle. He also poured out the coins of the money changers and overturned their tables. He told those who were selling the doves, "Take these things out of here! Stop making my Father's house a marketplace!" His disciples remembered that it was written, "Zeal for your house will consume me." The Jews then said to him, "What sign can you show us for doing this?" Jesus answered them, "Destroy this temple, and in three days I will raise it up." The Jews then said, "This temple has been under construction for forty-six years, and will you raise it up in three days?" But he was speaking of the temple of his body. After he was raised from the dead, his disciples remembered that he had said this; and they believed the scripture and the word that Jesus had spoken.

- The Jews understand "temple" to apply only to the building in which they are standing. Jesus, however, is applying the term to his own body and is prophesying his resurrection. This was to be the sign about which they had been asking.

- It seems that the Holy Spirit brings experience and understanding together when we are ready. The disciples understood and believed Jesus after he rose from the dead; then they remembered what he had taught them before. Events and teachings coalesced. When have you experienced a shift in your understanding about something you had heard or read many times before?

Saturday 10th November
Luke 16:9–15

"And I tell you, make friends for yourselves by means of dishonest wealth so that when it is gone, they may welcome you into the eternal homes. Whoever is faithful in a very little is faithful also in much; and whoever is dishonest in a very little is dishonest also in much. If then you have not been faithful with the dishonest wealth, who will entrust to you the true riches? And if you have not been faithful with what belongs to another, who will give you what is your own? No slave can serve two masters; for a slave will either hate the one and love the other, or be devoted to the one and despise the other. You cannot serve God and wealth." // The Pharisees, who were lovers of money, heard all this, and they ridiculed him. So he said to them, "You are those who justify yourselves in the sight of others; but God knows your hearts; for what is prized by human beings is an abomination in the sight of God."

- "Whoever is faithful in a very little is faithful also in much." Our faith grows with practice. Usually, we begin with small matters and then develop spiritually to where we can handle more important matters. God does not expect us to exercise faith we do not yet possess. Yet, we will determine the quality of our growth by the fundamental choices we make—which master we serve, for instance.

- To reflect on how your life is progressing is a valuable form of prayer, especially if it is done in the company of Jesus.

The Thirty-Second Week of Ordinary Time
November 11—November 17

Something to think and pray about each day this week:

Most Vulnerable—and Most Open

"Why is God so good?" I finally asked.

She laughed and recounted in great detail all the small events that had happened to her that day, until I agreed that God was indeed good. Many people who are poor have a greater appreciation of God's presence because they have a greater appreciation of their reliance on God. God is close to the poor because the poor are close to God.

I have also found that God meets us especially in those parts of ourselves that we would rather have go away. And here I'm not talking about the parts of our personalities that are drawn to sin, but the parts of ourselves that embarrass us, frustrate us, or even shame us—the parts that we wish to conceal from the world and that we spend so much time trying to hide. But it is here that we find ourselves most vulnerable and therefore most open to God.

—James Martin, SJ, *My Life with the Saints 10th Anniversary Edition*

The Presence of God
At any time of the day or night we can call on Jesus.
He is always waiting, listening for our call.
What a wonderful blessing.
No phone needed, no emails, just a whisper.

Freedom
Lord grant me the grace to have freedom of the spirit. Cleanse my heart and soul so that I may live joyously in your love.

Consciousness
Knowing that God loves me unconditionally, I look honestly over the past day, its events, and my feelings. Do I have something to be grateful for? Then I give thanks. Is there something I am sorry for? Then I ask forgiveness.

The Word
The word of God comes down to us through the Scriptures.
May the Holy Spirit enlighten my mind and my heart
to respond to the gospel teachings:
to love my neighbor as myself,
to care for my sisters and brothers in Christ.
(Please turn to the Scripture on the following pages. Inspiration points are there should you need them. When you are ready, return here to continue.)

Conversation
I know with certainty that there were times when you carried me, Lord. There were times when it was through your strength that I got through the dark times in my life.

Conclusion
Glory be to the Father, and to the Son, and to the Holy Spirit,
As it was in the beginning, is now and ever shall be,
World without end. Amen.

Sunday 11th November
Thirty-Second Sunday in Ordinary Time
Mark 12:38–44

As he taught, he said, "Beware of the scribes, who like to walk around in long robes, and to be greeted with respect in the marketplaces, and to have the best seats in the synagogues and places of honor at banquets! They devour widows' houses and for the sake of appearance say long prayers. They will receive the greater condemnation." // He sat down opposite the treasury, and watched the crowd putting money into the treasury. Many rich people put in large sums. A poor widow came and put in two small copper coins, which are worth a penny. Then he called his disciples and said to them, "Truly I tell you, this poor widow has put in more than all those who are contributing to the treasury. For all of them have contributed out of their abundance; but she out of her poverty has put in everything she had, all she had to live on."

- Widows are mentioned in both sections of this gospel reading. They represent the poorest and most vulnerable people in society. But those who "devour widows' houses," who multiply their sufferings, can be seen strutting around in public, even praying in public, seeking to be honored. Such hypocrisy is hateful to Jesus.

- Then Jesus sees a poor widow putting her last couple of small coins ("all she had to live on") into the temple treasury. He is astounded and contrasts her generosity with the disposition (which is not necessarily bad) of the rich who made large offerings "out of their abundance." Implicitly he may be criticizing the religious authorities for the pressure they put on people to part with what they cannot afford. Do I appreciate the qualities that can be found in the widows (and other poor) of my world?

Monday 12th November
Luke 17:1–6

Jesus said to his disciples, "Occasions for stumbling are bound to come, but woe to anyone by whom they come! It would be better for you if a millstone were hung around your neck and you were thrown into the sea than for you to cause one of these little ones to stumble. Be on your guard! If another disciple sins, you must rebuke the offender, and if there is repentance, you must forgive. And if the same person sins against you seven times a day, and turns back to you seven times and says, 'I repent,' you must forgive." // The apostles said to the Lord, "Increase our faith!" The Lord replied, "If you had faith the size of a mustard seed, you could say to this mulberry tree, 'Be uprooted and planted in the sea,' and it would obey you."

- Jesus tells us that despite our efforts to lead a good life, we are sure to stumble. He understands this and hence his lovely gift of reconciliation. But he warns us of the great damage we do if we are responsible for causing others to stumble. Our being together should be for our mutual support and not a cause for others to stray or lose faith.

- Be grateful for all those who, through the grace of God, have helped you live your faith.

Tuesday 13th November
Luke 17:7–10

Jesus said to his disciples, "Who among you would say to your slave who has just come in from plowing or tending sheep in the field, 'Come here at once and take your place at the table'? Would you not rather say to him, 'Prepare supper for me, put on your apron and serve me while I eat and drink; later you may eat and drink'? Do you thank the slave for doing what was commanded? So you also, when you have done all that you were ordered to do, say, 'We are worthless slaves; we have done only what we ought to have done!'"

- This text can be hard to understand. The central point would be that humble service done out of love for the Lord is its own reward. It can be helpful to compare the words of Jesus spoken at another time, when he was speaking of who is the greatest: "for who is the greater; the one at table or the one who serves? The one at table surely? Yet here am I among you as one who serves!"

- It can be hard to grasp the depth of the relationship that Jesus has with us if we fail to understand his great love of and service to us in his passion and death. Lord, help me grasp how generously you have acted toward me.

Wednesday 14th November
Luke 17:11–19

On the way to Jerusalem Jesus was going through the region between Samaria and Galilee. As he entered a village, ten lepers approached him. Keeping their distance, they called out, saying, "Jesus, Master, have mercy on us!" When he saw them, he said to them, "Go and show yourselves to the priests." And as they went, they were made clean. Then one of them, when he saw that he was healed, turned back, praising God with a loud voice. He prostrated himself at Jesus' feet and thanked him. And he was a Samaritan. Then Jesus asked, "Were not ten made clean? But the other nine, where are they? Was none of them found to return and give praise to God except this foreigner?" Then he said to him, "Get up and go on your way; your faith has made you well."

- Notice how Luke draws attention to the marginalized situation of the lepers. They are regarded as unclean and forced to live outside the towns and villages. Even when approaching Jesus, they keep their distance. Curing a leper restores not only the person's health but also restores the person to the community.

- All ten lepers have faith; but only one experiences deep gratitude. The Samaritan goes out of his way to thank Jesus in person. How much do we take God's many blessings for granted, or worse still, as our entitlement?

Thursday 15th November
Luke 17:20–25

Once Jesus was asked by the Pharisees when the kingdom of God was coming, and he answered, "The kingdom of God is not coming with things that can be observed; nor will they say, 'Look, here it is!' or 'There it is!' For, in fact, the kingdom of God is among you." // Then he said to the disciples, "The days are coming when you will long to see one of the days of the Son of Man, and you will not see it. They will say to you, 'Look there!' or 'Look here!' Do not go, do not set off in pursuit. For as the lightning flashes and lights up the sky from one side to the other, so will the Son of Man be in his day. But first he must endure much suffering and be rejected by this generation."

- The Pharisees' question presumes that the kingdom of God is yet to come and that it will be visible, like an earthly kingdom. Jesus replies that the kingdom is already present but is invisible: "The kingdom of God is among you." An alternative translation reads: "The kingdom of God is within you."

- Jesus encourages his disciples not to get worked up, or even overly curious, about the end times and the (second) coming of the Son of Man. Instead let them concentrate on the here and now, and ponder on Jesus' teaching: that the Son of Man "must first endure much suffering and be rejected by this generation." This they will soon see acted out in Jerusalem. Why do you think Jesus shifts the emphasis away from the end times?

Friday 16th November
Luke 17:26–37

"Just as it was in the days of Noah, so too it will be in the days of the Son of Man. They were eating and drinking, and marrying and being given in marriage, until the day Noah entered the ark, and the flood came and destroyed all of them. Likewise, just as it was in the days of Lot: they were eating and drinking, buying and selling, planting and building, but on the day that Lot left Sodom, it rained fire and sulphur from heaven and destroyed all of them—it will be like that on the day that the Son of Man is revealed. On that day, anyone on the housetop who has belongings in the house must not come down to take them away; and likewise anyone in the field must not turn back. Remember Lot's wife. Those who try to make their life secure will lose it, but those who lose their life will keep it. I tell you, on that night there will be two in one bed; one will be taken and the other left. There will be two women grinding meal together; one will be taken and the other left." Then they asked him, "Where, Lord?" He said to them, "Where the corpse is, there the vultures will gather."

- The stories of Noah and the flood and of Lot and the destruction of Sodom were part of the folk memory of Israel. Jesus wants his listeners to notice how life was going on normally—people were engaging in their everyday activities—when the disaster struck. There was no warning, no premonition, and no time to plan an escape! So too the Son of Man will come suddenly and unexpectedly.

- The only way to be prepared is to live a good life, one based on love. Then the coming of the Son of Man will not be a disaster but our final liberation. In what ways do I prepare for this future Jesus has described?

Saturday 17th November
Luke 18:1–8

Then Jesus told them a parable about their need to pray always and not to lose heart. He said, "In a certain city there was a judge who neither feared God nor had respect for people. In that city there was a widow who kept coming to him and saying, 'Grant me justice against my opponent.' For a while he refused; but later he said to himself, 'Though I have no fear of God and no respect for anyone, yet because this widow keeps bothering me, I will grant her justice, so that she may not wear me out by continually coming.'" And the Lord said, "Listen to what the unjust judge says. And will not God grant justice to his chosen ones who cry to him day and night? Will he delay long in helping them? I tell you, he will quickly grant justice to them. And yet, when the Son of Man comes, will he find faith on earth?"

- In telling this parable Jesus recognizes our need for encouragement in prayer, especially as we cope with disappointment. The interaction between the judge and the widow is vivid, psychologically believable, and there is an underlying humor. If even a despicable human being like the judge can be badgered into acting justly, how much more readily will the all-loving, ever-generous God respond to our needs when we present them to him?

- The concluding verse indicates that persistence in prayer is impossible without faith. But which comes first, prayer or faith? Does my faith grow as I pray, or do I pray more because my faith has increased? I bring these questions to you, Lord.

The Thirty-Third Week of Ordinary Time
November 18—November 24

Something to think and pray about each day this week:

We Cannot Stop at Thank you

Every November, my social media feeds are filled with posts and pictures of people doing "30 days of thanks." At first glance, I appreciate the way people are intentionally reflecting on their lives to say thank you for what they name as gifts and blessings. It reminds me of one of the steps of the Examen, where we pause and thank God for what we noticed in the last 24 hours.

St. Ignatius, though, did not suggest we stop our prayer at offering thanksgiving. He invited us to bring our entire lives before God, naming with honesty our thanks, our moments where we feel God, our lives' dark spots, and our sins.

The temptation to offer only prayers of thanksgiving to God is a common practice that I notice in my ministry of retreats and spiritual direction. We are afraid to bring our mess before God and fearful to be completely honest with God about what's going on in life.

I wonder how many of our human relationships would last if we kept all of our conversations at the level of thanks, like we sometimes do with God? Relationships move to a different level when we risk being vulnerable, when we have a deep sharing of heart, and when we have a space to voice not only what we are thankful for, but also our lingering questions, our desires, and our struggles. We cannot stop at thank you.

—Becky Eldredge on *dotMagis*, the blog of *IgnatianSpirituality.com*
http://www.ignatianspirituality.com/22822/
we-cannot-stop-at-thank-you

The Presence of God

Dear Jesus, as I call on you today, I realize that often I come asking for favors. Today I'd like just to be in your presence. Draw my heart in response to your love.

Freedom

God my creator, you gave me life and the gift of freedom. Through your love I exist in this world. May I never take the gift of life for granted. May I always respect others' right to life.

Consciousness

Dear Lord, help me to remember that you gave me life. Teach me to slow down, to be still and enjoy the pleasures created for me. To be aware of the beauty that surrounds me: the marvel of mountains, the calmness of lakes, the fragility of a flower petal. I need to remember that all these things come from you.

The Word

The word of God comes down to us through the Scriptures. May the Holy Spirit enlighten my mind and my heart to respond to the gospel teachings. (Please turn to the Scripture on the following pages. Inspiration points are there should you need them. When you are ready, return here to continue.)

Conversation

What feelings are rising in me as I pray and reflect on God's word? I imagine Jesus himself sitting or standing near me, and I open my heart to him.

Conclusion

I thank God for these moments we have spent together and for any insights I have been given concerning the text.

Sunday 18th November
Our Lord Jesus Christ, King of the Universe
Mark 13:24–32

"'But in those days, after that suffering,
 the sun will be darkened,
  and the moon will not give its light,
 and the stars will be falling from heaven,
  and the powers in the heavens will be shaken.'

Then they will see 'the Son of Man coming in clouds' with great power and glory. Then he will send out the angels, and gather his elect from the four winds, from the ends of the earth to the ends of heaven. // "From the fig tree learn its lesson: as soon as its branch becomes tender and puts forth its leaves, you know that summer is near. So also, when you see these things taking place, you know that he is near, at the very gates. Truly I tell you, this generation will not pass away until all these things have taken place. Heaven and earth will pass away, but my words will not pass away. But about that day or hour no one knows, neither the angels in heaven, nor the Son, but only the Father."

- We frequently hear the phrase, "the signs of the times." This Gospel passage deals with the signs of the end times. How do you balance, or reconcile the description of these events (taken in part from the Book of Daniel) and the last verse, which states that "about that day or hour no one knows . . . but only the Father"?

- Some Christians have been led astray by becoming fixated on signs of various sorts and prophesying the imminent end of the world. It may be more prudent to expect the unexpected and simply be ready to welcome the Son of Man whenever he comes. In the meantime, be consoled by Jesus' words: "Heaven and earth will pass away, but my words will not pass away."

Monday 19th November
Luke 18:35–43

As Jesus approached Jericho, a blind man was sitting by the roadside begging. When he heard a crowd going by, he asked what was happening. They told him, "Jesus of Nazareth is passing by." Then he shouted, "Jesus,

Son of David, have mercy on me!" Those who were in front sternly ordered him to be quiet; but he shouted even more loudly, "Son of David, have mercy on me!" Jesus stood still and ordered the man to be brought to him; and when he came near, he asked him, "What do you want me to do for you?" He said, "Lord, let me see again." Jesus said to him, "Receive your sight; your faith has saved you." Immediately he regained his sight and followed him, glorifying God; and all the people, when they saw it, praised God.

- I allow this vibrant, dramatic story to draw me into its action. I imagine myself as the blind beggar sitting helpless by the side of the road. All I can do is shout when I learn that Jesus is passing. Even when Jesus asks me to come forward, others have to lead me. How do I feel as I hear Jesus' respectful and sensitive question: "What do you want me to do for you?" Soon I will regain sight because of my faith and trust. I rejoice and give the praise to God.

- How can I treat beggars (representing all poor people) and the blind (representing all people with disabilities) with the respect and sensitivity that Jesus shows here?

Tuesday 20th November
Luke 19:1–10

Jesus entered Jericho and was passing through it. A man was there named Zacchaeus; he was a chief tax collector and was rich. He was trying to see who Jesus was, but on account of the crowd he could not, because he was short in stature. So he ran ahead and climbed a sycamore tree to see him, because he was going to pass that way. When Jesus came to the place, he looked up and said to him, "Zacchaeus, hurry and come down; for I must stay at your house today." So he hurried down and was happy to welcome him. All who saw it began to grumble and said, "He has gone to be the guest of one who is a sinner." Zacchaeus stood there and said to the Lord, "Look, half of my possessions, Lord, I will give to the poor; and if I have defrauded anyone of anything, I will pay back four times as much." Then Jesus said to him, "Today salvation has come to this house, because he too is a son of Abraham. For the Son of Man came to seek out and to save the lost."

- Jesus has come "to seek out and to save the lost." This final verse is the lens through which we are asked to contemplate the entire story. Zacchaeus is a high-ranking tax collector in the pay of the Roman occupiers. To his fellow Jews he is a traitor and, in their words, a sinner. Yet he is the man Jesus chooses to be his host during his stay in Jericho. What does this say about Jesus? About his ministry? About his priorities?

- Who would I be in this story? How would I react to the way Jesus deals with Zacchaeus?

Wednesday 21st November
The Presentation of the Blessed Virgin Mary
Luke 19:11–28

Jesus went on to tell a parable, because he was near Jerusalem, and because they supposed that the kingdom of God was to appear immediately. So he said, "A nobleman went to a distant country to get royal power for himself and then return. He summoned ten of his slaves, and gave them ten pounds, and said to them, 'Do business with these until I come back.' But the citizens of his country hated him and sent a delegation after him, saying, 'We do not want this man to rule over us.' When he returned, having received royal power, he ordered these slaves, to whom he had given the money, to be summoned so that he might find out what they had gained by trading. The first came forward and said, 'Lord, your pound has made ten more pounds.' He said to him, 'Well done, good slave! Because you have been trustworthy in a very small thing, take charge of ten cities.' Then the second came, saying, 'Lord, your pound has made five pounds.' He said to him, 'And you, rule over five cities.' Then the other came, saying, 'Lord, here is your pound. I wrapped it up in a piece of cloth, for I was afraid of you, because you are a harsh man; you take what you did not deposit, and reap what you did not sow.' He said to him, 'I will judge you by your own words, you wicked slave! You knew, did you, that I was a harsh man, taking what I did not deposit and reaping what I did not sow? Why then did you not put my money into the bank? Then when I returned, I could have collected it with interest.' He said to the bystanders, 'Take the pound from him and give it to the one who has ten pounds.' (And they said to him, 'Lord, he has ten pounds!') 'I tell you, to all those who have, more will be given; but from those who have nothing, even what they have will be taken away. But as for these enemies of mine who did not want me to be king over them—bring them here and slaughter them in my presence.'" After he had said this, he went on ahead, going up to Jerusalem.

- This is a puzzling parable. There are two parallel story lines. First, there is the hostility between the king and the citizens who want to be rid of him. Second, there are the interactions between the king and his slaves. The latter receive the most attention. The king himself is avaricious, tyrannical, and cruel. His only positive quality is his willingness to reward loyalty and initiative in his slaves.

- It is difficult to see what light the parable throws on the nature of the kingdom of God (which is what the introduction leads us to expect). Could it be teaching that our service of God is not to be minimalist, grudging, or fearful but generous, imaginative, and proactive? Is it teaching that we need a willingness to take risks when responding to God's mandate? That we must be ready to lose our life in order to find it?

Thursday 22nd November
Luke 19:41–44

As he came near and saw the city, he wept over it, saying, "If you, even you, had only recognized on this day the things that make for peace! But now they are hidden from your eyes. Indeed, the days will come upon you, when your enemies will set up ramparts around you and surround you, and hem you in on every side. They will crush you to the ground, you and your children within you, and they will not leave within you one stone upon another; because you did not recognize the time of your visitation from God."

- Luke's Gospel is structured around Jesus' journey to Jerusalem. The last stage of this journey turns into a triumphant procession (celebrated by us on Palm Sunday) from the Mount of Olives into the city. But at some point, Jesus pauses, overcome with emotion. He looks at the city skyline, dominated by the magnificent temple, and he weeps aloud.

- What does he see? What moves him so deeply? The whole history of Israel, his own people, unfolds before him. Everything leads to this day, to his own coming among them. But they are blind, obstinate, and unbelieving. They are rejecting their Messiah. Jesus also has a premonition of what this people will suffer during the siege of Jerusalem by a Roman army in 70 AD. Stand quietly beside Jesus and allow yourself to be drawn into his lament.

Friday 23rd November
Luke 19:45–48

Then Jesus entered the temple and began to drive out those who were selling things there; and he said, "It is written,

'My house shall be a house of prayer';
but you have made it a den of robbers."

Every day he was teaching in the temple. The chief priests, the scribes, and the leaders of the people kept looking for a way to kill him; but they did not find anything they could do, for all the people were spellbound by what they heard.

- John's Gospel places the account of the cleansing of the temple at the beginning of Jesus' public ministry. Luke, however, who supplies less detail, places it near the end. This allows him to link it with the plotting of Jesus' enemies against him. Luke is building up the atmosphere of hostility that will lead to the eventual arrest, torture, and death of Jesus.
- Can the Christian life ever be without tensions and conflicts? What in the church today needs cleansing?

Saturday 24th November
Luke 20:27–40

Some Sadducees, those who say there is no resurrection, came to him and asked him a question, "Teacher, Moses wrote for us that if a man's brother dies, leaving a wife but no children, the man shall marry the widow and raise up children for his brother. Now there were seven brothers; the first married, and died childless; then the second and the third married her, and so in the same way all seven died childless. Finally the woman also died. In the resurrection, therefore, whose wife will the woman be? For the seven had married her." // Jesus said to them, "Those who belong to this age marry and are given in marriage; but those who are considered worthy of a place in that age and in the resurrection from the dead neither marry nor are given in marriage. Indeed they cannot die anymore, because they are like angels and are children of God, being children of the resurrection. And the fact that the dead are raised Moses himself showed, in the story about the bush, where he speaks of the Lord as the God of Abraham, the God of Isaac, and the God of Jacob. Now he is God not of the dead, but of the living; for to him all of them are alive." Then some of the scribes answered, "Teacher, you have spoken well." For they no longer dared to ask him another question.

- The Sadducees make fun of the concept of resurrection. In this way, they avoid listening to the message of Jesus about the reality of the resurrection and how the resurrected state is a new creation in which we are sharing in the divine life of God.

- Our faith is nourished by our prayers and intercessions for our loved ones who have died. We pray frequently for the dead this month: "Eternal rest grant unto them, O Lord, and let perpetual light shine upon them. May they rest in peace. Amen." It's good to believe that this prayer will be said for us, when our time comes.

The Thirty-Fourth Week of Ordinary Time
November 25—December 1

Something to think and pray about each day this week:

Spiritual Clutter

The great purge of every nook and cranny of our home has begun. We are in the process of sharing-out toys, outgrown clothes, and superfluous belongings. We are letting go of the things we have held onto "just in case" and other things that have cluttered our lives just because we haven't had the time to clear things out on a regular basis. The resulting space that we are recovering in our home is freeing. There is more room to move and more room to live. There is more space to focus on the things that really matter—and those things are *not things*.

As we clear the clutter from our home, I am reminded that Advent is a great time to clear the spiritual clutter as well. I ask myself, when Jesus comes, will there be room for him to stay, or will he find my heart and soul too cluttered? Am I hanging onto things I don't need out of that "just in case" type of fear? Or, do I trust him enough to let everything go? Have I taken the necessary time to free up space for him? Is my priority, in fact, Jesus, or is it things or other attachments? When he comes, will I be able to respond to him freely, or will my movements be impeded by stuff that's holding me back? My soul-cleaning goal is to be able to fling open the door to my heart and fearlessly let go of all of those things that might get in the way of his entry. Can I do this?

—Rebecca Ruiz on *dotMagis*, the blog of *IgnatianSpirituality.com*
http://www.ignatianspirituality.com/23016/making-room-this-advent

The Presence of God
Dear Jesus, I come to you today longing for your presence. I desire to love you as you love me. May nothing ever separate me from you.

Freedom
Lord, grant me the grace to be free from the excesses of this life. Let me not get caught up with the desire for wealth. Keep my heart and mind free to love and serve you.

Consciousness
Where do I sense hope, encouragement, and growth in my life? By looking back over the past few months, I may be able to see which activities and occasions have produced rich fruit. If I do notice such areas, I will determine to give those areas both time and space in the future.

The Word
God speaks to each of us individually. I listen attentively, to hear what he is saying to me. Read the text a few times, then listen. (Please turn to the Scripture on the following pages. Inspiration points are there should you need them. When you are ready, return here to continue.)

Conversation
What is stirring in me as I pray? Am I consoled, troubled, left cold? I imagine Jesus standing or sitting at my side, and I share my feelings with him.

Conclusion
Glory be to the Father, and to the Son, and to the Holy Spirit,
As it was in the beginning, is now and ever shall be,
World without end. Amen.

Sunday 25th November
Our Lord Jesus Christ, King of the Universe
John 18:33b–37

Then Pilate entered the headquarters again, summoned Jesus, and asked him, "Are you the King of the Jews?" Jesus answered, "Do you ask this on your own, or did others tell you about me?" Pilate replied, "I am not a Jew, am I? Your own nation and the chief priests have handed you over to me. What have you done?" Jesus answered, "My kingdom is not from this world. If my kingdom were from this world, my followers would be fighting to keep me from being handed over to the Jews. But as it is, my kingdom is not from here." Pilate asked him, "So you are a king?" Jesus answered, "You say that I am a king. For this I was born, and for this I came into the world, to testify to the truth. Everyone who belongs to the truth listens to my voice."

- Jesus has to correct Pilate's understanding of Jesus' role: "My kingdom is not from this world" or "My kingdom does not belong to this world." In spite of this warning, we have sometimes celebrated this feast in a (worldly) triumphalist manner that does not harmonize with Jesus' understanding of himself.

- Why is it important to read a scene from the Passion today? Does it help us grasp what the kingship of Christ truly means? (Notice Jesus' stress on truth in this passage). How can Jesus be both king and suffering servant?

Monday 26th November
Luke 21:1–4

Jesus looked up and saw rich people putting their gifts into the treasury; he also saw a poor widow put in two small copper coins. He said, "Truly I tell you, this poor widow has put in more than all of them; for all of them have contributed out of their abundance, but she out of her poverty has put in all she had to live on."

- Jesus often shows himself to be an acute observer of what is going on around him. He also has the ability to present his teaching through commenting on what he sees—as he does here, while he sits in the temple. Lord, remind me to observe what happens around me and to listen for your wisdom.

- Jesus is surprisingly non-judgmental. He does not condemn the temple authorities for avarice, or the rich who give alms out of their surplus wealth. He simply points out that the poor widow gives more than anyone else because she gives her last penny. We do well to concentrate on the good works we see rather than others' weaknesses.

Tuesday 27th November
Luke 21:5–11

When some were speaking about the temple, how it was adorned with beautiful stones and gifts dedicated to God, Jesus said, "As for these things that you see, the days will come when not one stone will be left upon another; all will be thrown down." // They asked him, "Teacher, when will this be, and what will be the sign that this is about to take place?" And he said, "Beware that you are not led astray; for many will come in my name and say, 'I am he!' and, 'The time is near!' Do not go after them. // "When you hear of wars and insurrections, do not be terrified; for these things must take place first, but the end will not follow immediately." Then he said to them, "Nation will rise against nation, and kingdom against kingdom; there will be great earthquakes, and in various places famines and plagues; and there will be dreadful portents and great signs from heaven."

- Endings are sometimes welcomed, sometimes feared. Now that we are coming to the end of the Liturgical Year (Advent begins next Sunday) our Gospel readings will focus on the end times. Jesus begins by foretelling the end of the temple in Jerusalem (destroyed in 70 AD). Given the significance of the temple for Jewish religion and culture, this could be seen as symbolizing the end of their messianic hopes. It certainly led to the Jewish diaspora and to the Rabbinic Judaism that we know today. Nothing could ever be the same again.

- Did I have to deal with painful endings during the past few years? Did I face the deaths of loved ones, failed relationships, unemployment, breakdown of health, and so forth? Where was God for me during these crises? Were there also endings that I welcomed, which brought me freedom and opened up new opportunities?

Wednesday 28th November
Luke 21:12–19

Jesus said to his disciples, "But before all this occurs, they will arrest you and persecute you; they will hand you over to synagogues and prisons, and you will be brought before kings and governors because of my name. This will give you an opportunity to testify. So make up your minds not to prepare your defense in advance; for I will give you words and a wisdom that none of your opponents will be able to withstand or contradict. You will be betrayed even by parents and brothers, by relatives and friends; and they will put some of you to death. You will be hated by all because of my name. But not a hair of your head will perish. By your endurance you will gain your souls."

- Sporadic persecution of Christians had already begun when Luke was writing his Gospel. This situation may well be reflected in this passage. Similar persecution is also happening in many parts of the world today. Are those of us living in more tolerant countries sensitive to the sufferings of our fellow Christians who find themselves "hated by all because of my name"? Are we in effective solidarity with them? Do we pray for them? Do we engage in advocacy on their behalf?

- Jesus not only describes what his followers will have to endure, but he also offers assurance that he will support them and make them strong. To echo Saint Julian of Norwich: "All will be well, and all will be well, and all manner of things will be well."

Thursday 29th November
Luke 21:20–28

"When you see Jerusalem surrounded by armies, then know that its desolation has come near. Then those in Judea must flee to the mountains, and those inside the city must leave it, and those out in the country must not enter it; for these are days of vengeance, as a fulfillment of all that is written. Woe to those who are pregnant and to those who are nursing infants in those days! For there will be great distress on the earth and wrath against this people; they will fall by the edge of the sword and be taken away as captives among all nations; and Jerusalem will be trampled on by the Gentiles, until the times of the Gentiles are fulfilled.

"There will be signs in the sun, the moon, and the stars, and on the earth distress among nations confused by the roaring of the sea and the waves. People will faint from fear and foreboding of what is coming upon the world, for the powers of the heavens will be shaken. Then they will see "the Son of Man coming in a cloud" with power and great glory. Now when these things begin to take place, stand up and raise your heads, because your redemption is drawing near."

- Again there is the bringing together of two events: the destruction of Jerusalem and the coming of the Son of Man. One happens within history; the other marks the end of history. Notice how aware Jesus is of the horrors of war, especially how the innocent and vulnerable suffer.

- The Second Coming will be announced by strange cosmic happenings. These will cause terror and confusion among all the earth's peoples. But believers need have no fear. Indeed, they are to "stand up and raise their heads" because Christ's coming is the final stage of their redemption (or liberation). They actually desire his coming. "The one who testifies to these things says, 'Surely I am coming soon.' Amen. Come, Lord Jesus!" (Rev.22:20). Is this my desire today? Do I long to be with him?

Friday 30th November
Matthew 4:18–22

As Jesus walked by the Sea of Galilee, he saw two brothers, Simon, who is called Peter, and Andrew his brother, casting a net into the sea—for they were fishermen. And he said to them, "Follow me, and I will make you fish for people." Immediately they left their nets and followed him. As he went from there, he saw two other brothers, James son of Zebedee and his brother John, in the boat with their father Zebedee, mending their nets, and he called them. Immediately they left the boat and their father, and followed him.

- This scene offers us a paradigm of the way Jesus calls each of us. Note that the initiative is entirely his. As we read in Mark 3:13, he "called to him those whom he wanted." Jesus wants you and me to follow him, not just as companions but as sharers in his mission. "I will make you fish for people." Christian spirituality is not simply about "Jesus and me" but about "Jesus, me, and those to whom he sends me." Each of us is a fisher: a witness, a prophet, an evangelizer, a healer, and a communicator of the good news.

- What was it like for Andrew to hear his call? A mix of emotions? Delight in being singled out (we all want to be wanted!), but with maybe a bit of hesitation about leaving behind his means of livelihood? What is the cost of discipleship for me? Do I need to let go of anything?

Saturday 1st December
Luke 21:34–36

Jesus said to the disciples, "Be on guard so that your hearts are not weighed down with dissipation and drunkenness and the worries of this life, and that day catch you unexpectedly, like a trap. For it will come upon all who live on the face of the whole earth. Be alert at all times, praying that you may have the strength to escape all these things that will take place, and to stand before the Son of Man."

- Today is the last day of the liturgical year, tomorrow being the first Sunday of Advent when the cycle of the liturgical year begins again. In this text, Jesus reminds us of the passing aspect of life. In this way he urges us not to be caught unawares and to pay attention to fulfilling our desires for good.
- What do I desire in the coming year of the church—for myself and for my fellow Christians?

LOYOLA PRESS.
A JESUIT MINISTRY

Join a Worldwide Community of Prayer

Make a "Sacred Space" in your day with the worldwide prayer community at **www.SacredSpace.ie**. Inspired by the spirituality of St. Ignatius of Loyola, the daily updates help you pray anywhere, anytime.

Sacred Space is brought to you by the Irish Jesuits and Loyola Press.

Sacred Space
YOUR DAILY PRAYER ONLINE

Reading on Jesuits lives through the Ages

The Pilgrim's Story, by Brendan Comerford SJ, is an introduction to the life and spirituality of St Ignatius Loyola. Written from a pastoral perspective, this book reflects on Ignatius's description of himself as a pilgrim.

€12.95

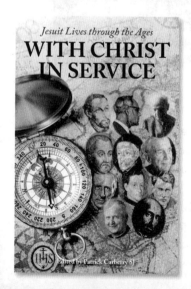

With Christ in Service, edited by Patrick Carberry SJ, is an inspiring and informative read for those who want to know more about the Jesuits and their inspiration.

€9.95

www.messenger.ie